RIVALS

ALSO BY BILL EMMOTT

20:21 VISION: TWENTIETH-CENTURY
LESSONS FOR THE TWENTY-FIRST CENTURY

JAPANOPHOBIA: THE MYTH
OF THE INVINCIBLE JAPANESE

THE SUN ALSO SETS: THE LIMITS
TO JAPAN'S ECONOMIC POWER

BILL EMMOTT

RIVALS

HOW THE POWER STRUGGLE BETWEEN CHINA, INDIA AND JAPAN WILL SHAPE OUR NEXT DECADE

HARCOURT, INC.   ORLANDO   AUSTIN   NEW YORK   SAN DIEGO   LONDON

Requests for permission to make copies of any part of the work
should be submitted online at www.harcourt.com/contact or mailed
to the following address: Permissions Department, Houghton Mifflin
Harcourt Publishing Company, 6277 Sea Harbor Drive, Orlando,
Florida 32887-6777.

www.HarcourtBooks.com

Library of Congress Cataloging-in-Publication Data
Emmott, Bill.
Rivals: how the power struggle between China, India and Japan
will shape our next decade/Bill Emmott.—1st ed.
p. cm.
Includes bibliographical references and index.
1. Asia—Foreign relations.   2. Balance of power.
3. International relations.   I. Title.
JZ1720.E52   2008
327.1'12095—dc22   2007052804
ISBN 978-0-15-101503-0

Text set in AGaramond
Designed by April Ward

Printed in the United States of America
First edition
K J I H G F E D C B A

FOR CAROL

CONTENTS

A NOTE ON NAMES

ASIAN NAMES CAN BE CONFUSING because of varying practices of Westernization. In this book, Chinese names are given in the standard Chinese order, with family name first and given name second, as in Deng Xiaoping. Some Chinese people, in particular those working in Western institutions, follow the Western naming order, but this is not yet standard practice. For Japanese names, however, the Western order is used virtually universally when dealing with foreigners, and so that is followed here: e.g., Junichiro Koizumi, where Koizumi is the family name. For Korean names, the family name is used first, as in Kim Jong-il. In Singapore, for people of Chinese extraction (such as Lee Kuan Yew), the Chinese naming order is used; for others, such as Kishore Mahbubani, the Western order is used. For Indians, the given name is first and the family name is second.

1. ASIA'S NEW POWER GAME

FEW OF HIS CONTEMPORARIES think of George Walker Bush as a visionary American president unless they are using the term to imply a touch of madness. Such is the legacy of his misadventure in Iraq, of the continued instability in Afghanistan, of the worldwide decline in the reputation of the United States during his administration, that many would rank him as having been the worst American president since Richard Nixon (1969–74), or Herbert Hoover (1929–33), or even, for his harshest critics, since the founding of the republic. It has not been for want of ambition. In the two years following the terrorist attacks of September 11, 2001, President Bush appeared to form the grandest of grand foreign-policy strategies, seeking nothing less than a transformation of the Middle East and Central Asia, the regions from which the terrorism seemed to have originated, with democracy—or at least accountability—replacing dictatorship. John Lewis Gaddis, a Yale professor of grand strategy and the doyen of cold-war historians, described this as "the most fundamental reassessment of American grand strategy in half a century."[1] And so it was. But it collapsed in ruins. Whoever is elected as America's next president, in November 2008, is likely either to reject the Bush strategy altogether or to distance themselves from it by several hundred miles.

Except in one respect. That respect represents one of the few points of continuity between the Bush administration's first few months in office, when a rising China had been considered America's principal foreign-policy concern, and the post-September 11 world. In September 2002 the Bush administration stated that one of its aims would be to "extend the peace by encouraging free and open societies on every continent."[2] Early in his second term, George Bush sought to do just that, in the most rapidly changing continent of all, the one that is home to half the world's population and to its fastest-developing economies: Asia. He did it by launching a bold initiative to try to establish closer American ties with the world's biggest democracy, India.

That act may eventually be judged by historians as a move of great strategic importance and imagination. It recognized that while al-Qaeda and its sort pose the biggest short- and, perhaps, medium-term challenge to America, in the long term it is the expected shift in the world's economic and political balance toward Asia that does promise, as the Bush team originally thought, to have the greatest significance. It was the culmination of a process that was begun by his then-new secretary of state, Condoleezza Rice, on a visit to Delhi in March 2005, and was sealed by President Bush himself during his own visit to India exactly a year later. With India's professorial prime minister, Manmohan Singh, President Bush signed a deal to cast aside forty years of hostility and suspicion between the two countries, ending almost a decade of tension over India's 1998 nuclear-weapons tests, by agreeing to commence collaboration over civil nuclear energy and to sweep aside decades of practice in nuclear nonproliferation agreements. India was being made a very special case, in a manner designed to help boost both its economic strength and its military capacity. And that exception was being made for a very special reason: the rise of China.

China is used to being treated as a special case. Richard Nixon's presidency was dominated at the time by the final failed years of the Vietnam War and by Watergate, but memories of it now are dominated by a diplomatic act, not a military or judicial one: his dramatic

opening of relations with China in 1971–72, which brought to an
end more than two decades of bitter estrangement between the
United States and the People's Republic. Watergate may have given
us a suffix to be attached to each and every scandal that occurs in
Washington, but the opening to China has lived on even more
strongly in the imagination, yielding operas, plays and books, as well
as a term (*Nixon-to-China*) now generically used to denote a meeting of minds between political extremes. Shocking though it seemed
at the time, with hindsight Nixon's courting of Mao Zedong and his
regime made perfect sense, helping to preserve and exploit the isolation of the Soviet Union. After Mao's death in 1976 and the ascent
to power of Deng Xiaoping, it can even be said to have made possible the process by which China chose to emulate America's capitalist
system, albeit as "socialism with Chinese characteristics" in Deng's
delicious phrase, and thus to launch what we now call globalization:
the huge rise in trade, investment and other forms of connectedness
between almost every country in the world but especially involving
the two most populous, first China and later India.

George Bush's rapprochement with India cannot rival Nixon's
trip to China for its sheer shock value, nor for the drama with which
it was unveiled. Indeed, its initial phase in 2005 was hardly noticed
outside India. Moreover, although the 2006 nuclear pact caused an
uproar in Washington and in arms-control circles in Europe, the
dominant argument about it concerned an issue too arcane to catch
the public imagination: namely, the effect of the deal on the global
regime designed to prevent the spread of nuclear weapons. Nor was
the rapprochement entirely new, for it built on discussions begun almost a decade earlier by President Bill Clinton's administration, and
especially by his deputy secretary of state, Strobe Talbott.[3] But the
final step taken by the Bush administration was a big one, a step
that his predecessor had not been willing to take.

It amounted to a sidelining of nuclear-proliferation concerns
in pursuit of a much grander and more strategic goal: a close and

enduring friendship with India, a country that had aligned itself with the Soviet Union during the cold war. It was a country whose economy was by then growing strongly, that had shed much of its anti-Western ideology and that wanted both acceptance as a global power and assistance to become one. Its status as a democracy was thus being given a higher priority than fears about nuclear proliferation: A democracy, the deal implied, could be trusted not to spread nuclear weapons, even if it refused to sign the nuclear nonproliferation treaty or to forgo the right to test further nuclear weapons, as India continued to do. Most crucially, India was a country with the potential to balance the rising power of China. George Bush's recognition of that fact was his Richard Nixon moment. Where Nixon had used China to balance the Soviet Union, Bush was using India to balance China. Like Nixon's move, with hindsight Bush's approach to India made perfect sense.

China, not surprisingly, was far from happy about it. Neither America nor India has wanted to say explicitly that China is the reason for the U.S.-India nuclear deal, but there cannot really be any other explanation for India's exceptional treatment. India's economy could have been supported, or its democracy encouraged, in any number of less contentious ways, if those had been the true aims. The Chinese government is certainly aware of what is going on, though it has not complained loudly about the deal, presumably because there is little that it can do about it and because the deal is not directly aggressive toward China.

One comfort for China is that during 2007 the nuclear deal did not have an easy political ride in either America or India, as both countries' governments were becoming weaker for other reasons, and their opponents were becoming emboldened. Plenty of left-wing Indians hate the idea of cozying up to Uncle Sam, and plenty of Americans still distrust India enough to object to giving it a free pass on nuclear-weapons testing, on its decision to shun the 1968 Nuclear Non-Proliferation Treaty, or on its relatively friendly relations with Iran, one of America's keenest foes. The Communist parties that in India provide essential parliamentary support for Dr. Singh's Congress Party–led coalition threatened in 2007 to withdraw that support if the nuclear deal were to be implemented. They argue that the deal restricts India's sovereignty too much, by, for example, threatening that America could in the future withdraw its nuclear technology if India were to test another nuclear weapon. Nevertheless, the deal continues to stumble forward.

The Bush administration's desire to give India such an exceptional status—supplying it with nuclear fuel and technology despite it not signing the NPT and despite the fact that under the deal only fourteen of its twenty-two nuclear reactors are to be subject to inspections by the International Atomic Energy Agency—sparked criticism in Europe, too.[4] Would this deal not encourage other budding nuclear powers, who could well conclude from this arrangement that they can expect to avoid long-term punishment if they test weapons? Would it not embolden North Korea, which ratified the NPT in 1985 but withdrew from it in 2003, and Iran, which remains a signatory but is widely believed to have broken its rules? Or Egypt, another American ally that wants to have a nuclear-power program and may feel obliged to extend it to weaponry if Iran does the same? What about Pakistan, the other South Asian nuclear-weapons state that is outside the nonproliferation regime? Wouldn't it have been better to seek a package deal to encompass both nations?

Those are perfectly reasonable questions. The future status of the global nonproliferation regime, the nuclear programs of North Korea and Iran, and policy toward Pakistan will be especially important preoccupations of whomever becomes America's next president in January 2009. But none of these is likely to mean that the new president will repudiate the civil nuclear deal that President Bush has signed with India, nor the wider effort President Bush has made to snuggle closer to America's old cold-war foe. The behavior of North Korea and Iran, and the nuclear tests conducted in 1998 by Pakistan and India, all suggest that the NPT regime was already failing before the India deal was mooted. Some Pakistani generals have threatened a nuclear arms race with India in response to the U.S.-India deal, but Pakistan is likely to remain too beholden to America to risk such a move, unless its government is overthrown by Islamic fundamentalists, in which case the NPT would be the least of the world's worries.

Another concern is that Pakistan might now receive stronger nuclear support from China to balance the American deal with India, but there is no sign of that happening. In any case, a matching China-Pakistan deal would probably be beside the point: Pakistan does not need civil nuclear energy in the way that India does, and the wider significance of the U.S.-India deal will lie in the overall strengthening of America's relationship with India rather than in the specifics of India's nuclear status. The Indian rumor mill has also been spinning with stories that an agreement between China and India's eastern neighbor, Bangladesh, formerly East Pakistan, to help Bangladesh set up a nuclear-power program could lead to weaponry too. Bangladesh's military government confirmed in October 2007 that it plans to go ahead with a nuclear plant, but since it has signed the Non-Proliferation Treaty and the Comprehensive Test Ban Treaty there is no reason why this should lead to nuclear-weapons development. That, however, doesn't stop Indian commentators from speculating about it.[5]

There is bipartisan support in America's Congress for a closer relationship with India, even if the Democrats there have quibbled over the details of the nuclear deal. In the chair of the Senate's Indian-American caucus is none other than Senator Hillary Clinton, which is why when her main opponent for the Democratic presidential nomination, Barack Obama, found that one of his campaign staff had sent out a memo lampooning Senator Clinton for being the member for "D-Punjab," he had to disown it hastily. With more than two million people of Indian origin living in the United States, generally quite prosperously, Indians have become prominent campaign contributors.

In any case, that India and the United States are serious about each other, whatever the domestic politics of the nuclear deal, was shown by another agreement they made in June 2005: a joint "defense framework," which was labeled as envisaging a ten-year program of expansion of the military relationship between America and India. It is likely, for the first time, to lead to arms sales by American defense companies to India, ending a long period of Indian reliance on Russia and France for its most sophisticated weaponry. Writing in May 2007, Robert Blackwill, who was George Bush's ambassador to India in 2001–03, stated that "it is safe to say that the alignment between India and the United States is now an enduring part of the international landscape of the twenty-first century."[6]

Why did George Bush think it was so urgent to establish such an alignment that he was prepared to risk destroying—or at least disrupting—the global nuclear antiproliferation system? You might dismiss it as typical Bush administration recklessness, but for the fact that the stakes in nuclear proliferation are huge, according to President Bush himself. The danger of nuclear materials falling into the hands of terrorists had played a central part in his speeches during his first term, most notoriously the Axis of Evil speech given in his January 2002 State of the Union address, and had also been one of the main justifications given for the invasion of Iraq in 2003. The nonproliferation regime has been one of the main bulwarks against that sort of danger ever since it was set up in the 1960s.

There are two principal explanations. One is that the Bush administration had had so many foreign-policy failures in its first term that by 2005 it was desperate for a success, and India offered an unbeatable feature of being strategically significant while also being a democracy. The other is that, despite the understandable focus after September 11, 2001, on the Middle East and Central Asia, the most important long-term trend in world affairs does indeed remain the shift in economic and political power to Asia. As countless books have put it, China is doing what Napoleon forecast two centuries ago: "shaking the world."[7]

This trend will encompass many presidencies, not just Mr. Bush's, bringing Asia a much greater say in world affairs during the next quarter century and beyond. The most cited long-run forecasters are the economists at Goldman Sachs, owing to their coining the acronym BRICs to denote the future impact of the four big emerging countries, Brazil, Russia, India and China, and the firm's boldness in producing forecasts reaching as far ahead as 2050. They reckon that if it carries on with progrowth policies and manages its economy reasonably well, China could overtake the United States as the world's biggest economy as soon as the late 2020s.[8] By 2050, India might also overtake the United States, if it pursues vigorous economic reforms during the current decade and beyond. Neither China nor India will have average living standards anywhere near as high as those in the United States or Western Europe in 2050, but China's income per head could by then be roughly the same as America's is now.

The Goldman Sachs analysis, which is more or less shared by economists at the World Bank, holds that both China and India can sustain their current rates of annual gross-domestic-product growth of 8–10 percent for a further ten to fifteen years, following which China's growth will slow to still impressive annual rates of 5 percent or so, but India's will carry on at 10 percent or more as its population will still be growing and still be predominantly young. Even over just the next ten to fifteen years, both countries could almost triple their economic output.[9] Such forecasts are plausible, even if the actual dates and figures are bound to be wrong: There are too many uncertainties even over a few years let alone over four decades or more.

Interruptions and discontinuities, such as that experienced by Japan since its financial crash in 1990, can throw out the most well-meaning and most soundly based of long-range predictions.

Even so, the direction is clear: Asia is going to carry on getting richer and stronger, probably for a long time to come. Asian companies are going to become more and more prominent in international business, as competitors for Western ones, as purchasers of Western assets and as sources of new technology. That will be painted as a threat to American and European livelihoods by many politicians, but in truth the effect will be positive, even if the competitive pressure hurts some individual Western companies. The trade and innovation that are generated will make the West richer and stronger, too, just as the rapid postwar growth of Western Europe and Japan helped enrich the United States during the half century that followed. But it will change the relative balance of power in the world. Neither America nor Europe will be able to dominate world affairs in the manner to which they have become accustomed. Asia is going to demand an equal seat at the table.

Even so, this trend is not as simple as it looks. There is no single entity called Asia, one that will in the future demand equality of treatment and influence with America and Europe. Asia is divided. And the process of rapid economic development is going to divide it still further, in political terms. The rise of Asia is not just, or even mainly, going to pit Asia against the West, shifting power from the latter to the former. It is going to pit Asians against Asians. This is the first time in history when there have been three powerful countries in Asia, all at the same time: China, India and Japan. That might not matter if they liked one another, or were somehow naturally compatible. But they do not, and are not. Far from it, in fact.

In the past, one country has always been dominant, either in the region as a whole or in its own part of it. Since 1945, the United States has dominated Asia because of its military presence, its importance as a market and a source of foreign investment, and its close alliance with (some would say, control over) Japan, Asia's richest country and hitherto its only candidate for global power. The rise of China has changed that, especially during the 1990s and the present decade, giving rise to a belief that during the twenty-first century China could eventually emerge to challenge America for global leadership. China's growth has been so relentless, and has so often been described as "awesome" by Western visitors, that it may come to seem as if Asia and China are one and the same—especially during 2008, the year of the Beijing Olympics. Yet they are not. Japan's political and economic sway have declined since its financial crash in 1990, but as chapter 4 will argue there is no reason why that decline should be permanent. And during the past five years a third country has begun to emerge with both the aspirations and the capabilities of exercising regional and even global power: India.

India's emergence, shown by the acceleration of its annual economic growth rate to nearly 10 percent in 2007 and by the rapid expansion of its trade, means that the balance between these three regional powers is going to become the crucial determinant of whether Asia's rise will be one of peace and prosperity or one that brings conflict and turbulence, both to the region itself and to the world as a whole. It also means that, increasingly, the behavior of each of these three countries is being determined by a consciousness of the others' goals, interests, and actions, for Japan, China and India are increasingly looking like actual or potential impediments to one another.

In other words, Asia is becoming an arena of balance-of-power politics, with no clear leader, rather as Europe was during the nineteenth century. China may emerge as the most powerful of the three, but like Britain in the nineteenth century it is unlikely to be capable of dominating its continent. A new power game is under way, in which all must seek to be as friendly as possible to all, for fear of the consequences if they are not, but in which the friendship is only skin-deep. All are maneuvering to strengthen their own positions and maximize their own long-term advantages.

That is what the Bush administration had spotted when it sought to strengthen India and to strengthen America's own alignment with India. It was playing Asia's new power game. It did so in its own interests, of course: A stronger India would usefully limit China's freedom of maneuver in the region, and help to prevent it from using a dominance of Asia to rival America at a global level. Although China is not currently posing any threat to America, the alignment with India may help to discourage it from doing so, or else help defer the day when it does so. A more even balance of Asian power is also, though, in the interests of the rest of the world as well as of Asia itself, for it would stand a chance of keeping the region's natural rivalries under some sort of check. For once, President Bush's unilateral instincts actually served multilateral interests, too, although it would have been better if he had at the same time produced a coherent proposal for how to deal with nuclear weapons proliferation in light of his deal with India—just as it would have been rather better if he had pushed harder for peace between Israel and Palestine at the same time that the U.S. was invading Iraq.

Human affairs never have a sole driver or explanation, and it will be the same in Asia: The new power game between China, Japan and India is not going to shape everything that happens during the next few decades. But it is going to shape an increasing amount of what happens. Indeed, it is already doing so. Once you look at Asia through the prism of this balance-of-power game, many things start to make more sense.

Why, for example, did Japan make India its largest recipient of overseas aid, beginning in 2004? Why did it finance much of the construction costs of the Delhi underground railway system, and why is it planning to repeat that effort for a new freight transport route between Kolkata, Delhi and Mumbai? Like America, Japan wants to strengthen India in order to make Asia more comfortable for Japan's own interests. Why, in 2005, did other Asian countries push for India to be included in a new pan-Asian grouping, the East Asia Summit, despite the fact that it plainly is not situated in East

Asia? Japan, Singapore and Indonesia were the main countries pressing for India's inclusion, with American encouragement, and their
aim was to prevent China from dominating Asia's intergovernmental institutions.

China tried to resist that effort and to keep the East Asia Summit truer to its intended name by limiting it to Southeast Asian
members plus China, Japan and South Korea in Northeast Asia.
But it lost that argument, and so India, along with two other non-
East Asians, Australia and New Zealand, took its place at the inau-
gural summit in Kuala Lumpur in December 2005. Why, on the
other hand, did China block Japan's candidacy for permanent membership in the United Nations Security Council in 2003–04, and
with it India's candidacy, too? The reason was that it did not want
its Asian rivals to gain a global status equivalent to its own.

Why, to take a case from the middle of 2007, did neither India
nor China join the widespread international condemnation of the
military regime in Myanmar, the erstwhile Burma, when it mur-
dered and jailed thousands of Buddhist monks and other dissidents
after they protested against its disastrous rule? India is intensely
proud that it is a democracy, and was brought to independence from
Britain in 1947 by nonviolent campaigns by Mahatma Gandhi of
just the sort that the Burmese monks were attempting. For decades,
it has claimed—sometimes gratingly—to be occupying the moral
high ground in global affairs. Yet it essentially ignored the tragic
events that were taking place just across its border. The reason is
that it is engaged in a contest for influence in Myanmar with that
country's eastern neighbor, China: Both have been investing in
Burmese oil and gas fields, both have been building and repairing
roads, and both have been selling weapons to the military regime.[10]
India felt it could not risk alienating the Burmese military by
protesting about its repression, for fear of encouraging Myanmar to
fall entirely under Chinese control.

Beyond the two former cold war contestants, Russia and America, four countries or entities have serious and fairly advanced pro-

grams designed eventually to send men into space. Why are three of them—Japan, India and China—from Asia? (The other is the European Union's joint program.) In September 2007 Japan launched an unmanned lunar orbiter; the following month, China did the same. India has said that it plans to do so during 2008. In 2003 China proudly became the first Asian country to send a man into orbit around the Earth using its own rocket. All three countries have said they hope to send a manned mission to the Moon at some point during the 2020s. Yet to do so will cost a fortune, and most scientists think manned space flight is an extravagance given how much more can be learned through cheaper and more frequent unmanned missions. For all their recent economic successes, China and India remain among the world's poorest countries, with annual incomes per head of just $2,500 and $800 respectively in 2007, compared with more than $40,000 in the country that pioneered manned space flight, the United States.

Prestige no doubt plays a big part in space exploration, but prestige is also a relative concept: Each of the three countries is doing this because the others are, too. Moreover, all three believe that space will be the next military battleground, and all three believe that to be both safe and powerful they need to develop their own space technology. If either Japan or India had any doubt on that point they will have been convinced by China's shooting down, in January 2007, of one of its satellites orbiting the Earth, in a test or demonstration of its capability to do so. It did so without giving any warning, nor did it offer any explanation afterward.

It would be an exaggeration to say that there is an arms race underway in Asia.[11] But all three of Asia's great powers are strengthening their military forces in ways that suggest that awareness of one another is one of the prime motives. Japan, for example, is limited by its American-imposed post–World War II constitution to maintaining military forces only for self-defense, a stipulation that successive governments have interpreted as meaning that defense spending should be equivalent to no more than 1 percent of GDP

(America spends more than 4 percent of GDP). For the past decade, Japan has been investing in higher and higher military technology—notably surveillance satellites, submarine detection equipment, and advanced warships—rather than expanding the size of its forces. But in 2001 it made another significant change: The law governing the Japan Coast Guard, which stands outside the main defense budget, was revised to permit it to use force to prevent maritime intrusions. Since then the Coastguard has been given a sharply increased budget, which now totals Y187 billion or about $1.65 billion. It has a fleet of eighty-nine armed patrol ships of over 500 tons each, equivalent (according to Richard J. Samuels, an expert on Japan based at the Massachusetts Institute of Technology) to about 65 percent of the total tonnage of China's naval ships. Two of its newest boats are roughly two-thirds the size of a destroyer.[12]

Why has the Japan Coast Guard been expanded in this way? It is not just because of the risk of piracy, or because Japan consists of a large archipelago of islands. It is because the ownership of some of the most distant of those islands is disputed with China, and because naval power is expected by defense planners to be the principal conventional means by which Asia's great powers compete and flex their muscles. A bigger coast guard helps to free up the real navy, the Maritime Self-Defense Force, to range more widely, helping (until November 2007) to refuel American ships in the Indian Ocean and taking part in military exercises with India, America and Singapore in September of that same year.

That point also lies behind India's desire to expand its existing fleet of aircraft carriers, which currently consists of a single vessel, to three ships by 2020, and its desire to upgrade its air force by buying advanced American fighters and surveillance aircraft. In the past, such a program would have been pigeonholed as being driven just by India's longstanding conflict with Pakistan. But that is no longer the sole, or even main, concern for Indian strategists. That position is held by China. The Chinese do not yet return the compliment to

India. But just as India's military budgets can no longer be explained by Pakistan, so the 17.8 percent rise in China's official military budget in 2007 could not be explained in the traditional way as a reflection of China's determination to display overwhelming power to its foes across the Taiwan Straits. China now has larger preoccupations: in space, as already noted; under the sea, with its expanding fleet of submarines; and with its surface fleet. It does not yet have an aircraft carrier. But it has bought two from the former Soviet Union for research and training purposes. And it will be no surprise when it starts to build aircraft carriers of its own.

Such a preoccupation with military hardware should not leave the impression that the thesis of this book is going to be that Asia's great powers are destined for conflict, in the same way as Europe's nineteenth-century balance of power descended into the carnage of the twentieth century's two world wars. Conflict is not inevitable. Indeed, China, India and Japan are not currently showing aggression toward one another. There has been plenty of tension between Japan and China, especially in 2004–06, over their tragic history in the twentieth century and, to a lesser extent, over undersea resources and disputed islands. There has been some tension between India and China, over their own much larger territorial disputes in the Himalayas. But none of that tension has looked like it would provoke a conflict.

Nevertheless, the relationship between China, India and Japan is going to become increasingly difficult during the next decade or more. A whole array of disputes, historical bitternesses and regional flash points surround or weigh on all three countries. Conflict is not inevitable but nor is it inconceivable. If it were to occur—over Taiwan, say, or the Korean peninsula, or Tibet, or Pakistan—it would not simply be an intra-Asian affair. The outside world would inevitably be drawn in, and especially America given that country's extensive military deployments and alliances in Asia. Such a conflict could break out very suddenly, as chapter 8 will show. That is why George Bush's sense of urgency in seeking closer ties with India makes sense: Preparations need to be made well before tensions arise. Managing the relationship between China, India and Japan promises to be one of the most important tasks in global affairs during the next decade and beyond, comparable in importance to the need to find peaceful ways to manage the relationships between Europe's great powers during the twentieth century. The opportunity, in terms both of commerce and of human welfare, is tremendous, if the relationship is handled well. But so is the danger, if the relationship were to go wrong.

Managing this relationship will also be difficult because as both India and China grow and expand their trade and overseas investment, those countries' economic and political interests are going to overlap more and more, with each encroaching increasingly on what the other considers to be its natural backyard. The overlapping of interests is already happening, as China reaches across to Africa through the Indian Ocean for resources and as India reaches across to East Asia, through the Malacca Strait between Indonesia and Malaysia, for markets and commercial partners.

The most basic point, though, is that even without overt hostility, the politicians and strategic planners of all three countries will feel obliged, by their sense of national responsibility and of historic opportunity, to compete for advantage, to prepare for the worst, to build alliances and networks against one another—just in case circumstances change. A senior official at India's Ministry of External Affairs in Delhi, one of the least hostile men possible, put this especially appositely in an interview in March 2007. He said: "The thing you have to understand is that both of us [India and China] think that the future belongs to us. We can't both be right."

The future does, however, belong to Asia. By common consent, this promises to be the Asian century, an era during which the economic rise of the region's two giants, China and India, along with their numerous smaller neighbors in East and Southeast Asia, will lead to a commensurate transfer of political power and intellectual influence away from the West. Those worried about jobs, who agree that *The World Is Flat,* in the book title by Tom Friedman of the *New York Times,* and are not as enamored as he is about globalization, see this process as a threat to American and European living standards that is being posed by all the Asian countries, as factories and offices slide across a flat world to exploit their cheap hands and brains.[13] Those with more of a grand historical bent, such as Niall Ferguson, a British professor at Harvard, see this process as signifying "the descent of the West," the title of the final chapter in his recent history of the twentieth century, a period during which the end of Western dominance of Asia may well, in his view, prove to be that century's most important upheaval.[14]

The common consent is not entirely right, however. Mr. Ferguson's emphasis on the word *dominance* has the merit of fitting the facts, while *descent* does not—at least not on present evidence. The European empires in Asia have all gone. The Japanese empire that sought to emulate them proved short-lived. First Japan; then the four Asian "tigers" of South Korea, Taiwan, Hong Kong and Singapore; then a Southeast Asian cluster of Malaysia, Thailand and Indonesia; then China, then India, then Vietnam—all have succeeded in achieving economic development that has propelled them much higher in the global rankings of nations. Such countries can no longer be bossed about in the way they once were. They can no longer be dominated by outsiders.

On any measure, Asia has become stronger, more important, richer and more impressive. Home to almost half the world's population, including six of its ten largest countries, Asia by 2006–07 accounted for more than a fifth of the world's GDP, almost 30 percent of world exports and a third of its crossborder capital flows.[15] (In these figures, Asia includes everywhere east of Iran but excludes Australia and New Zealand.) The region includes the world's second, fourth, twelfth and thirteenth largest economies, in Japan, China, South Korea and India respectively; and its third, fourth, eleventh, twelfth, fourteenth and seventeenth largest goods and services exporters (in turn China, Japan, Hong Kong, South Korea, Singapore and Taiwan). The two countries holding far and away the largest foreign-exchange reserves in the world are China ($1.4 trillion, as of mid-2007, but rising rapidly) and Japan ($916 billion). There is plenty of room to debate whether it is really beneficial to hold such large reserves, most of which have in effect been lent to the United States through the purchase of U.S. Treasury bonds. But it certainly means that neither country can be held to financial ransom.

Taken as a whole, Asia's income per capita rose sevenfold between 1950 and 2005. Exploiting a world now open for trade in goods and technology, all the Asian success stories have raised their incomes much faster than did America and Britain during their own nineteenth-century take-off periods. It took Britain nearly sixty years to double its per-capita income during its industrial revolution after 1780; America took about fifty years to do the same after 1840. South Korea, Taiwan and China all managed to double their per capita income during merely their first decade of take-off, and have managed to do it again even more rapidly during their second decade.

What is also striking, however, is how far Asia still has to go before it reaches what might reasonably be called its natural position in world affairs. According to Angus Maddison, the greatest living historian of economic data, in 1820 China and India alone accounted for nearly half of world output.[16] After all its success in the past half century, Asia as a whole remains less than halfway back to that relative share, a share that would be roughly proportionate to Asia's share of world population. In fact, the raw statistics suggest that the idea of a "shift of power to Asia" is something of a myth. As the chart shows, between 1990 and 2006, for all the excitement about Chinese and recently Indian growth, the region's share of global GDP has risen merely from 20.6 percent to 22.3 percent, which is hardly spectacular. America's share has actually gone up, from 25.5 percent to 27.5 percent, not down as many gloomy Americans seem to believe. The West has seen no "descent."

This is partly the result of using broad, continental definitions in such figures. The shares of global output held by America and the European Union have been sustained by the decline in the shares accounted for by Latin America, Africa and the Middle East—i.e., the "rest of the world." Those shares were especially depressed until 2002–03 by low world prices for energy and other commodities, many of which are produced in those countries, but prices have since then been rising again, in some cases sharply. Asia's share, which has grown surprisingly little during these sixteen momentous years, disguises a shift within Asia from stagnating Japan to China, India and other fast-growing economies.

There is, however, another reason why no major shift can be found in the statistics:

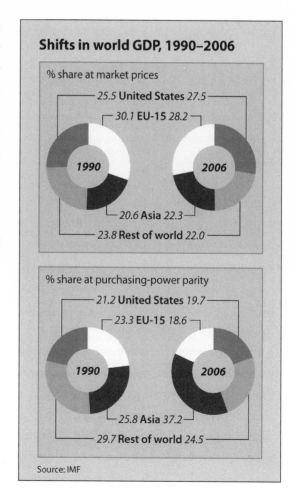

Shifts in world GDP, 1990–2006

% share at market prices

25.5 United States 27.5

30.1 EU-15 28.2

1990   2006

20.6 Asia 22.3

23.8 Rest of world 22.0

% share at purchasing-power parity

21.2 United States 19.7

23.3 EU-15 18.6

1990   2006

25.8 Asia 37.2

29.7 Rest of world 24.5

Source: IMF

It is that the cheap-currency policy followed by China has had the effect of preventing it from happening. The Japanese currency has also been weak or falling in value, mostly by accident but sometimes deliberately. Comparisons of global GDP have to be expressed in a common currency, usually dollars, so the fact that the dollar was generally strong against Asian currencies during the sixteen years in question has tended to restrain the shift in shares of global output. America's Congress has been calling for China to revalue its currency, the renminbi, by at least 27.5 percent against the dollar. Despite a surplus on the current account of its balance of payments of more than 10 percent of GDP, a condition that would normally bring about a currency appreciation, the renminbi had by early 2008 risen in value against the dollar by only 14 percent since the beginning of 2005. The result is that if China were actually to obey Congress' demand, the shift in the global GDP statistics would be dramatic: America's share would fall sharply, while the share of China, and any other Asian countries whose currencies rose alongside the renminbi, would climb.

The distorting effect of currencies can be countered by using a different set of statistics, ones in which the GDP numbers have been adjusted to take account of differences in prices between countries, a process known to economists as purchasing-power parity, or PPP.[17] On PPP measures, as the lower half of the chart shows, Asia's relative size has grown much larger: On the IMF's reckoning, in 2006 Asia made up 37.2 percent of world GDP at PPP, compared with 25.8 percent in 1990. The shares accounted for by the U.S. and the then-fifteen European Union members have dropped from 21.2 percent and 23.2 percent in 1990 to 19.6 percent and 18.6 percent now respectively. That PPP share is much closer to Asia's natural, population-based share. Over the long run, currencies can be expected to move to reflect such price differences, albeit approximately, so in theory Asian currencies should rise in value relative to the dollar and the euro. Thus while the PPP share of 37.2 percent of world GDP in 2006 overstates Asia's global impact at that particular time, it may offer a reasonable indication that the region's impact will become greater.

However the longer they resist the pull of both theory and politics, the more that currency markets have accentuated a bizarre state of affairs in the world economy, one that is being reflected in a new sort of power tussle, one expressed in financial markets and share ownership rather than with guns or navies. Normally you would expect that rich, mature countries, in which economic growth and hence returns on investment had slowed, would accumulate capital and then invest it in faster-growing, poorer, developing countries, in which the returns on investment are higher. In recent years, however, the opposite has been happening: Poor countries' capital has been flowing to America.

The flow was broadly normal during the first half of the 1990s, when the fall of the Soviet Union and the liberalization of economies in Asia, Latin America and Eastern Europe encouraged Western money to move to what by then were called "emerging markets." Returns in those markets were volatile but high. Most did not have enough of their own savings to finance their growth and so were glad to import capital. In 1997–98, however, that process came to grief when East Asia had a financial crisis, led by Thailand, Indonesia and South Korea, and when Russia defaulted on its sovereign debts. Those countries had been importing capital (i.e., borrowing abroad), but on an assumption of rigid exchange rates that proved to be false. When currencies dropped, the debts became unpayable, defaults began and lenders ran scared. Emerging market investment went out of fashion for a while. But also, many of the emerging markets themselves transformed their economic structures, becoming exporters of capital rather than importers of it. Hence the bizarre outcome: Vast pools of capital have since been accumulated in China, Singapore, Malaysia, Taiwan, Russia and the oil producers of the Gulf, and much of it has been lent to or invested in the richest, most advanced country of all, the United States of America. China's current-account surplus of more than 10 percent of GDP has had as its counterpart America's current-account deficit of more than 6 percent of GDP.

This strange state of affairs may not last. Sharp moves in currencies, a financial crisis and recession in America or Europe, slower expansion of trade in Asia, a fall in energy prices: All or some of those could cause the seesaw to swing again, ending or reducing the great torrent of capital that has been flowing from poor to rich. The seizing-up of credit markets in America and Europe in August 2007, the accelerating decline of the dollar, the first nationwide fall in American house prices: These events together suggested that the swing of the seesaw might have begun. Meanwhile, however, a side effect of the capital imbalances has threatened to bring about a clash between American, European and Asian governments. This was the emergence of huge state-controlled funds, partly financed by those foreign-exchange reserves but also financed out of the profits of state-owned companies, all with a mandate to invest in Western companies and stock markets—as well as companies and assets in other developing countries.

These so-called sovereign wealth funds have been seen before: Oil producers began to make similar investments during the oil boom of the 1970s; Libya, for instance, bought a slice of Italy's national car producer, Fiat. Most of all, though, they carry an echo of the controversy that broke out in the late 1980s over Japanese purchases of high-profile assets in America such as Rockefeller Center in New York, the Pebble Beach Golf Links in California, Columbia Pictures in Hollywood and the Firestone tire company in Ohio. Those purchases were demonized as evidence of a Japanese takeover of the United States. But there is a crucial difference: Those acquisitions were by private companies. Even if they were resented and feared (wrongly, as it turned out, since the buyers lost billions on the deals, and the private fears were never shared by government), such companies could at least be assumed to be making their investments for normal capitalistic purposes, namely profit.

Sovereign wealth funds may well be seeking profit, too, but it is not as safe in their case to assume so, nor in the case of purchases by state-owned enterprises. With such state-held entities reasonable suspicions may arise that an investment has a national strategic purpose instead, such as the securing of technology or some security advantage, or is intended to distort a market by controlling a competitor in the same way as a state subsidy may distort competition unfairly. Reasonable suspicions, moreover, have a habit of being exploited by unreasonable protectionists as a tool of national and international politics.

Most of all, investments by sovereign funds will reek of power and influence whenever they bring control of an asset rather than just a minority investment. The ability to purchase and control foreign assets could soon become the most potent symbol yet of the shift of economic and political power to Asia—if it is allowed to occur. The problem in working out a coherent public policy for dealing with sovereign funds is that no one wants to turn away capital, and it is widely accepted that liberal capital markets have played a big part in the world's current period of growth and prosperity. Yet control by one country's state of assets in another may stretch support for liberalism beyond the breaking point. The right approach at a national level will be to set up review procedures for foreign purchases by state-linked entities that involve control rather than being a portfolio investment; and at the international level, probably through the Organization for Economic Cooperation and Development (OECD), a code of practice needs to be agreed on to prevent distortions to competition and retaliation against perceived competitive unfairnesses.

Such purchases, or attempts to purchase, have already made political waves in Europe and America. But if Germans, French or Americans can imagine sinister political motives behind Chinese investments in their countries, just think what would be the reaction if such purchases were to occur inside Asia, inside the three regional powers. Would a Chinese state-owned firm be allowed to buy Nippon Steel, say, or Toshiba? Or a prominent Indian firm? You can bet your bottom renminbi that it would not be. China, India and Japan are rivals. They have good reason to be suspicious and jealous of one another. Sovereign wealth funds capturing assets in one anothers' markets would feel, to many people, like a modern equivalent of invasion or colonization.

Where will it all lead? The West, we already know, can no longer have its own way anything like as easily as it did during the nineteenth and twentieth centuries: Power has become more evenly distributed across the globe. Nor will the West be the only important shaper of global or regional affairs in future: Other countries, including China and India, will also be capable of wielding influence. Indeed, they already are. Africa's new leaning toward China for aid and trade is but one example.

Military power, in which America still holds a huge preeminence, has become less effective now that public opinion in a televisual and Internet age resists war and that nuclear weapons make war between the world's great powers feel unimaginably costly. The "unipolar moment" described by an American neoconservative commentator, Charles Krauthammer, when the fall of the Soviet Union in 1989–91 left America as the lone superpower, will soon be over, if it is not already, and for reasons more fundamental and enduring than America's post-Iraq weakness.[18] That weakness might turn eventually back into strength, just as it did after America's previous debacles in Vietnam and Iran in the 1970s. But rather than American weakness it is a question of rising Asian strength, and the fact that as their strength grows the new Asian powers will all demand a bigger say in world affairs.

The forecasters say that Asian economic strength will continue to rise. Yet whether they are right or wrong, such forecasts anyway miss the most important things. They focus on an apparent outcome, a predicted end point, and one too far ahead to be of much practical use. A more important and immediate point is that economic growth is a process, not a destination, and that to achieve the forecasted outcome requires countries to change dramatically: in social, political, educational, economic and even military and diplomatic terms.

Economic growth at a pace that doubles an economy's size every seven or eight years is not a process that simply requires a country to maintain a steady course and a constant pressure on the accelerator. It is a process that requires a country to maintain itself in a constant state of radical transformation. In business, people have become used to talking enthusiastically about "disruptive technologies." Asia is going to be full of disruptive transformations. They are already disrupting the world, causing anxiety about jobs from the American Midwest to the Italian Mezzogiorno. But they are also going to disrupt Asia itself, and all the countries within it, as well as all those countries' relationships with one another. That process of internal Asian disruption could prove to be the most earthshaking of all.

Imagine, if you can, how different China is today from the country that existed at the time of the Tiananmen Square protests and massacre in 1989. Chiefly, it is different physically, in terms of the size, number and appearance of its cities, its roads, its ports, its airports, in terms of the quality of the clothes people wear and the material things they possess. The most visible change in Tiananmen Square, or at least the neighboring roads, is the replacement of the then-ubiquitous bicycle by the now-ubiquitous and polluting motor car. China is also very different, though, in terms of the education of its children or at least of its elites' children, now that many have been sent abroad, chiefly to Western countries, for part of their schooling or their university education. That was barely possible before Deng Xiaoping came to power in 1978, but in the twenty-five years to 2003 more than 700,000 Chinese were educated abroad; now more than 130,000 are studying abroad at any given time. The eighteen years since Tiananmen have also transformed the air that the Chinese breathe and the water they drink, making it much, much dirtier. They have transformed the structure of economic life, as between state-owned enterprises and private ones, between public provision of services such as health and education and private provision, between companies listed on stock exchanges and those held privately, making China much more capitalist and privately owned than before. But they have also made the country much more unequal between the rich and the poor, between the rural areas and the urban ones.

China today is utterly different from the China of two decades ago. China in ten, fifteen or twenty years' time is going to be utterly different once again. If it isn't, it will not have been able to achieve the sort of sustained rates of economic growth that are currently expected of it. A similar process of change can be expected in India— if it succeeds in sustaining rapid economic growth.

Rather than projecting ahead to see what might be the raw economic rankings between the nations in 2020 or 2050, the more important questions to ask are about the process that these rapidly developing Asian countries will experience: How might the countries have to change to realize the futures that are expected of them? How smooth is that process of change likely to be? What sort of effects are these internal changes likely to have on the country's relations with its neighbors, with others in Asia, on regional politics and economics as a whole and on the rest of the world?

Those changes, those pressures, those reactions are what this book will attempt to chart and, to a degree, to predict. How might the experience of growth, the awareness of increased strength, the probable new pressures from domestic public opinion affect how India, China and Japan view one another, and how each of them views the West? What might be the implications for Asia's hottest spots, in Taiwan, the Korean peninsula, Kashmir and others, all of which will be affected by the transformations underway, by any domestic political instability and by the rivalry between these three?

How will these disruptive transformations affect the planet as a whole, given (almost) everyone's worries about climate change, natural resources and the rising demand from Asia's new giants for everything that can be grown on the soil or dug up from below? Meanwhile Asia's two giant onlookers, Russia and the United States, will be buffeted by these changes and will be seeking all the while to influence them. Amid all this disruptive transformation, Asia is being created, before our eyes. So is the twenty-first-century world.

2. **A CONTINENT CREATED**

POLITICS WILL SHAPE TOMORROW'S ASIA, an Asia of great-power rivalry, of suspicion and of strategic maneuvering, the beginnings of which can already be seen. Today's Asia has been shaped by economics, and it is an Asia of increasing prosperity, of interdependence and of global financial influence. This is the first time since the Mongol Empire established by Genghis Khan in the thirteenth century that Asia has become truly interconnected across the 6,000 kilometers (4,000 miles) that separate Japan in the east from India in the west, or even as far as Iran (8,000 kilometers, 5,000 miles). Economics, rather than nomadic horsemen, is the force that is now turning Asia into a coherent entity, and it consists of more than simply the long-haul aircraft, the mobile phones and the Internet that are connecting the whole world. The commercial links that are emerging inside Asia are producing the deepest and most extensive integration that Asia has ever seen. They are bringing about the very creation of Asia. They are, in effect, creating a new continent.

That may seem a rather odd thing to say. Asia is not new. Trading links have connected the countries at Asia's extremes before, whether along the so-called silk road carrying goods and travelers from China, through India and Afghanistan and the rest of central Asia into the Arab, African and European worlds for more than 2,000 years, or through the region's network of trading ports, or via the merchant ships that were exploring not just the region but the globe at the same time as or even before their European counterparts in the fifteenth and sixteenth centuries. Links even between countries as far apart as India and Japan have existed for more than a millennium, with Buddhism having traveled to Japan from India via China and Korea. Some of the older Japanese temples contain outstanding Sanskrit archives, and have statues and other iconography that are based directly on Hindu gods and goddesses, and on Chinese ones, too. One of the most famous Japanese camera brands, Canon, is living evidence of this legacy. It was named by its founder in the 1930s after the Buddhist bodhisattva of compassion, Kwannon, a name derived from the Chinese Guanyin, which in turn is based on the bodhisattva Avalokitesvara from India. Tibetan Buddhists believe that their spiritual leader, the Dalai Lama, is a reincarnation of that same bodhisattva, or enlightened being.

Asia's history was, it is true, distorted by more than two centuries of European colonial empires. For centuries before then, China had been Asia's centerpiece, its hegemon, to use a favorite modern Chinese term albeit borrowed from Greek, though only of Asia east of the Himalayas; India, especially under the Moghuls after the sixteenth century, was the dominant power on the other side of that mountain range. Older Chinese parlance referred to China as the "middle country," often reworded as "middle kingdom," given that the country that saw itself as at the center of things was run by an imperial government and deployed a tribute system, with other Asian countries expected to act as vassal states, paying regular tribute to the Chinese emperor and with their leaders even expected to visit China for their status and titles to be affirmed. In China's large immediate neighborhood only Japan (except briefly in the fifteenth century) refused to pay this tribute.

The crumbling of China's Qing Dynasty in the nineteenth century opened the way to the domination of Asia by the European colonial powers, with Britain in the lead. Entrenched in India since the early eighteenth century, Britain sought to control Asia using naval power from its strategic positions in India, Hong Kong and Singapore, and to gain access to China's trade by means of port enclaves extracted from Chinese control. That imperial control united Asia in a strategic sense but divided its main nations into colonial fiefs held principally by Britain, France, Portugal and the Netherlands. What imperialism eventually did, however, was to produce the first flowering of pan-Asianist ideas, chiefly in Japan, from the mid-1880s onward, as it became the first non-Western nation to modernize. That pan-Asianism was defined by its opposition to Western colonialism: What united Asians, in the minds of the intellectuals who fostered this body of ideas, was their desire to be free of European oppression. Kakuzo Okakura, an influential Japanese artist and scholar, published a book in English called *The Ideals of the East* as the century began. The opening sentence is, "Asia is one."[1] He went on:

> The Himalayas divide, only to accentuate, two mighty civilizations, the Chinese with its communism of Confucius, and the Indian with its individualism of the Vedas. But not even the snowy barriers can interrupt for one moment that broad expanse of love for the Ultimate and Universal, which is the common thought-inheritance of every Asiatic race.[2]

Okakura believed that Europeans were interested only in material things rather than spiritual ones, in the means rather than the end of life. Beyond their unity in spiritualism, however, Asia was unified, in Okakura's view, chiefly by being colonized, by being humiliated and by failing to achieve its own form of modernization.

Rabindranath Tagore, a Bengali poet who in 1913 became Asia's first Nobel laureate and as a result an instant Asian celebrity, had become a friend of Okakura's when the Japanese scholar visited India in 1901. Tagore developed ideas along similar lines. In 1916 he paid a visit to Japan to study Asia's only successfully modernizing power. Tagore disliked what he saw as the homogenizing urban materialism of the West, taking root in Japan. Like Okakura, he was concerned that Japan might emulate Western imperialists and materialists rather than using its Asian spiritual heritage to improve on the West. Stephen Hay, in *Asian Ideas of East and West: Tagore and His Critics in Japan, China and India,* reports that in Tagore's lecture in 1916 at the Tokyo Imperial University, to an estimated 2,000 listeners, he presented a colorful sight:

> Robed in white, his flowing grey beard carefully combed, wearing the tall Taoist cap which Okakura had given him (no doubt as a symbol of Asian unity), . . . the poet made a splendid picture. In his high, melodious voice he began to intone his lecture, "The Message of India to Japan." He spoke as usual in English, but apparently without an interpreter. This must have added to the mystification of his audience, only a fraction of whom were able to understand his words.[3]

Nevertheless, Tagore's lecture was published in full in translation in the main Tokyo newspapers the following day. But it did not go down well. Tagore's attacks on materialism, on nationalism and on the use of power for imperialism in Asia went completely against the Japanese grain, which was bent on fostering all three of those isms. He was widely dismissed as being "the beautiful flower of a ruined country." What, in other words, did proud, independent Japan have to learn from a visitor from a country that had already been oppressed by Britain for more than a century?

Not surprisingly, Tagore's ideas about Asian unity went down a bit better in what was then another ruined country, China. But Stephen Hay reports that when Tagore toured China in 1924 the response was still lukewarm: His emphasis on spiritualism as the essence of Asianness was taken as a recipe for weakness rather than strength, and Chinese intellectuals took a dim view of the notion that Indian philosophy had much relevance to China.

Sun Yat-sen, the first provisional president of China following the republican revolution that in 1911–12 overthrew the Qing Dynasty, was also firmly Sinocentric but promoted a similar idea of pan-Asianism in a speech delivered in Kobe, Japan in November 1924, the same year that Tagore visited China. Like many in Asia, Sun Yat-sen had taken heart from Japan's defeat of Russia in 1904–05, the first time in which an Asian country had succeeded in defeating one of the Western imperialist powers, indeed one of those that had been engaged in occupying part of northeast China. Sun Yat-sen argued in his speech that the essential difference between occidental and oriental civilizations was that in Europe a cult of force had emerged from that continent's scientific materialism, bringing about "the rule of Might"; in the Orient a superior civilization prevailed, one based on "benevolence, justice and morality," or, as he also put it, "the rule of Right."[4] It was a neat reminder of the essential hypocrisy of the European (and American) colonialists, contrary to all their claims to be civilizing influences and to be carrying "the white man's burden."

On this view, pan-Asianism represented "the cause of the oppressed Asiatic peoples" and their desire to restore morality, rather than force, as their ruling principle. But Dr. Sun's chief concern at that time, which was the reason why he gave the speech in Japan, was whether Japan itself was going to become a Western-style oppressor, following the rule of Might, as many of its actions during the previous two decades—including the colonization of Korea and Taiwan, and the assumption of German and Russian colonial rights in China—suggested it would. Alternatively, he said, Japan could be "the tower of strength of the Orient," pursuing the rule of Right.

Japan did not follow Sun Yat-sen's advice. The history of the 1930s and 1940s was a history of a divided Asia, not a united one.

Japan chose to follow the rule of Might, even though some Japanese intellectuals continued to cloak their country's imperial actions in quite Utopian, pan-Asianist language, such as that of the "greater East Asia co-prosperity sphere." With Japan's defeat in 1945 and the beginning of the end of European empires in Asia—though the imperial death rattle continued to sound for two more decades—the pan-Asianist idea returned, again in an Indian form. Jawaharlal Nehru, India's first prime minister, held the Asian Relations Conference in Delhi in March 1947, even before India had become formally independent of colonial power. He wanted the countries of Asia to see one another as friends or even relatives, now that they were becoming free again.

Once again, it didn't happen. One reason was political. China was then fighting a civil war, but in any case neither Mao Zedong's Communists nor Chiang Kai-Shek's Kuomintang nationalists wanted India to take the lead in Asia: That was China's rightful role, in their view. After the Communist victory in 1949, that political reason turned ideological, too: Mao was interested more in exporting revolution, both for its own sake and as a tool of Chinese power, than in fostering Asian unity, with China supporting insurgent Communist parties all over the region. Rows between China and India, in the formidable personal forms of Nehru and Mao's prime minister, Zhou Enlai, disrupted attempts in the 1950s to repeat the 1947 conference and to foster Asian cooperation. The two even fought a border war in 1962, which humiliated India and left a legacy of bitterness and suspicion that still endures.

Another reason, though, was economic, albeit with a political underpinning. It was that both of Asia's demographic and territorial giants chose to close their economies to trade until the 1980s and '90s. For different reasons, they wanted to exclude (or, in India's case, limit) outside influences. But they shared an economic ideology that turned out to be ruinous: that central planning, within a closed and controlled economy, would be the best route to economic development. The region's one existing economic giant, Japan, did open itself to trade. But until the 1980s, its trade was overwhelmingly with America and Western Europe, the world's richest markets, rather than with poor Asia. Economic exchanges in turn shape the extent of cultural interplay and the movement of people for tourism, study, migration or other purposes. Since those exchanges were limited or even declining, Asia did not really exist during the first few postwar, and postcolonial, decades.

There is, however, a further, more fundamental point. Despite the dreams of the pan-Asianists, Asia itself has historically been indifferent as to its own existence. Taken as a cartographical whole, Asia has in reality always been a Western, or European concept, not an idea born or fostered in the region itself. Asia was an idea created in classical Greece, one that was used to refer to everything to the east of that country, the direction from which the sun rises. The Greek notion that the world consisted of three continents, Europe, Africa and Asia, led to the definition of Asia that persists today, with a dividing line between Europe and Asia that runs through the Bosphorus at Istanbul, the Black Sea and the Ural Mountains to the north, and through Suez and the Red Sea to the south. It was thus a negative definition, not a positive one.

As such, Asia makes no particular ethnic or racial sense, for there is as much or as little connecting together the peoples of Japan and Asian Turkey (i.e., east of the Bosphorus) as there is the peoples of China and France. Nor does it make any linguistic sense: Many European languages claim stronger ties to India than Indian languages do to Korean or Japanese. Politically, only in the Mongols can be found a thread that has tied the whole of Asia together, because of the success of Genghis Khan and his descendants in conquering and maintaining a thirteenth-century empire that spread from Georgia and Persia in the west to China and part of eastern Russia. Even the Mongols failed to bring Japan under their sway, however: It was a typhoon known as the kamikaze, or divine wind, that thwarted their attempted invasion of Japan in 1281 and gave its name to suicide pilots seven centuries later. But they did provide a later form of Asian continuity for India when in the sixteenth-century Muslim rulers descended from Genghis Khan took control of that subcontinent, forming what came to be known for three further centuries as Moghul or Mughal India: *Moghul* was the Persian word for *Mongol.*

Even so, Asia, taken in full, has largely been meaningless to most Asians. It has just been a convention, a choice imposed by European cartographers and reinforced by scholars and political taxonomists. The word is at least preferable to *Far East, Middle East* and *Near East,* which all define areas entirely by reference to Europe. But the still widespread use of those terms reveals the lack of any other definition.

A set of countries arranged around two large oceans, Asia has no clear boundaries, no obvious beginning, middle and end, and no obvious divisions according even to the points of the compass. The American continent, by contrast, is clearly delineated, and pretty much everyone knows what is meant, respectively, by North, South and Central America. Europe prompts a bit more debate and ambiguity, due to the sheer breadth of its landmass and to the classical division between Europe and Asia: Europeans and Turks are currently divided over whether Turkey can be considered part of Europe, as a matter of geography, of religion and, most important, of future membership of the European Union. But there is little doubt over what is meant by Western, Central and Eastern Europe, though the line between the latter two was distorted by the forty-year divide between the Soviet and capitalist countries during the cold war. Asia has no such neat divides or certainties.

What most Europeans and Americans currently think of as Asia is better described as East Asia: a huge area encompassing China, the Korean peninsula and Japan to the north; Indonesia and Papua, New Guinea, to the south; with those two groups of countries enveloping Malaysia, Singapore, the Philippines, Thailand and the nations of Indochina. Much of that region is farther south than the area generally known as South Asia: the Indian subcontinent, Pakistan, Sri Lanka, Bangladesh, Nepal and Bhutan, all of which are well north of the equator.

Cartographers include the Arabian peninsula, the eastern Mediterranean extending up to Turkey, and all the troubled countries in that area (Iraq, Syria, Israel, Lebanon, Jordan, Saudi Arabia, the Gulf states, Iran) as the westernmost part of Asia, but only Indians today seem commonly to refer to it as West Asia, no doubt as a postcolonial rejection of the Europeanist term *Middle East*. And Central Asia, generally recognized as the six "stans" caught between the Caspian Sea, Russia and China (i.e., Afghanistan, Turkmenistan, Kyrgyzstan, Kazakhstan, Uzbekistan and Tajikistan), is very far from being central to Asia itself. That is, no doubt, because of the vast geographical and political presence of China.

In the region itself, uses of the term *Asia* have rarely been truly continental, even in modern times, when new modes of transport and communication have connected together places that previously felt far apart. For example, when Singaporean and Malaysian political leaders claimed in the mid-1990s, in an echo of the pan-Asianists and of Dr. Sun Yat-sen, to have identified a set of "Asian values" about which they began to brag, values that put a lower premium than Western ones did on human rights and democracy but that nevertheless were making many Asians richer, their Asian values were derived from China's Confucian tradition, and so were strictly East Asian. Even such hubristic people as Singapore's Lee Kuan Yew and Malaysia's Mahathir Mohamad thus had no intention of including the world's most populous democracy, India, in their idea of Asia and of those shared values; nor did they wish to imply that the Wahhabi clerics of Saudi Arabia shared their values, even though for Dr. Mahathir the Saudis are fellow Muslims—and technically they are Asians, too.

Way back in 1947, when Nehru held his Asian Relations Conference in Delhi, the Arab countries were indeed represented. But since then few Arabs, whether leaders or led, have thought of themselves as Asians. The Arab League is their organization, not any pan-Asian body, since their sense of Arabhood stretches from the Arabian peninsula right across into North Africa. The Asian Development Bank, a lending institution with a mandate to assist national and regional economic development, has no members from the Arab world. Perhaps inevitably, virtually the only organizations that reflect the full geographical definition of Asia are sporting ones: the Asian Games (which in 2006 was held in the Gulf state of Qatar) or the Asian Cup for soccer. In sport, the more teams the better, especially for the sale of television rights and sponsorship. That also explains why Israel has taken part in the Eurovision song contest, despite being counted by cartographers as being in Asia.

This is more than just a semantic point. Asia has been not so much a continent as an array of subcontinents, or subregions, dotted across thousands of miles of ocean and land, whether in the minds of its residents, of military strategists, of economists, of international relations scholars or of Asia's own politicians. That fragmentation owed a lot to geographical reality but also to culture. The Chinese language, art and culture have played a powerful pannational role, but that role has been felt in Korea, Japan, Indochina and parts of Southeast Asia, rather than across the whole of Asia. Asia has never had a single dominant religion to serve as a unifier in the European manner: Buddhism can be counted as the world's first pannational religion, for it was the first to spread beyond the society within which it was created, but today it is not the dominant faith in any of the region's larger countries, and across the region it sits alongside Islam, Hinduism, Christianity and many other faiths. If Asia is unified by religion it is by religious tolerance, by the way in which religions have coexisted and even influenced one another in the region. That is an admirable characteristic, but it is not a unifying one.

Some would say that Asia does now have a unifying religion: money. A better way to put it would be that the continent's unifying religion is economic development and the accompanying reduction of poverty. For, first and foremost, Asia has in recent decades become united—or, rather, more united than ever before—by an ambition and an achievement: the ambition of economic development and the fact that so many countries in the region have been achieving that ambition. It has become united, in other words, by the very thing that Rabindranath Tagore hoped to unite it against.

Asia has become known as the region containing the world's fastest-growing economies, a batch of newly affluent countries with China now at their center. But rather than arriving all at once, this affluence and growth has spread in phases to a steadily larger group of countries, while that expanding group of successful countries has shared some of the same broad features and policies. In simplified form, those features could be summarized as follows: a substantial (but not complete) openness to trade, especially of manufactured goods and components; rising domestic savings to finance a high and rising level of investment; some guiding role for government, but amid highly competitive domestic markets; political and social stability; and an emphasis on education. There have been many differences between Asia's development successes, but those features have been shared.

Another common feature may be the role and attitude of the elites in these countries. Kishore Mahbubani, formerly a senior Singaporean diplomat and now a prominent writer about Asia and its emergence, suggests that the developmental success of many countries in the region can be ascribed to the fact that their elites have typically been "productive" rather than "parasitic": they may have been authoritarian and in many ways self-centered, but they have seen their interests and that of their societies as being mutually reinforcing rather than in contradiction.[5] The implicit contrast is with elites in many African and Latin American countries. Corruption has been seen everywhere in Asia, but it has been prevented by these productive elites from overwhelming the basic thrust of economic growth and from provoking social conflict. In some countries, such as Bangladesh and Pakistan, perhaps it still does. In India, it may be that the balance between parasitic and productive elites has finally tipped in the productive direction.

This analysis is perceptive but has the drawback of being somewhat circular: essentially it says that countries prospered because their elites pursued good policies, in the national interest, rather than bad ones, in their own interest. But why did they? As long as the group of success stories remained small, it was possible to find a common cultural explanation: Confucianism, or the ancient Chinese philosophy that assigned moral responsibilities to state officials and other rulers, rather than simply rights and powers, and that recommended the use of meritocracy to select and promote bureaucrats. That Chinese heritage—the "Asian values" promoted by Mr. Mahbubani's former boss, Lee Kuan Yew, and Malaysia's Dr. Mahathir in the 1990s—is shared most clearly by Japan, South Korea, Taiwan, Hong Kong and Singapore: the first development successes. Now, as success spreads, it is harder to find such a cultural explanation.

The prime features of Asian economic growth were pioneered by Japan in the late nineteenth century. Having been a deliberately closed society and economy for more than two centuries under the Tokugawa shogunate, after 1866–68, when the shogunate fell and imperial rule was restored, Japan opened itself up to foreign trade, investment, technology and ideas, and invested public money in a national education system. "Rich country, strong army" was the modernizers' slogan.[6] And the pattern of Japanese growth in that period bears many comparisons with that of China after 1978, once it, too, ended its isolation and sought capitalist economic development, especially in terms of the roles given to foreign investment, to a smooth relationship with the then-established superpower of Great Britain, and to the development of big industrial and trading conglomerates.

That phase of Japanese development yielded wars with China (1894–95) and Russia (1904–05), and the colonization of Taiwan (1895), Korea (1910) and Manchuria (1931), culminating in the devastating wars in China and the Pacific in 1937–45. No wonder, looking at Japan and at its contemporaneous rising power, Germany, in the late nineteenth century, many people conclude that when new powers emerge, conflict inevitably follows. Such a view might suggest that China is also destined for overseas military adventures and consequently for conflict with established powers as it gains in strength and ambition. But that parallel would be simplistic and almost certainly wrong.

The circumstances today, both external and domestic, are different. The age of empires, so rampant in the late nineteenth century and so influential on Japan's thinking about its hoped-for great-power status, is long over; and world markets are pretty open and efficient, so natural resources can be bought for money rather than sought by military means as in Japan's twentieth-century case. The risks and costs of conflict are higher now, and the benefits fewer. What should, however, be drawn from this analogy is how early in the process of modernization and of a rise in global status today's China still is. If 1978 is taken as a starting point comparable with 1866, then China's three decades of change by 2007–08 take it only to the equivalent of Japan in the mid-1890s. Time, with today's open markets and technological progress, may now be thought to move faster, in the developmental sense. But just as Japan did then, China is now sizing up its chances of becoming a true global power and trying to decide what might be necessary, in today's and tomorrow's circumstances, for it to become one. And just as for Japan then, the first priority for China now is domestic economic development: rich country first, strong army later.

When Japan rebuilt itself after its defeat in 1945 and occupation by America in 1945–52, it followed an amended version of the economic model that had previously brought it success. Trade, and in particular the exploitation of rapidly growing and liberalizing markets in Western Europe and the United States, continued to be important ingredients of Japanese growth, but investment by foreign companies was given a more limited role. Technology was imported through licensing, but management control was kept for Japanese companies. Capital, being scarce for at least the first decade of Japan's postwar recovery, was allocated by the government and through the banking system rather than through open capital markets. As before, the state played an important guiding role, even if the emperor was now playing much less of one: Public spending was kept low, but state influence, through licensing, finance, regulation and coordination was nevertheless important.

The Japanese currency, the yen, had a fixed exchange rate as part of the postwar system of currencies known as Bretton Woods, under which all were tied to the dollar, which in turn was backed by gold. During the 1960s, that combination of a fixed exchange rate, regulated capital markets and state involvement in credit allocation helped to drive investment to higher and higher shares of GDP, reaching a peak of nearly 40 percent by the end of the decade. By way of comparison, in America in 1970 investment accounted for a mere 18 percent of GDP. Like China now, Japan was an awesome and extraordinary anomaly in the world economy of that time.

It was ceasing, however, to become an anomaly in terms of its success and trajectory. Rapid economic development spread to South Korea, Hong Kong, Taiwan and Singapore in the 1960s and '70s; then to Thailand, Malaysia and Indonesia in Southeast Asia; and, in the 1980s, to China. The economies in the region that have enjoyed the most sustained periods of economic growth have shared, with Japan, the characteristic of high levels of investment as a share of GDP (now 45 percent in China's case), and a strong reliance on export growth. Some countries, notably South Korea and Taiwan, also imposed restrictions on foreign multinationals and have given the state a big role in guiding the country's often infant industries.

Hong Kong and Singapore, however, have relied much more on foreign investment and less on state guidance, though in Singapore state ownership was, and remains, quite high. Foreign investment has also been important in Southeast Asia's rapid developers, such as Malaysia, Thailand and more recently Vietnam. Until the mid-1990s, most used capital controls and a fixed exchange rate, just as Japan had done, but then a hasty liberalization to encourage capital inflows led to a boom, devaluations and a debt-laden bust in the 1997–98 East Asian financial crisis that was described in chapter 1.

China, though, has blended the pre- and postwar Japanese models: It retains capital controls and a tightly managed exchange rate, but encourages foreign direct investment and, at least since entering the World Trade Organization in 2001, has opened its economy to trade much more than Japan did in its early decades of postwar development. China's growth path was thus not, despite the claims of some enthusiasts, unprecedented either in terms of policy or of speed of achievement.

Now that it is possible to look back at the past half century, this process by which economic development spread to a wider group of countries appears quite natural, orderly and even inevitable. It has become known as the "flying geese" pattern, an idea first developed by a Japanese economist, Kaname Akamatsu, in the 1930s and then revived in articles in 1961 and 1962.[7] Under this theory, Japan was the lead goose, pioneering export-led industrial development; but as costs and living standards rose in Japan, so some lower-value and lower-technology industries would be moved to other countries, who would then fly in formation behind Japan rather like geese, passing industries on to one another in turn. In its initial form in the 1930s, the flying geese model gave a benign pan-Asianist backing to Japan's imperialist expansion toward a "Greater East Asia Co-Prosperity Sphere." By 1962 it had lost its imperialist trappings. Mr. Akamatsu was by the 1960s both more optimistic and more prescient than Gunnar Myrdal, a Swedish Nobel Prize–winning economist who wrote in his *Asian Drama* that Asian countries were

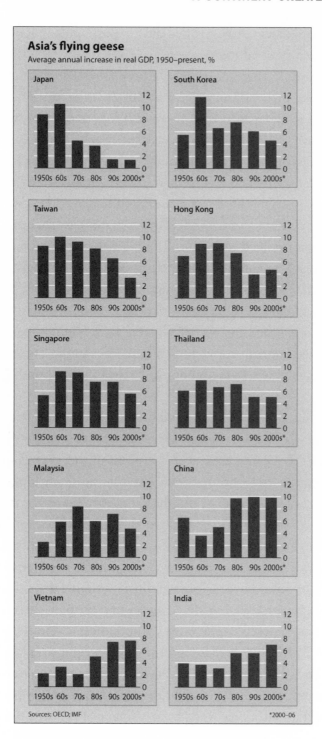

Asia's flying geese
Average annual increase in real GDP, 1950–present, %

Japan, South Korea, Taiwan, Hong Kong, Singapore, Thailand, Malaysia, China, Vietnam, India

Sources: OECD; IMF

*2000–06

doomed to remain impoverished due to overpopulation, inadequate savings and poor education.[8]

It has not, however, generally been obvious which countries would take their places as geese in this Asian formation. In 1960, by which time Japan was strongly flapping its postwar wings, few would have chosen South Korea as a likely and imminent follower, even though it had been a Japanese colony in the first half of the twentieth century and is Japan's nearest neighbor. South Korea was then barely seven years beyond the ceasefire that had ended the Korean War without a peace treaty; it was as poor as Ghana or Sudan, and even considered economically weaker than its Stalinist enemies in North Korea; and its capital city, Seoul, was beset with violent demonstrations. Now it is far richer than those troubled African nations. For follow it did, during that very decade, under the dictatorship established in 1961 by General Park Chung-hee, due to a determined effort to copy much of Japan's example. So, from similarly unfavorable starting points, did Taiwan, Singapore and Hong Kong.

In 1993, the World Bank published what became a landmark study of East Asian economic development, called *The East Asian Miracle,* to track and explain the motions of these geese, but it excluded China from the analysis. That exclusion now looks bizarre. In a sequel to that study published in 2007, called *An East Asian Renaissance,* the authors explained that China had not been included in the 1993 study "because the transition experience there was considered sui generis." The Tiananmen massacre that took place in 1989 may have had some influence on that decision, though the authors are too diplomatic to say so, and the political balance inside China between conservatives and economic reformers looked uncertain until Deng Xiaoping threw his weight publicly behind reform on a tour of Southern China in 1992. In the new study, China takes center stage, even though the "renaissance" in the book's title refers to East Asia's recovery from a financial crisis in 1997–98 in which China played no direct part. But now, the study says, "China is the biggest development story in the world today and a major economic presence in the region, representing one-half of developing East Asia's GDP and one-third of its exports."

This latest judgment is surely sound. China and Japan, as Asia's two biggest economies, biggest import markets and biggest exporters of capital, are now, in their different ways, both central to the region's economic evolution. The geese, if they are in a formation, have more than one leader. But might another country now be notable for its exclusion from the World Bank's new study? That country is Asia's other big development story, India, which receives barely a mention in the 2007 book. Like China's in 1993, India's experience is presumably considered to be sui generis.

That is understandable, given the very different structure of India's economy to that of the typical East Asian countries and its relative lack of participation in East Asia's trading network. Whereas in China in 2003 industrial output (including both mining and manufacturing) accounted for more than 50 percent of GDP and services for only a little more than 30 percent, in India it was the other way around, with services providing about 55 percent of output and industry less than 30 percent. Trade, too, has played a smaller role in India than in China, with exports and imports being equivalent to about 35 percent of GDP in India in 2003, compared with 66 percent in China.

To borrow the language cited earlier from Kishore Mahbubani, the Singaporean diplomat, India could also be said to have had a parasitic elite during its first three or four decades of independence, rather than a productive one: It produced some rich people and companies, but the nation as a whole grew painfully slowly. That changed with liberalization led by Rajiv Gandhi in the 1980s and then, from 1991, by Narasimha Rao and his finance minister Manmohan Singh, who became India's prime minister himself in 2004. This elite has no Confucian heritage, but it has become a more productive one. Even so, from 1991 until 2003 the share of investment in GDP refused to take off, ranging between 23 percent and 27 percent, far below "East Asian" levels. India became famous worldwide for information technology and for the outsourcing of business services, not for manufacturing. The world is flat, as Tom Friedman noted, but for India it has seemed flat for the outsourcing of services, not for goods. Even if India has been growing, it has not seemed to fit the East Asian pattern.

Yet this may now be changing. In 2003–06, as the chart shows, investment shot up to 34 percent of GDP in India. Manufacturing output began to grow faster even than IT and business services. The overall economic growth rate rose from the annual 5–7 percent typical in the 1990s to more than 9 percent in 2006 and 2007, years in which manufacturing output grew by more than 12 percent. Trade has risen well beyond the equivalent of 40 percent of GDP. It

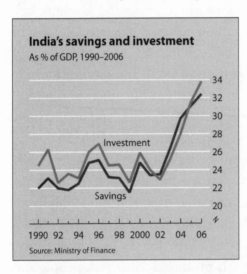

India's savings and investment
As % of GDP, 1990–2006

Investment

Savings

34
32
30
28
26
24
22
20

1990 92 94 96 98 2000 02 04 06
Source: Ministry of Finance

is still early, but India is looking more "East Asian" all the time, and could be about to pass through an economic evolution similar to the one that China passed through during the 1990s, albeit with a more freely floating currency and with looser capital controls. If the World Bank should publish another sequel to its 1993 study of Asian economies in a decade's time, it may then have to explain why India was previously omitted.

Because of the flight of all those geese, and especially because of China's increasing openness to both trade and foreign investment, the commercial links between Asia's culturally and politically diverse and geographically dispersed countries have become remarkably close. Multinational companies, both Asian and Western, are coming to treat the region as a single economic space, at least as far as production is concerned. It is nowhere near being a single market, but it has become a tightly connected pannational supply chain.

If you include Australia and New Zealand as part of Asia (as those countries would prefer you to) but exclude the Middle East (as geographers consider part of Asia but economists don't), then in 2005 according to the World Trade Organization more than 51 percent of all Asian merchandise exports went to other Asian countries. (Excluding Australia and New Zealand lowers the figure to 48.4 percent.) The proportion has risen by nine percentage points since 1990 and is heading toward the level of economic integration (55.8 percent) found in North America between the United States, Canada and Mexico. Those three countries share long land borders, however, with many cities in proximity to one another, so economic integration should come more naturally than in Asia. Both regions are less integrated than the European Union (two-thirds of its trade was between its twenty-five members in 2005). But unlike both the EU and North America, Asia lacks a single free-trade area or a customs union. If it were to achieve such a regional free-trade agreement, and if Indian manufacturing now becomes connected to the production network that has developed in East Asia, Asia would become much more integrated still.

Asia is thus becoming more like Europe in the way in which its economies are integrated with one another. It is also becoming more like Europe in the way in which its biggest countries' interests—both political and economic—are spreading across the continent and overlapping one another. But it has little of something Europe now has in abundance: unifying regional institutions, through which countries can settle disputes, build confidence in one another and agree on common rules and approaches for activities such as trade, investment, policing, the environment and, most critically, security.

Europe has the European Union (EU), which now contains twenty-seven member countries, and it has the North Atlantic Treaty Organization (NATO), which puts twenty-four European countries (including Turkey) in a collective security alliance along with Canada and the United States. It also has the looser but useful Organization for Security and Co-operation in Europe (OSCE), which is a regional security grouping of fifty-six countries spanning Europe, Central Asia and North America. The OSCE began life during the cold war as a forum through which the West and the East, the capitalist and communist worlds, could talk to each other. Now it is still intended to encourage communication, as well as to provide early warnings of potential conflicts. By comparison, Asia has plenty of organizations and so plenty of acronyms, but the organizations offer neither deep integration nor broad inclusion. They are generally subregional in scope and shallow in terms of commitment.

Mind you, that is not so different from the way in which the European Union has evolved. It has been given the shorthand name of Europe ever since it began with the formation of the European Coal and Steel Community in 1951, and then in 1957 with what was at first called the European Economic Community and is now the EU. But both of those entities consisted initially of only six countries, and so not even all of Western Europe, let alone the continent as a whole. The desire to prevent a repetition of the twentieth century's two great European wars was the prime motivation for the formation of these communities, but another security concern—namely, the cold war—meant that the membership necessarily had to be narrow. Europe's security organization, NATO, was a body expressly formed in opposition to the other half of Europe, the so-called Warsaw Pact, formed by the Soviet Union. Only now, in the first decade of the twenty-first century, fifty years since the initial communities were founded, are the EU's twenty-seven members truly representative of the continent, and only now are they coming together to form joint foreign and security policies.

Asian institutions have also been similarly local or regional, by and large. For example, the South Asian Association for Regional Cooperation, SAARC, brings together countries with a historical link, namely those that were directly or indirectly part of the British Raj in India until 1947: India, Pakistan, Bangladesh, Nepal, Bhutan, Sri Lanka, the Maldives and, since 2005, Afghanistan. Sports, especially the popularity of cricket, no doubt also cements a sense of South Asian identity. But these are countries whose main external political problems have been with one another: in religious divides between Muslims and Hindus, in three wars involving India and Pakistan and over the creation of Bangladesh (formerly East Pakistan), and in a dispute over Nepali relations with China that led to an Indian economic blockade of Nepal in 1989. The point of SAARC has been to try to encourage dialogue between the South Asian countries' politicians and officials, to make disputes less likely and to encourage trade. But little progress has been made.

For much of its history, the same was true of the Association of Southeast Asian Nations. Southeast Asia possesses the most venerable and durable of Asia's regional institutions in the form of ASEAN, which was founded in 1967 by five countries, Indonesia, Malaysia, Singapore, Thailand and the Philippines. In effect, it was a cold war grouping: These were America's allies in a region split both by the Vietnam War and by the confrontation between the United States, the Soviet Union and Mao's China. Only once Indochina was at peace and the cold war had ended did ASEAN have the chance to change and expand, adding Brunei in 1984, Vietnam in 1995, Laos and Myanmar in 1997 and Cambodia in 1999. Those ten countries give ASEAN a larger population (569 million) than the European Union's twenty-seven countries (490 million). But it is a much looser organization, which avoids the pooling of sovereignty that is the EU's main tool, and has a deliberate and much-emphasised policy of noninterference in each member country's domestic affairs.

Where the EU uses treaties and laws to regulate interchange between its members, ASEAN uses purely intergovernmental agreements, which are not legally binding. Although trade barriers between ASEAN members have been lowered substantially in the past decade, the group has no customs union. There are ambitious aspirations to move further toward a genuine single market for the membership by 2020, but progress so far has been slow. All ASEAN members signed up to a new charter in November 2007, supposedly with the aim of increasing the use of binding obligations and tougher rules, and promoting human rights and democracy, but the fact that dictatorships such as Myanmar, Vietnam and Laos are among the signatories makes the aim seem rather far-fetched.

There has also been talk of extending free trade and other cooperative work to an entity known enigmatically as ASEAN Plus Three, the three being Japan, China and South Korea. Those countries already send representatives to ASEAN's meetings. After the East Asian financial crisis of 1997–98, the finance ministers of ASEAN plus three established a monetary cooperation agreement called the Chiang Mai Initiative, under which the members agree to swap foreign currency reserves between one another's central banks, in case of renewed currency crises. But the Chiang Mai Initiative is vague, the swap agreements are small and there is no operational mechanism. Nor is there any secretariat or other institutional identity for ASEAN Plus Three in its nonfinancial form.

Nevertheless, ASEAN itself is now a fairly close-knit group. Few people probably love it (does anyone ever love acronymic institutions?), but Southeast Asians are becoming gladder that it exists. The reason lies not in regional solidarity—though the countries do share some common concerns, such as dealing with piracy in the seas that surround them—but in a collective sentiment of being overshadowed by others: Japan to the northeast, the United States across the Pacific, but above all China, which sits all around their northern boundaries. Their problem, in other words, is of being small fish in a sea dominated by big ones. Whether those big fish are sharks or whales is a matter of speculation. Fortunately for ASEAN however, none of these potential predators currently wants to be seen to be bossing the others around, so all are willing to give ASEAN a central role in whatever regional community-building may occur.

The ASEAN Regional Forum, ARF, was set up in 1993 as an adjunct to ASEAN to provide a means or a process through which regional security issues and disputes might be discussed, defused and even resolved. Some regional officials say it was originally a Japanese idea, but memories of Japan's historical security role as an imperialist meant that the forum had no chance of developing under Japanese leadership, and so it fell to ASEAN. Now, though, it has caught on and there are twenty-six participants in the ARF's meetings, ranging as far and wide as Australia, Canada, Russia and the European Union, but also India, China, the United States, Japan and even North Korea. That breadth of membership, though, provides a clue to the entity's effectiveness. Although it may have useful discussions about uncontentious issues such as piracy and disaster relief, it is not a grouping within which the big powers or the main troublemakers have so far chosen to discuss and negotiate the truly contentious topics.

Such topics tend to not be discussed at all, as in the case of Taiwan, or are limited to smaller, more local organizations. One example is the Shanghai Cooperation Organization, or SCO, which originated in a meeting held in 1996 between China, Russia, Kazakhstan, Kyrgyzstan and Tajikistan to discuss security in their border regions. Formalized in 2001 as the SCO with the addition of a further Central Asian state, Uzbekistan, the point of the organization arises essentially from two things: common fears of terrorism and other forms of Islamic extremism, with for China and Russia a particularly strong fear of separatist movements; and China's desire to exert influence in Central Asia and to avoid it being simply a Russian sphere, in order to secure access to energy supplies from the Caspian Sea region. Some Western commentators have taken the SCO as a nascent anti-American or anti-Western grouping, especially now that Iran, Pakistan and India have joined SCO meetings as observers. But this is to overinterpret the organization. It does reflect China's new ability to take initiatives and to persuade other countries to join in. Mainly, though, it reflects the existence of genuine shared concerns in Central Asia, and a certain competitive spirit between Russia and China in that region.

To China's east there lies, of course, an even larger concern, shared between Western powers and China: North Korea's nuclear-weapons program. That issue has also given rise to a new entity, or at least a new process: namely, six-party talks involving both Koreas, China, Russia, the United States and Japan. This is the only official forum within which China, the rising power, and America, since 1945 the main force providing regional security within Asia, have had direct and substantive discussions about security. Although it remains premature to describe the six-party talks as having been a success, given that North Korea still retains its nuclear-weapons program, there has been much speculation that this six-party format could offer a basis for a future security organization or forum covering a wider set of topics. If so, it would have the undoubted advantage of having brought together six countries whose future stability, role and ambitions will be vital to Asia's security and peace. But it would have the disadvantage of excluding others that are also likely to play an important role: Australia, because its armed forces are experienced in regional peacekeeping and disaster-relief operations; and India, because its armed forces are among Asia's largest.

Hence Asia's newest institutional creation: the East Asia Summit, launched in Kuala Lumpur in 2005. Fortunately, that title superseded the previous clunky nomenclature for this grouping, which was ASEAN Plus Three Plus Three: i.e., the ten members of ASEAN plus Australia, New Zealand and India, along with China, Japan and South Korea. Yet though an improvement, East Asia Summit is hardly a gem of clarity or accuracy as a name. On no possible definition of East Asia can a gathering of all these countries truly qualify as an East Asian summit. To use the term is like describing France as part of Eastern Europe.

To see Asia as a genuine region, stretching from Mumbai across to Tokyo and as far south as Sydney and Wellington, remains premature. But the creation of the East Asia Summit is an act of anticipation—of the emergence of security concerns, shared economic-policy problems, rivalries and ambitions across the whole of Asia. It is even an act of anticipation of a time when Asia will be seen not simply as a set of single countries, each preoccupied with their domestic affairs, but also as a collective entity. For the moment, though, the region's great powers need to be considered separately.

3. CHINA: MIDDLE COUNTRY, CENTRAL ISSUE

ONCE UPON A TIME, all the most famous slogans about politics and policy in China came from Mao Zedong's Little Red Book or the Great Helmsman's other works: political power growing from the barrel of a gun, letting a hundred flowers blossom, and so forth.[1] Nowadays they all seem to come from his fellow Long Marcher Deng Xiaoping, although in the absence of a little book from Deng, scholars of modern China spend a fair amount of time trying to work out whether he really said all the famous things attributed to him. There is Deng's description of capitalism as "socialism with Chinese characteristics," as cited earlier; or his statement that "it doesn't matter whether a cat is black or white, so long as it catches mice," to justify the market economy he was introducing during the 1980s. He advised that you should "cross the river by feeling the stones," to denote the need for pragmatism in public policy. His most apt description of China's foreign policy, however, was an adaptation of an old Chinese saying, that China should "disguise its ambition and hide its claws" or, in its milder version, "keep a cool head and maintain a low profile."

Whether or not Deng actually said it, this piece of wisdom happens to describe accurately what China has been doing during much of the past fifteen years. The effort has been successful, even if some foreign observers of China have still claimed to see claws whether or not they are hidden. Yet times are changing. They are changing for China's foreign policy and will almost certainly change for its economy too. It is going to get harder for China's profile to stay low and for its head to stay cool. That in turn is going to make China a more awkward neighbor for Asia's other great powers, India and Japan, and a tricky counterpart for America.

What China has been doing, ever since the Tiananmen Square massacre of 1989, is concentrating on economic development and on making sure that foreign tensions and entanglements do not obstruct that goal. Using what a professor of international relations at Renmin University in Beijing, Shi Yinhong, has nicely called "smile diplomacy," China focused during the 1990s on making sure that its Asian neighbors did not fear it and increasingly, as aid, trade and investment began to be added to the smiles, that its neighbors welcomed it more and more.[2] As one notable result, South Korea, a country with whom China had no diplomatic relations until 1992 due to cold war estrangement and the legacy of the Korean War of 1950–53, is now one of China's biggest trading partners, with two-way trade exceeding $100 billion a year. More than 600,000 South Korean citizens now live in China, whether for work or for study.

During the cold war, many countries in Southeast Asia were allied quite closely with the United States—Singapore, Indonesia, the Philippines—while Vietnam and Cambodia both suffered either under direct Chinese attack (in the 1979 war with Vietnam) or from Chinese support for the deadly dictatorship of Pol Pot in Cambodia. So although that pair was estranged from America because of the Vietnam and Cambodian wars, they were also estranged from their Chinese neighbor, who had been promoting revolution through local Communist parties, and who after the American retreat in 1975 posed a more immediate threat, anyway. The Association of Southeast Asian Nations, ASEAN, was set up in 1967 essentially as an anti-Communist grouping. China's rapid economic growth in the 1990s then led to a new set of fears, especially in

Malaysia, Thailand and Singapore, that the region's economies might be hollowed out by the shift of manufacturing in general and multinational investment in particular to China.

So China has been seeking to neutralize this legacy and those fears, using aid, soft loans and investment by state-owned or -guided companies to support Southeast Asian economies, and using diplomacy to spread reassurance and to defuse territorial disputes in the South China Sea. China has lowered its trade barriers in ways that have proved helpful to its southern neighbors, signed ASEAN's Treaty of Amity and Cooperation (under which countries pledge not to attack one another) and launched negotiations about a free-trade arrangement with ASEAN in 2001, jumping ahead of both India and Japan in the effort to strike such a deal. In 2007, however, Japan jumped back ahead when it signed a free-trade pact with ASEAN that covered not only goods and services as China's did, but also investment.

This smile diplomacy has been extended to China's Himalayan neighbor, India, even if in that case the smiles have been rather more forced. Three-way summits have begun to be held regularly between China, India and Russia, and the Chinese and Indians have also been exchanging high-level bilateral visits by their leaders, have been promising to boost their trade, and have been swearing everlasting friendship. Some panicky Western observers have even seen in these two-way or three-way exchanges the beginning of some sort of anti-Western alliance. But that is far-fetched, both for reasons of historical enmity and because each recognizes the other two as large, autonomous countries with a clear and ambitious sense of their self-interest. China and India continue to have a big dispute over their mutual borders, a dispute which led to a fierce war in 1962.[3] China claims an entire Indian state, Arunachal Pradesh, as being rightfully its own; at 84,000 square kilometers, Arunachal Pradesh is roughly the size of Hungary or Portugal, though its population is only a little over one million. Meanwhile India claims that China is occupying

38,000 square kilometers of what is rightfully India, in Aksai Chin, high in the Himalayas, and also in part of neighboring Kashmir that was ceded to it (illegally, in India's view) by Pakistan. Aksai Chin is roughly the same size as Taiwan, though it is virtually uninhabited.

On the face of it, the two sides have made progress on these border disputes, setting up regular negotiations between senior officials to discuss them. But those officials have so far talked only about issues of process, not about the borders themselves. A border crossing was opened to trade in 2006 at Nathu La, between China and the Indian state of Sikkim, for the first time since the 1962 war, yet only for a limited range of goods, and the crossing was not in one of the disputed areas. And while India has tried to remain diplomatically optimistic that a compromise will be reached, China has repeatedly underlined the firmness of its own position, so much so as to call into question agreements the Indian side thought to have already been struck, notably an apparent deal that whatever eventual border settlement is agreed on it will not necessitate the movement of people. In 2006, the Chinese ambassador to Delhi caused an outrage by publicly stressing that China claims the whole of Arunachal Pradesh, not just a share of it, just before China's president, Hu Jintao, was due to come to India in the first visit by a Chinese president for a decade. Such a claim would certainly suggest that people would have to be moved, unless they all simply agree to be Chinese. In May 2007 a "confidence-building" visit to China by more than 100 Indian officials had to be cancelled after China acted in a typically provocative way: It refused to grant a visa to one member of the Indian delegation who happened to come from Arunachal Pradesh itself, on the grounds that he is therefore Chinese and doesn't need one. Such uncompromising behavior may represent an attempt by China to punish India for its nuclear dalliance with the United States and to encourage internal opposition to that dalliance. Or it may simply be that China sees no benefit in compromising. It may think that time, because of its growing economic strength, is on its side.

All that said, Chinese policy toward India has been successful in the past fifteen years in a way that is consistent with its broader foreign policy: China has ensured that relations are warm enough to facilitate trade, and that tensions and disputes are by and large kept under control. China's Asian neighborhood has thus been made safe, friendly and economically advantageous in ways that enabled the country to maintain a low global profile. During the first decade of the twenty-first century, however, Chinese foreign policy has begun to change, because the Chinese economy has demanded it. As Chinese industry became more advanced, especially heavy industry such as steel and chemicals, so its demand for natural resources grew apace, a demand that could not be satisfied from domestic mines and oil wells. At the same time, abundant Chinese savings enabled the country to accumulate capital, and gave China's big state-owned mining and oil companies the wherewithal to invest abroad. So as well as buying oil, iron ore and other commodities from the Middle East, Latin America, India and elsewhere, Chinese firms began to invest directly in mines and oil fields, most notably in Africa, in order to increase the supply of those products. In that way, Chinese interests came to spread well beyond its Asian neighborhood: across the Indian Ocean to the Middle East and Africa; across the world to Latin America, Australia and Canada.

As a result, the low profile recommended by Deng is no longer feasible. China's interests have become global, with investments often in the world's most war-torn and unstable places. But a cool head, and the careful hiding of claws, remain desirable. Broader commercial interests bring a broader political and diplomatic exposure for China. When President Hu Jintao has been making his extensive foreign tours of Africa and Latin America in recent years, that exposure has looked rather positive—as if those regions now court the Chinese and their money as a welcome alternative to the West. There is much truth to that view: It is always good to have an alternative, a point that African governments have made clear when their leaders have flocked to Beijing for summits and pledges of aid or loans, which unlike those from the World Bank or Western governments come with no political strings attached—though they do generally come with commercial strings, tied to contracts for Chinese companies.

The exposure also brings negative results, too, however. Big investments and resources-supply contracts in African countries such as Angola, Zambia, Nigeria, Ethiopia, Somalia and above all Sudan have confronted China with a new set of dilemmas. In Sudan, in particular, China has found it hard to reconcile its traditional stance against interference in any other country's sovereign affairs with its other now-traditional stance of supporting the decisions of multilateral institutions such as the United Nations. In recent years, the UN has wanted to send peacekeepers to the western Sudanese province of Darfur, to prevent further genocide, and the Sudanese government has refused to accept them. At first, the Chinese response to this was to do nothing and hope the world would look the other way. But in 2007 the Darfur issue threatened to damage China's image in the run-up to the 2008 Beijing Olympics. Steven Spielberg was caught in the middle: The famous film director was acting as a consultant on the Olympics opening ceremony and on a film being made about the games. Hollywood hit out at Hollywood: Mia Farrow asked in an article in the *Wall Street Journal* whether Mr. Spielberg wanted to be "the Leni Riefenstahl of the Beijing Games," a painful comparison to the woman who made a film for Hitler about the 1936 Berlin Olympics.[4] Stung by such publicity, the Chinese government has started to try to persuade the Sudanese to comply with the UN request and in February 2008 Spielberg quit.

Nevertheless, China has stationed 4,000 of its own troops in Sudan, to protect its energy and minerals investments there. Its oil firms own 40 percent of the Greater Nile Petroleum Operating Company, though an Indian state-owned firm also owns 25 percent. India suffers less criticism for its involvement with the Sudanese government because it does not have a permanent seat on the UN Security Council and so is an onlooker for UN decisions rather than a direct participant. Meanwhile, China is increasingly concerned about how to protect the flow of those resources from Africa and the Middle East to China. In effect, what sailors call its "sea lanes of communication" (SLOCs) for those resources are currently protected in the Indian Ocean by the American and Indian navies. The ocean is large but those SLOCs pass through a bottleneck on their way to China and the rest of East Asia, namely the Malacca Straits between Indonesia, Malaysia and Singapore. That strait could easily be blocked by a hostile power such as the United States in the event of a military confrontation over Taiwan, or India.

To get around that bottleneck, China is creating other means of access for itself to the Indian Ocean, and sources of influence there. It is financing and building a deep-water port at Gwadar in Pakistan that is for commercial use but could also help China's navy, and is rebuilding and widening a road through Pakistan to Western China, the Karakoram Highway. It has supplied arms to the governments of Nepal and Bangladesh. It has installed surveillance facilities on islands off the Myanmar coast, is building a road linking its own Yunnan province to the Bay of Bengal through Myanmar, and is building and upgrading ports and naval bases in Myanmar. China's desire for that access through Myanmar, and for intimate relations with Myanmar's military regime, produced another foreign-policy predicament when large demonstrations by Buddhist monks and ordinary citizens threatened to topple the regime in September 2007 and were followed by a violent crackdown. China quietly supported the dispatch to Myanmar of a negotiator from the United Nations, while presumably hoping that he did not achieve very much or that his visit would not lead to further, more awkward action by the UN Security Council.

Meanwhile, China is increasing its development aid to the island countries of the Indian Ocean, including Sri Lanka, the Seychelles and the Maldives. In January 2007 President Hu Jintao made a tour of eight African countries and at the end of it visited the Seychelles. Unlike with the other countries, the purpose of this visit was not to discuss resources trade or investments. Nor was he there, like most visitors, for the snorkeling. His purpose was to build relations with the Seychelles so that in the future Chinese naval ships will be able to call in on that country's ports, just as Indian and American ships do.

That policy, being pursued largely for economic reasons, is ringing alarm bells among Indian strategists and could well become a new source of tension between China and India. Indians have long been hypersensitive about Chinese support for their archenemy, Pakistan, which has included the supply of conventional arms and nuclear technical assistance. They see it as part of China's effort, pursued ever since the 1962 war, to keep India tied down through regional conflicts. More recently, however, Indian military officials and strategic thinkers have become increasingly concerned about China's incursions into the Indian Ocean. Brigadier Arun Sahgal of the United Service Institution of India, a research body for India's armed forces, refers to these activities as China's "strategy of concirclement."[5] And he concludes that China sees such activities in an asymmetrical manner: that it feels entitled to expand its sphere of influence and activity, but that it is likely "fiercely to resist India's attempts at usurping its [i.e., China's] perceived strategic space." A policy of engagement, he says, "will always be on Chinese terms with India a junior partner."

Foreign policy is becoming considerably more difficult, as China's interests spread and its dilemmas mount up. For the moment, China is avoiding being the focus of world criticism because that role is being played by America. The decline in the international reputation and influence of the United States since the invasion of Iraq has limited America's chances of leading any global effort to turn China into a "responsible stakeholder," i.e., one that faces up to its dilemmas by acting in the global interest rather than solely in its own interest.[6] China is also being helped by its surplus of capital, which is giving China a generous reputation all around the world. Most of all, it is helped by the strength of its domestic economy, which is increasing its global capabilities, its global importance and its global image all at the same time. That economic strength, with an annual growth rate in GDP of more than 11 percent in 2007, disguises a turbulent process of economic and social change all over the country. It could not be otherwise, if growth rates that fast are to be achieved: They always involve rapid change. There is, however, more change ahead. It promises to be even more turbulent.

The question has been posed in different ways by different observers at different times during the 1990s and the current decade: Is China's growth real? Can it carry on like this? Might a crash be imminent? What will happen if a crash occurs? And the related but also vital question: Will all this economic growth, creating as it is a large group of affluent urbanites, generate unstoppable pressure for political reform, too?

China's economy retains the capacity to provoke shock, awe and puzzlement because the country is so big and unfamiliar. Expectations of an imminent collapse are often, however, based on a pair of false premises: that the rapidity of China's development is unprecedented and therefore exceptional, requiring exceptional explanations; and that the course of that development has so far been remarkably, nay suspiciously, stable, as if China had repealed the laws that describe how economies go through cycles of strength and weakness.

The only way in which China's economic development has been unprecedented is that such growth has never happened before in a country as large in population and geography. Given that there is no other country that matches China's scale, this is not surprising. India is the only one that comes close, and the salient fact about India over most of the past thirty years is how disappointing its economic performance has been, compared with its evident potential. Only in this current decade has India begun to show its mettle. It is rare, though, to hear even India's recent growth being described as "remarkable" or "awesome," as one does with China. This may be because India is a democracy with large numbers of English speakers and a legal system based on British common law, so expectations of it in the West are higher than for a communist country that only eighteen years ago sent in tanks and machine guns to the center of its capital city to quell a rebellion. But perhaps many people who themselves live in democracies also have a sneaking admiration for the way dictators—or, rather, in China's case, authoritarian systems—are able to make decisions and make things happen, the modern equivalent of Mussolini's supposed success in making the trains run on time in 1920s Italy. The results of that decisiveness in China are highly visible: new roads, airports, container ports and skyscrapers. India's infrastructure, by comparison, remains meagre and looks outmoded, the unripe fruit of its democratic indecisiveness.

As chapter 2 showed, China's pattern and pace of growth has been pretty similar, in its basic outline, to the periods of rapid growth seen in earlier decades in Japan, South Korea, Taiwan and some other Asian countries. China's growth has gone on now at an annual average rate of real GDP increase of 8–10 percent for almost thirty years. That is excellent but not exceptional. China's "renegade province" of Taiwan sustained average GDP growth rates of around 8 percent for forty years. Singapore averaged 9 percent in the 1960s and '70s, and almost 8 percent in the 1980s and '90s. Japan's high growth period lasted for more than twenty-five years, a period during which it had no serious economic setback—which cannot be said of China's first quarter century of rapid development.

When Deng Xiaoping began to allow market forces into agriculture in the late 1970s, and then permitted the creation of small, profit-oriented companies called "township and village enterprises," which were formally owned by local authorities but acted as if they were private, he was launching a great period of Chinese growth but from a very low base. China's GDP in 1978, expressed in current prices, was just $228 billion, and its GDP per head was $240. By 2006, almost three decades later, GDP had increased twelvefold to $2.7 trillion and GDP per head had risen tenfold.

Or had it? The reason for the belief that China's growth has been pretty stable is that the official GDP figures say as much. But China's official statistics are notoriously unreliable. The basic statistic used in appraising and comparing economies, gross domestic product, is in China's case the most unreliable of all. And the figures mislead in two directions. They are unreliable in defining the low base from which China's growth spurt began in 1978 as well as in charting its course since then. They may now even be understating the size of the economy. All the former communist countries in Central and Eastern Europe turned out to have much lower GDPs in 1991, after the Soviet Union had been dissolved, than they had had in 1988, when it still existed. The reason for this was not just the political disruption of a change of regime. It was that the Soviet-era GDP figures had been false, based as they were on volumes of production rather than on any concept of value added. Since production volumes were based on government-set targets, there were clear incentives to report that the targets had been met or exceeded, even if they hadn't been. It was the same in China. Almost certainly, China's GDP in 1978 was much lower than the official figures claim—which could mean that China's growth since then has been even faster than is officially recorded.

It isn't quite as simple as that. For although market forces have taken hold in China, some of the legacy of statistical mystery lives on. In 2005, for example, the national GDP growth rate was 10.4 percent. The country is divided into twenty-two provinces, five so-called autonomous regions (e.g., Tibet, Inner Mongolia, Xinjiang) and four municipalities administered directly by the central government (Beijing, Shanghai, Chongqing and Tianjin): thirty-one regions in all. In 2005, fully twenty-nine of those thirty-one regions reported GDP growth rates that were higher than the national one; only two, Hainan and Yunnan, crept in below it. It is like the children in Garrison Keillor's fictional Lake Wobegon: Everyone is above average. So either those provincial figures are false, or the national ones are—or possibly both.[7]

Confused? We all should be. The GDP figures remain grossly unreliable. It is, however, possible to crosscheck GDP figures in two main ways: by comparing them with figures for "gross national expenditure" that, as in all national accounts, forms the counterpart of production statistics, based on surveys of what money is being spent on; and by tracking some of the components of GDP, such as industrial output and other statistics that underpin economic activity, such as trends in power consumption. Neither of these crosschecks is entirely reliable, but at least they can provide some evidence of trends. Economists who have crosschecked China's official GDP data in this way conclude that the Chinese economy has not been consistently over-valued or under-valued in recent decades—the growth is real, and not a mirage—but that what has happened is that the data have been smoothed out, so that bad times have been made to look less bad, and good times less good.

What the official data show is that ever since the mid-1990s annual growth has always been somewhere between 8 percent and 12 percent. That is a much better record than the volatile 1980s, when a boom in the early reform years of 1982–84 brought annual growth as high as 15 percent, followed by a hiccup in 1986, a brief renewed boom, and then a slump in 1988–90. That late-1980s slump featured consumer-price inflation of almost 20 percent, panic withdrawals of bank deposits and then the mass demonstrations in Beijing and many other big cities by students and ordinary workers that culminated on June 4, 1989, in what has become known as the Tiananmen Square massacre, although most of the killings took place elsewhere in Beijing. Prodemocracy idealism did play an important part in those events, but the economic background needs also to be borne in mind: slumping growth, a bank panic and high inflation all served to feed discontent with Communist Party rule.

The party itself has certainly borne those points in mind. When China was again hit by high inflation and slumping growth in the late 1990s, these setbacks did not appear in the GDP figures. Officially, China enjoyed 8 percent GDP growth in both 1998 and 1999—admittedly slower than earlier in that decade but still quite comfortable. Consumer-price inflation had hit 25 percent in 1994, which brought on draconian measures by the government to get it back under control. It is known that masses of the most inefficient state-owned enterprises were closed, putting tens of millions of people out of work. Yet neither of these could have happened while maintaining an unchanged 8 percent growth rate. Previously, growth in electricity consumption had tended to move more slowly than GDP growth during boom periods and to outpace it during slumps. In 1998–99, growth in electricity consumption dropped to less than 3 percent, which implies that GDP growth might have been even slower than that. Yet officially it was five percentage points faster.

Potential demonstrators and rebels do not base their mobilizations only on data from the national accounts, of course. Killing off inflation, which affects the savings of ordinary people as well as their faith in the money they use every day, may well have been more important politically than avoiding a recession. But the Communist Party has at its core a belief in the power of information to shape public behavior, so manipulating the GDP statistics will have come naturally to it. Engineering a rapid economic recovery to create new jobs to replace some of the millions—roughly 30 million—lost in that period will have been even more important, however.

No one knows what an accurate series of GDP statistics would look like for China. Nevertheless, one thing is clear: that far from having enjoyed steady growth, China's economy has actually been a roller-coaster affair. The chart shows the pattern as depicted by Jonathan Anderson, chief Asia economist of UBS Securities, who is one of the region's most respected outside observers. UBS chooses to estimate China's GDP growth by using expenditure-side figures, deflating them to allow for price movements, and adjusting them at times when other statistics suggest the

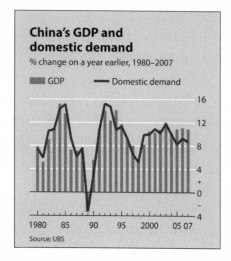

China's GDP and domestic demand
% change on a year earlier, 1980–2007

GDP   —— Domestic demand

Source: UBS

data may be badly awry. Mr. Anderson's figure for 1998, note, shows a bit more than 5 percent growth, which is well below the official figures but above the estimates of some gloomier economists. His figures also show fairly stable rates of growth in 2005–07, while official numbers have shown an acceleration.

Will this roller-coaster economy now make another stomach-churning descent? No one can be sure. But it is clear that in 2007 and 2008, the Chinese economy came to exhibit some extreme and unusual characteristics. Those features look unsustainable. They are harbingers of change.

One of the things that marks China out as different even from other East Asian success stories was outlined in chapter 2: its very high level of investment. At 40–45 percent of GDP, all that spending on factories, buildings, infrastructure and other capital assets is considerably higher than in other East Asian economies, and has been the biggest force behind China's overall growth rate. Of course, as has just been shown, those statistics may be unreliable: If GDP is being incorrectly estimated, then the ratio may be overstated (or indeed understated). There are also questions about whether China's definition of investment is entirely comparable to that used elsewhere; certainly, this measure includes some items that other countries would not categorize as investment, such as land sales.

Nevertheless, the definition has not changed significantly in recent years, so we can at least be fairly sure about investment's trend. And that trend has been strongly upward, with annual increases in real gross fixed capital formation (the fancy term for investment) of 27.7 percent in 2003, 26.8 percent in 2004, 26 percent in 2005 and 24 percent in 2006. The rate of increase has been falling slightly, but in all those years investment grew more than twice as fast as recorded GDP. The purpose of investment should, in principle, be to enable output to increase in future; in other words, to raise the rate of GDP growth. But this does not seem to be happening, at least not to any great extent. If it were occurring, China's growth rate would be hitting 15 percent or more. The higher investment seems to be increasingly inefficient.

Another unusual feature, which is the flip side of this investment boom, is China's very high level of savings, by both households and companies. If there are plenty of savings to finance the investment then inefficiency is not a danger per se; it represents a lost opportunity to grow even faster, rather than signaling a risk of a future financial crisis, for instance. When East Asian economies had their financial crisis in 1997–98 the cause was reckless borrowing from abroad, on assumptions that exchange rates against the dollar were fixed, which they proved not to be. China has no need for foreign borrowing and so will not face a crisis of that sort. Its semifixed exchange rate may cause other problems, but not a debt crisis like those in South Korea, Thailand and Indonesia.

The nature of Chinese savings is important, however. In Japan, South Korea and Taiwan, savings have also been high during their periods of rapid economic development, but those countries' supersavers were mainly households. That has also become true in India in the past few years. In China, while household savings rates are considerably higher than in rich Western economies, the main source of savings has recently been companies. The gross national savings rate in China increased by ten percentage points from the late 1990s to 2005, reaching almost 50 percent of GDP; of that increase, 60 percent of it was generated by companies making higher profits and paying down debts—i.e., by increasing their savings. A big reduction in the government budget deficit also helped, as tax revenues grew rapidly.

Much of China's investment has been financed straight out of companies' own earnings and from bank loans. Steven Barnett and Ray Brooks of the IMF have calculated that retained earnings have been financing more than half of the investment, with bank lending (including for personal mortgages) accounting for a further quarter.[8] Foreign direct investment by multinational firms, although much trumpeted, has played only a minor part: It accounted for about 4 percent of investment in 2005, according to Barnett and Brooks. The high level of savings is therefore a result primarily of high and rising corporate earnings, which in turn finance most of the investment. If those earnings were to fall, so might national savings, and so might investment.

Chinese companies, whether private or state owned, pay very little to their shareholders as dividends. The banking system remains in state ownership. Although many of the big banks have now floated their shares on the Hong Kong stock market, the bulk of the shares remain in state hands. The result is that the cost of money is not being set in modern financial markets, according to supply, demand and risk: Instead the cost appears to many users to be low or possibly zero. The interest rate on bank loans is not actually zero (it is around 7 percent for one-year loans), but the true cost of borrowing also depends on whether interest rates and debt repayments are ultimately going to be enforced. When the 1990s downturn occurred, many companies, especially state-owned ones, stopped paying interest on their debts, leaving the banks carrying huge portfolios of what bankers call "nonperforming loans," the bulk of which were written off thanks to injections of capital by the government. In effect, that money came free of charge from the government. If there is another downturn, will this happen again? No one can be sure, especially now that many big banks have some foreign share-holders. But if you were a state-owned, state-guided or state-favored company borrowing today to finance a new factory or building, you might well bet that in extremis there will be another bailout. If you are right, your cost of capital will indeed be zero.

This underpricing of credit and capital is being reinforced by another of China's exceptional features: its vast foreign-exchange reserves. At $1.4 trillion, these are now the largest foreign reserves that have ever been accumulated (Japan's are the second largest, at $916 billion). They have become so large because the exchange rate of China's currency, the renminbi (also known as the yuan) has not been allowed to rise even though the income from exports and other transactions has vastly exceeded the outflow of money to pay for im-ports. In other words, China has a large and growing surplus on the current account of its balance of payments—the surplus exceeded 10 percent of GDP in 2007, an exceptional proportion for such a large economy—which would normally cause the currency to rise.

Although China is now associated popularly with having a very large trade surplus, this surplus has risen very recently and suddenly. China's overall trade ran only a fairly small surplus until 2004, when it suddenly rocketed upward. The reason was a big drop in imports as new Chinese factories began to replace foreign suppliers of steel, machinery and other goods. In the three years 2004–07, growth in net exports—i.e., in the trade surplus—accounted for about a third of China's overall GDP growth. The most dramatic effect, though, was seen on capital flows and the foreign reserves.

Rather than allowing the renminbi to rise according to market demand, the central bank, the People's Bank of China, has absorbed these capital flows by buying foreign securities, mainly American Treasury bonds, and adding them to the foreign reserves. To avoid that process simply adding to the domestic money supply (because the bank is, in effect, printing more renminbi in order to buy those foreign securities), the central bank also has to "sterilize" it by selling renminbi securities to Chinese banks and thus withdrawing liquidity, or by requiring banks to hold larger and larger reserves of their own against their lending. But the rise in foreign reserves is making it harder for the central

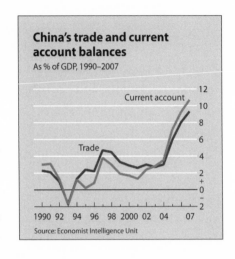

China's trade and current account balances
As % of GDP, 1990–2007

Source: Economist Intelligence Unit

bank to sterilize the inflows entirely. In 2007, reserves were rising at a rate of around $45 billion a month, or $550 billion a year.

So far, sterilization has been successful. But it has come at a cost: that in recent years the People's Bank of China has had to sacrifice monetary policy to currency policy. The need to concentrate on the exchange rate and on sterilizing the growth in foreign reserves, at a time when the trade and current-account surpluses have ballooned, means that the central bank has been unable to use the normal tools of interest rates to try to restrain lending and to control inflation. The impact of all that unrestrained liquidity is seen in two main places: in the growth of fixed-asset investment, already discussed; and in rising prices for investible assets, which essentially means real estate and share prices. The effects can also be seen in more esoteric markets, such as for the finest Pu-er tea from Yunnan (a 100-gram brick of sixty-year-old tea sold for a record of RMB 300,000, i.e., more than $38,000, in January 2007, at the Guangzhou Tea Cultural Festival).

The supply of real estate has been rising rapidly in urban areas thanks to that investment boom and the construction it has stimulated. If you tour any Chinese city you will see rows and rows of apparently empty buildings. Nevertheless, residential prices have risen on average, nationwide, by well over 50 percent since 2000 despite that oversupply. In 2007, land prices were rising at an annual rate of 15 percent.

The impact on share prices in China's two main domestic stock markets, Shanghai and Shenzhen, has been even clearer, as the chart shows. The supply of shares on domestic stock markets has been fairly limited, as the big primary flotations of state-owned banks and other enterprises have taken place in Hong Kong; Chinese investors are not officially permitted to buy shares in Hong Kong or other foreign exchanges, and foreign investors have only restricted access to the Shanghai and Shenzhen exchanges. The main investors on those exchanges are Chinese companies and state agencies, using some of their surplus of cash, although retail investors have also flocked to buy shares during 2006 and 2007, as the returns on shares have come to look a lot more attractive than those on bank deposits. Companies have become engaged in what is a circular process: In 2006–07, well over half the growth in earnings reported by listed companies on the Chinese exchanges was coming from equity and property investments, whose value was driven higher by retail investors betting on that very earnings growth. The result has been the simplest sort of asset-price inflation: a 130 percent rise in the Shanghai composite index in 2006 and a further 107 percent rise by the end of September 2007.

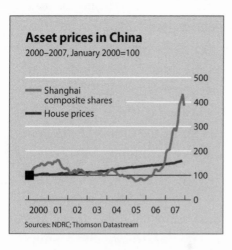

Asset prices in China
2000–2007, January 2000=100

— Shanghai composite shares
— House prices

Sources: NDRC; Thomson Datastream

If property and share prices were to fall sharply, as they did in Japan during the 1990s following that country's asset-price bubble, the direct effects on the economy would be fairly modest. Ownership of shares, in particular, is quite limited, so that rises in prices do not boost household consumption noticeably and falls in prices would not hurt it noticeably, either. Those retail investors who lost lots of money might, though, become angry and hold protests in the streets of Shanghai or Beijing, depending on whether they felt the authorities were somehow to blame.

Companies and state agencies investing in the stock market would feel their own pain, however: Their earnings would be hit, and they would have less money to invest in physical assets. A real-estate slump would be more damaging still for companies, for it is corporate investors who have been building most of the skyscrapers and apartment blocks. Ultimately, though, the real damage would be felt by the lenders: in other words, China's big banks. Their losses, resulting from a big increase in their portfolios of nonperforming loans, would partly hurt their investors, which in the case of the big banks includes some foreign banks and Western institutional investors. Mainly, though, the bulk of the losses would fall on the banks' main owners: the Chinese government.

Asset prices are a worrying sort of inflation, for their booms and busts can cause financial crises. But they are not China's only inflation concern, nor its most fundamental worry. This marks an important change: Although China had two episodes of damagingly rapid consumer-price inflation in recent decades, in 1985–89 and in 1994–98, the country has for a decade been more associated with falling prices than rising ones. Chinese factories, famously, are the reason why America's Wal-Mart can meet its promise of "every day low prices." The use of Chinese, Indian and other Asian labor to make tradeable goods has contributed to a downward pressure on goods prices worldwide since the mid-1990s, counteracting a rapid rise in prices of energy and raw materials since 2002. The "China price" has been a synonym for the world's lowest-cost source of products and hence of downward pressure on global inflation.

So it has become reasonable to assume that the huge supply of labor represented by the hundreds of millions of Chinese of working age who are still living in rural areas will mean that wages will remain repressed for years, especially as productivity in Chinese factories is rising as technology and management improve and is being helped by all that capital investment. But the assumption is turning out to be wrong. The idea of permanently cheap Chinese labor is plausible only relative to wage levels in rich Western countries. Chinese wages (like Vietnamese and Indian wages) will remain well below Western wages for a long time to come. That does not mean that wages will not rise in China. Indeed, they are rising already, and the rise appears to be outpacing productivity growth.

One reason for rising wage levels is the sheer demand for labor resulting from the rapid growth of the economy, and of the construction industry in particular. That demand could wane just as fast as it has waxed. But there are also two other more enduring and deeper reasons: agricultural reform and demography.

Farmers' incomes lagged badly behind the rest of the economy in the late 1990s and the early part of this decade as food prices were falling and the tax burden imposed on them by local governments was rising, which made it more attractive to migrate to urban factories in search of work and income. Relaxation of the national residency permit system, a legacy of Mao that was designed to control mobility, made this easier. But the widening gap between rural and urban incomes worried the government, which became concerned that urbanization might be proceeding too rapidly and that the risk of social instability in rural areas might increase. So in 2004 new measures were introduced to help farmers: agricultural taxes and fees were cut or abolished, and subsidies for food production and farm equipment were in-

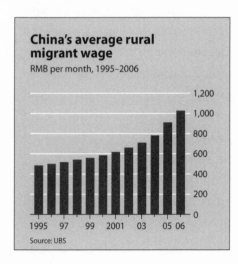

China's average rural migrant wage
RMB per month, 1995–2006
1,200
1,000
800
600
400
200
0
1995   97   99   2001   03   05 06
Source: UBS

creased substantially. This injection of public money coincided with a rise in food prices as domestic demand for grains and meat rose and as world food prices also climbed. Urban development and industrialization have steadily reduced the amount of land available for farming. Consequently rural incomes have

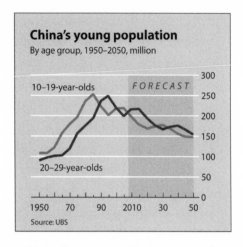

China's young population
By age group, 1950–2050, million

been rising strongly—which is making fewer people want to migrate. Or, to put it another way, it has become necessary to offer higher wages to persuade them to do so.

Much of the huge supply of unskilled or low-skilled labor in recent years has consisted of young Chinese in rural areas who go to the cities for a few years before returning to their villages. Surveys suggest that about 60–70 percent of migrants later return in this way. The so-called one-child system of population control that was introduced in 1979 truly lived up to its name only in the cities, but it still had the effect of reducing rural birth rates. As a result, the number of people entering the age groups likeliest to migrate in search of work—those in their twenties—has peaked and is now falling, especially in rural areas. The number of young people in China's countryside now is about 100 million, according to UBS's Jonathan Anderson, but within two decades the number will probably have fallen to around 60 million.[9] The supply of cheap factory-fodder labor is now falling. It is not that there is suddenly going to be a labor shortage, of course: It is that the supply of younger workers is falling, gradually, and the demands they are making are rising gradually.

The combination of fast monetary growth and rising wages can really only mean one thing: the return of inflation. It is not

returning as hyperinflation, but its return is likely to be a remorse-
less one, unless measures are introduced to deal with it. The danger
that inflation will produce popular dissent and even protests makes
it very likely that the authorities will feel obliged to cure it, which
in turn mean one thing: change. A change in monetary policy, a
change in currency policy, which together will change the country's
economic course. The more difficult questions are how and how
smoothly; what impact this process could have on Chinese politics
and on social stability; and what impact such change might have
on China's foreign interests, influence and relationships.

The idea that China is going to change course, or should change
course, ought not to be a controversial one. None other than Premier Wen Jiabao said in a press conference at the National People's
Congress in March 2007 that "there are structural problems in
China's economy which cause unsteady, unbalanced, uncoordinated
and unsustainable development." By making that statement, Premier Wen was simply reiterating the position taken by the leadership as long ago as December 2004, at its annual Central Economic
Work Conference, to the effect that China's growth strategy needed
to be altered. Premier Wen wasn't just referring to inflation: He was
also expressing concern about the inequality between rural and
urban China that his government has been trying to moderate
through its agricultural reforms since 2004, and about the environmental damage being done by the present course of Chinese growth.
Energy use and air pollution, including the greenhouse gases that are
thought to cause global warming, have risen more rapidly than either Chinese or Western forecasters expected during the past few
years. The reason is that investment has been higher than expected,
and that Chinese companies have been engaged in low-tech, labor-
and energy-intensive manufacturing for longer than expected.

Economists in Chinese government think tanks also say so. In
October 2006, for example, I spoke to Yu Yongding, director of the
Institute of World Economics and Politics at the Chinese Academy

of Social Sciences and a member of the monetary policy committee of the central bank, the People's Bank of China, in 2004–06. His view was that the abnormalities in China's economy—excessively high rates of investment and savings, a current-account surplus then approaching 10 percent of GDP, a trade-to-GDP ratio of 65–70 percent, China's status as a huge net exporter of capital, foreign exchange reserves then of more than $1 trillion—were all signs that change is needed. China must, he said, restore the central bank's control over monetary policy, and thus avoid a damaging financial bubble like that seen in Japan during the 1980s; must improve the quality of investment and reduce pollution; and must move companies and investment out of low-profit sectors such as textiles. Such a change can, and should, be accompanied by increased public spending on health and education.

It is, though, easier said than done—which is why it hasn't yet happened, despite being talked about since that Work Conference in December 2004. In principle, it should be straightforward: A sharp revaluation of the renminbi against the dollar, perhaps by as much as 30–40 percent, should stop the inflow of short-term capital that is inflating the foreign-exchange reserves and causing excessive monetary expansion, and would enable the central bank again to use interest rates to govern the creation of credit and to keep a lid on inflation. That could be done with a one-off revaluation or by making the currency convertible and allowing it to float freely. Being cautious and reluctant to give up controls that would be hard to restore, the authorities are likely to reject the bold option of full convertibility and to go for a revaluation. But they are reluctant to do even that.

Such a sharp move would devastate low-profit export industries such as textiles. In the long term that would be a good thing, Yu Yongding argues: China "shouldn't be competing with Bangladesh and Africa." Higher interest rates for bank loans would also threaten property developers and other speculative investors, which include a lot of state-owned companies, state agencies, and provincial and municipal governments. They rather enjoy using cheap capital to build new cities and industrial parks. They don't want that to come suddenly to an end—which is why the call by Premier Wen to change economic course has so far gone unheeded. Too many companies and local governments are benefiting from the investment boom. Surely, however, the party leadership can order the change to take place? It is not so simple. The leadership itself may well be divided on the matter. But also, although there is no democracy or pluralism in China as a whole, within the Communist Party there is a sort of controlled conflict. Interest groups vie with one another. A consensus needs to form before a decision can be made and, just as important, implemented. Meanwhile the asset bubble continues to inflate.

This situation is not, however, unprecedented. The patterns of growth in Japan, South Korea and China have been strikingly similar during comparable periods of economic development, with investment rising steadily to reach a peak as a share of GDP of about 40 percent before falling gradually following some sort of a crisis. The closest parallel is with Japan in the late 1960s and early '70s. By then, Japan had considerably higher living standards than China does today: In 1970 its GDP per head was more than $10,000 expressed in today's prices, which is four times as high as China's $2,500. But its macroeconomic imbalances bore a close resemblance to China's, as did its industrial structure—apart from the fact that agriculture by then played a far smaller role in Japan than it still does in China's economy.

In 1970, Japan's investment rate was at its peak of 40 percent of GDP; its rapid industrial growth was causing severe problems of pollution; its current-account surplus grew to more than 2 percent of GDP; and its currency came to look especially undervalued. That surplus sounds small by today's Chinese standards. But at the time, exchange rates were fixed against the dollar and gold under the system that had been agreed on at Bretton Woods at the end of the

Second World War, and capital did not move as freely as it does now, making surpluses and deficits as large as China's and America's of 2000–07 simply impossible. But in 1968–71, Japan's surplus and America's deficit still caused a considerable amount of political friction, as the U.S. struggled to finance its war in Vietnam.

It was in 1971 that Japan's enjoyment of a fixed and undervalued yen came to a sudden end when President Richard Nixon unilaterally abandoned the Bretton Woods system and forced other countries, including Japan, to negotiate revaluations of their exchange rates with the dollar. That shock for Japan was followed swiftly by a second blow, the sharp hike in oil prices due to the Arab oil embargo in 1973, which also caused inflation in Japan. The combination of those two shocks forced a change: In-

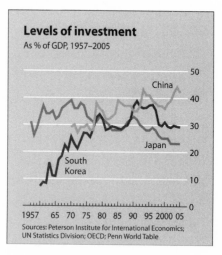

Levels of investment
As % of GDP, 1957–2005

Sources: Peterson Institute for International Economics;
UN Statistics Division; OECD; Penn World Table

vestment gradually came to play a smaller part in the Japanese economy, industry moved upmarket and out of low-tech goods, and a sizeable public budget deficit was used to support the economy during the transition. The chart shows the way in which investment waxed and waned in both Japan in the 1970s and later in South Korea in the 1990s.

At that time, however, Japan did not have the asset-price inflation that China now has. Japan's asset-price bubble—much, much larger rises in property and share prices than China has yet seen—did not take place until the late 1980s. That China has a combination of both a huge investment oversupply and an asset-price bubble means that the longer a change in economic policy and direction is delayed, the bigger the risk that mere adjustment turns into something more dramatic.

In China's case, the prompt for change will be different: Where Japan's currency in 1970 was in effect controlled by America, China today can make its own choices. It, too, is under pressure from rising oil prices though, and worried about their impact on inflation: $100 per-barrel oil could be today's equivalent for China of the oil embargo for Japan, a pressure that, in combination with other causes of inflation, forces the Chinese government to revalue the renminbi and to focus its monetary policy on inflation rather than the currency.

The Chinese government is, however, in a good position to follow the Japanese example of the 1970s by using public spending and borrowing to support demand and to ease the adjustment process. A decade ago, the government was struggling to raise enough revenues, with tax revenues only around 10 percent of GDP. By 2007, that figure had doubled, to just over 20 percent. The budget deficit is about 1.2 percent of GDP; that is about a fifth as large as India's budget deficit and is similar to the deficit being run by the United States, except that China has abundant savings with which to finance its government borrowing, unlike America. Government debt is only around 20 percent of GDP. The party leadership has already promised to expand public spending on health, education and other social services. The buoyant state of the public finances means that there should be enough scope to carry out that promise as well as to use public borrowing to support the economy more broadly. In the event of the more wrenching sort of economic recession, resulting perhaps from a collapse in asset markets, the budget deficit and government debt might both become much larger than the current figures, given that state banks would suffer from a big rise in non-performing loans and would demand more public money to bail them out. The public finances are, however, probably in good enough shape to cope with that.

But is Chinese society in good enough shape to cope? It is a commonplace now to observe that the legitimacy of the Chinese Communist Party depends not on ideology but on economic growth. It is also a commonplace that in all countries social and political stability come under threat at times of economic hardship and change.

The Tiananmen protests of 1989 that brought protestors on to the streets not only of Beijing but in a total of 341 Chinese cities took place at just such a time. Inflation and then recession cast doubt on the competence of the Communist leadership; discontent about corruption and injustice, always somewhere near the surface, broke through it. The protestors were not just some idealistic university students, though such people were at the center of it all in Tiananmen Square and were the ones in front of the cameras of the Western media. More worrying still for the Communist Party was the participation of ordinary workers, supposedly the party's core supporters. Bruce Gilley, a Canadian journalist turned academic at Queen's University in Ontario, estimates that as many as 100 million people may have participated in the protests at one time or another during the roughly six weeks during which they took place in all those cities.[10] Mr. Gilley argues that "like Budapest in 1956, Prague in 1968 and Warsaw in 1981, Tiananmen in 1989 was a failure that foretold later success."

Does it foretell the future? Whether China will eventually become some sort of democracy is a perennial debate, especially (though not only) among westerners, but one to which there can be no confident answer. Some, like Mr. Gilley, argue that it is only a matter of time. Democracy, on this argument, is a universal virtue, a universal human desire, one that the Chinese people showed in 1989 that they share and that will eventually prove necessary if China is to achieve lasting stability. Pei Minxin, a scholar at the Carnegie Endowment for International Peace in Washington, D.C., writes that far from being a boost to economic growth, Communist Party rule is actually holding it back and will do so even more in the future as corruption and cronyism spread even further.[11] Gordon Chang, who worked in China as a lawyer for many years, stands for a similar diagnosis, albeit taking the view that the Chinese Communist regime will collapse by the end of this decade rather than China simply being held back.[12] Susan Shirk, who was deputy assistant secretary of state responsible for America's relations with China during the Clinton administration and is now a professor at the University of California at San Diego, describes China with the title of her 2007 book *Fragile Superpower,* because of China's volatile internal politics.[13]

Others, such as Andrew Nathan of Columbia University in New York, argue to the contrary, that China exhibits what he has called "resilient authoritarianism," and that the authoritarian Communist Party regime looks strong enough and resilient enough to remain in power for the foreseeable future. Arthur Kroeber, editor of *China Economic Quarterly,* concurs with that view, arguing that although corruption is a problem it is not extensive enough to threaten a government that has shown itself to be "administratively competent and in many ways meritocratic."[14]

Daniel Bell, a Canadian political philosopher now at Tsinghua University in Beijing, argues that liberal democracy is anyway not the universal value that westerners claim it is, and that the Confucian tradition in China and other Chinese-influenced parts of East Asia may offer an alternative source of justice, human rights and accountability, based around a meritocratically selected bureaucratic elite.[15] James Mann, a journalist who was Beijing correspondent for the *Los Angeles Times* in the mid-1980s, describes the idea that democracy is inevitable as *The China Fantasy,* in the title of his polemical 2007 book: It is a fantasy used, he claims, by successive American presidents to justify their policy of "engagement" with China, and in particular of liberalizing trade without pressing China about human rights.[16] Like Mr. Nathan, Mr. Mann reckons that Communist rule in China does not look fragile at all: The best working assumption, he argues, is that it is here to stay.

Hope may spring eternal for many observers, inside and outside China, but there is certainly no sign that the party leadership intends to bring in anything that westerners would recognize as democracy any time soon. The word does pop up in speeches by Hu Jintao and Wen Jiabao, but with a time horizon attached that is many decades into the future—usually fifty years or more—or with an implication that Chinese democracy would not mean pluralism. What exactly it would mean has never been made clear. Often, indeed, the gnomic sayings of the leaders imply that democracy does not mean very much, for in their terms China already has a democracy. On June 25, 2007, for instance, in a speech at the Party School in Beijing, President Hu said that China should "continue to expand orderly political participation of our citizens, and perfect our democratic system." In this context, the term is as far from pluralism as it was in the name of the former German Democratic Republic (aka East Germany) or still is in the name of the Democratic People's Republic of Korea (aka North Korea).

One strong argument for why political change may occur in China rests on the fact that economic change has been occurring so rapidly and disruptively. As a result of modernization and growth, many elements that are independent of central government, including big businesses, rich individuals, local governments and even moderately affluent urbanites, have become more powerful and have developed interests that sometimes come into conflict, as well as property rights that they are ever keener to protect. A proxy for this theory is the emergence of a middle class that owns property and holds savings, both of which give it powerful motivations to demand justice, accountability and good governance. As issues and interests become more complex they become harder to manage in a rigid authoritarian system. Such complex, more affluent societies will tend to have a growing middle class, for companies and civic organizations will be employing those sort of educated and relatively affluent people. This theory does not, however, tell us what sort of political change might occur to enable these interests to be more easily reconciled, nor whether such change will take place in a gradual, orderly way or in a more disorderly manner. Another way to look at China, moreover, is as a country with an orderly central government and party system, but with a whole series of mafias or mobs ruling at local level, often with as much thuggery and other coercion as any rules or principles. Such a situation makes evolutionary theories hard to apply, at least in a thoroughly convincing way.

The obvious countries to use as points of comparison for China are its two neighbors that have previously made the transition from authoritarian government to electoral democracy, namely Taiwan and South Korea. Both did so in the early 1990s. Either or both are sometimes dismissed by China buffs as special cases: Taiwan, because its status as a largely unrecognized country, with independence de facto but not de jure, may have produced exceptional pressures; South Korea, because of the influence there of its ally the United States. America happily left South Korea as a military dictatorship throughout the cold war, but may have put more pressure on it to democratize as the cold war came to a close. Those dismissals are rather patronizing to Koreans and Taiwanese, who doubtless had their own reasons for favoring a move to democracy and taking to the streets to demand it. Even so, taking GDP per head as a rough measure of economic development, affluence and the likely rise of a middle class, it is possible to widen the comparison to take in other countries that have swapped dictatorial regimes for democracy.

The table shows thirteen countries that have done so and the levels of their GDP per head, expressed in dollars, at the time when they made the transition. The transitions marked, it should be noted, are those to full democracy; many of these countries began earlier with partial, often rigged democracies, which would be the way in which China would presumably do it, if the Communist Party were to choose to do so via a gradual, or orderly change.

Although GDP or income per head may be only a rough proxy both for middle classes and for democracy, it is worth noting that of the world's fifty richest countries by GDP per head, only a handful of microstates (including Hong Kong) and oil producers are not democracies. For oil producers such as Saudi Arabia or Brunei, GDP per head is a poor proxy for middle-class development in any case, as both GDP and wealth are heavily concentrated in one industry and a few hands.

Democracy and living standards

	Year of full democracy	GDP per head at market prices, dollars	GDP per head at PPP, dollars
India	1947	120*	742
Philippines	1986	533	2,360
Indonesia	1999	746	2,776
Russia	1991	1,866†	6,077
Brazil	1985	1,903	5,020
Portugal	1976	2,107	8,786
Chile	1989	2,204	4,425
Greece	1974	2,480	9,693
Argentina	1983	3,544	7,038
Spain	1977	3,568	11,957
Mexico	1991	3,709	6,532
South Korea	1993	8,195	10,361
Taiwan	1992	10,513	12,604
China in 2007	n/a	2,460	6,290

Sources: IMF; Penn World Tables   *1950 †1994

The first thing the table should tell us is that there is no obvious pattern. Put another way, every country has special circumstances of some sort, and it is rare for democratic change to occur organically. The table omits all the new democracies that emerged in central Europe after the fall of the Soviet Union on the principle that their timing was determined by events in the imperial power that had been occupying them rather than at home, although the same might be said to have applied to India, which is why it introduced democracy in 1947 when it became independent from Britain and was one of the world's poorest countries. There are two other Asian outliers that also turned democratic when they were very poor: the Philippines, when "people power" led to the overthrow of Ferdinand Marcos in 1985–86; and Indonesia, when the East Asian financial crisis led to the downfall of that country's longtime dictator, Suharto, in 1998 and full democracy a year later.

In Spain and Portugal it took the deaths of longtime dictators, respectively Francisco Franco and Antonio de Oliveira Salazar, to enable democratization to occur, though in neither case did it do so immediately. In Latin America a failed war (Argentina) and the regional debt crisis (Brazil) may explain the timing in those two countries; Chile is an unusual case in which a dictator (Augusto Pinochet) handed over power voluntarily, though under the assumption, subsequently proved wrong, that he would be immune from prosecution for human-rights abuses committed during his dictatorship. The other unusual case is Greece, where a military junta's dictatorship collapsed in ignominy in 1974 and was replaced by democracy—but the junta itself had overthrown Greece's previous, short-lived postwar democracy in 1967.

As well as telling us that there is no clear rule, however, the table has another message. It is that if there is any general relationship between GDP per head and adoption of democracy, then China is still pretty early in that process. Such a process is not going to be a linear one anyway, since there can be no simple connection between affluence and constitutional change. Some people, especially Russians keen to justify under Vladimir Putin's leadership their move away from a fully free democracy, have recently argued that China's success poses a challenge to the idea that modernization and development are necessarily associated with democracy. But China is certainly not unusual in still being authoritarian at its current income level.

If you use the purchasing-power parity method to adjust the figures according to relative price levels and living standards, then China begins to look more advanced though still not anomalously so. Its current GDP per head at PPP moves it above the four Latin American countries when they democratized, although Mexico had been holding rigged elections for years before it adopted a properly free and open system. The way its ruling party, Institutional Revolutionary Party (PRI), held a monopoly of power amid quasielections until 1991, and still did not lose the presidency until 2000, could even be something of a model for the Chinese Communist Party.

Another problem with the theory that democracy develops when a middle class emerges is that there is no clear definition of what is meant by a middle class.[17] The term is relative, rather than absolute, and has different meanings for different purposes, anyway. It can be defined by profession, by income, by consumption patterns, or by self-identification. Probably, for political purposes, what matters is a combination of income, property ownership and savings that might lead people to demand accountability, rights and remedies at times of economic or other stress. With China's still-low GDP per head, the number of such people remains small. But as urbanization proceeds and as the economy grows, this group is likely to expand. The chart shows estimates made by the McKinsey Global Institute, a think tank attached to the McKinsey consultancy, of how and when various levels of middle-class urban citizenry, measured by income, might emerge.[18]

In 2005, if the McKinsey analysis, based on figures from the National Bureau of Statistics, is correct, China had 191 million urban households, which could equate to 400–600 million people. Of those, however, more than 77 percent had annual incomes of less than RMB 25,000, which at 2007 exchange rates means less than $3,300. Note that even that is higher than the national GDP per head, confirming that even poor urban incomes are higher

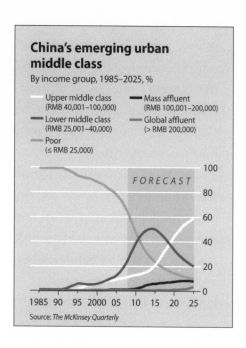

China's emerging urban middle class
By income group, 1985–2025, %

— Upper middle class (RMB 40,001–100,000)
— Lower middle class (RMB 25,001–40,000)
— Poor (≤ RMB 25,000)
— Mass affluent (RMB 100,001–200,000)
— Global affluent (> RMB 200,000)

FORECAST

100
80
60
40
20
0

1985 90 95 2000 05 10 15 20 25

Source: *The McKinsey Quarterly*

than rural ones. About 12.6 percent were considered lower middle class, with annual incomes of RMB 25,001–40,000, which at 2007 rates means $3,300–$5,250. Only 10 percent of households were earning more than that. Those numbers were a bit lower than those claimed in a report by Xinhua, China's official news agency, in June 2007, which said that China now has 80 million people in a middle class that it defines as being in households with an annual income of between RMB 60,000 and 500,000 ($7,800–$66,000).

By 2015, however, McKinsey forecasts that urban Chinese will have not only become more numerous—280 million households— but also considerably more affluent. Nearly half will be earning the inflation-adjusted equivalent of RMB 25,001–40,000; more than a quarter will be earning more than that. Those particular forecasts may prove to be over- or underestimates. But the point remains: the number of people with middle-class interests to protect will be in the hundreds of millions, not the tens of millions as is the case today.

Yet will they be angry with the Communist Party? A big reason for the resilience of Communist authoritarianism in the face of the roller-coaster economy of the 1980s and '90s, and all the disruption economic change has brought to Chinese society, is the one cited by Mr. Kroeber of the *China Economic Quarterly:* that it has shown competence and become more meritocratic. People may have occasionally been discontented but they have not often been angry, at least not since 1989.

A crucial change in the Communist Party and its governing bureaucracy since the 1980s has been that it has instituted rules and procedures for appointments and terms of office that have made it less likely to become ossified and to appear blatantly self-serving. It is no longer run by octogenarians, as it was under Deng Xiaoping, and the elders and seniors have become less able to favor their own families, as they did in the 1980s and still in the early '90s. The average age of the twenty-five members of the party's Politburo, following new appointments in October 2007, is just over sixty-one; the much larger Central Committee has an average age of fifty-five.[19] Most positions, in central and provincial government, have de facto or even de jure term limits. Leaders do retire, rather than just going on until death.

Generational change has been institutionalised: Hu Jintao's administration is known as the "fourth generation" of leaders (Mao was the first; Deng the second; Jiang Zemin's group in the 1990s the third). Following the Seventeenth Party Congress in October 2007 it has already become conventional wisdom that the leaders in the fifth generation, when Hu steps down in 2012 as he is expected to, will be Xi Jinping, the former party secretary in Shanghai, and Li Keqiang, the former party secretary in Liaoning province, who were both promoted at that congress. The party is not a meritocracy in the sense that leaders are chosen by exam or pure talent, nor in the sense that inheritance counts for nothing: The party does not yet fulfill the meritocratic, objective model envisaged by Professor Bell of Tsinghua University, mentioned earlier. But at least promotion does generally depend on ability rather than cronyism or nepotism, even if the ability rewarded may sometimes be of a distasteful sort.

Since political opinion polls cannot properly exist in China, it is not possible to know what people think about the Communist Party today. It is plausible to think that many are cynical about it— it is many years since idealism or ideology generated loyalty—but may not feel actively hostile. Living standards are rising. Wealth is being accumulated, even by quite ordinary people. Episodes of incompetence or malfeasance, such as the spread of HIV/AIDS through blood transfusions, or the initial cover-up of the SARS respiratory disease, or water contamination through toxic industrial spills, or of corruption, have been so far been too local to produce a national revolt or else have been remedied swiftly enough to deter widespread protest. The SARS crisis in 2003 was probably the riskiest recent episode. And there is one important and often overlooked way in which the state and the party have left urban households alone: They have not taxed them, or at least not heavily.

In the mid-1990s, as was previously noted, government tax revenues totaled only 10 percent of GDP. In the past decade, that figure has been doubled—but without resort to much taxation of urban households. Farmers had been a traditional source of taxes, especially for provincial governments, but their burden was cut sharply in 2004–06. So where has the money come from? The table shows that it is being levied largely on companies.

The category labeled "other" includes all sorts of taxes that ordinary people pay, such as stamp duties on share trading, or levies on property transactions. But individual income tax has accounted for only a little more than 7 percent of total tax revenue, and in recent years that proportion has been declining. In 2006 it came to RMB 245.4 billion, or 7.1 percent of the total. If Xinhua's figures are correct, then the 80 million middle-class people paid only RMB 3,000 (about $390)

Sources of China's tax revenue

%

	1995–2000, ninth 5-year plan	2001–05, tenth 5-year plan
State-owned enterprises	52.3	28.3
Collective enterprises	13.3	5.2
Enterprises listed on a stock exchange	10.3	29.4
Private companies	2.2	7.1
Foreign companies	14.5	20.5
Other	7.4	9.5

Source: China Statistical Book, quoted by Francesco Sisci, La Stampa, March 2007

each in income tax in 2006, and that calculation assumes that China's other 1.2 billion people paid nothing. Yet according to the tax law, even those at the bottom end of Xinhua's range (RMB 60,000) are supposed to pay 35 percent of their income in tax, which would mean RMB 21,000 a year. The law is not being enforced.

In 2006, the government announced that it would be. It introduced a new requirement that anyone earning more than RMB 120,000 a year (in other words, quite wealthy by Chinese standards) would have to file an income-tax return by the beginning of April 2007. Despite threats of hefty fines, however, the new law was widely ignored. Officials estimated that at least 6–7 million people should qualify for this requirement. But only about 1.6 million complied.

This does not matter, as long as the government is not short of money. It has pledged to spend much more on both health and education, since expectations for hospitals and schools are rising and weaknesses in them are a commonly cited grievance both in cities and in the countryside. As long as the economy remains buoyant the government's revenues will do so, too, and it will have a ready option to raise more cash from state-owned enterprises by forcing them to pay the state a larger dividend from their profits. (That would have the added benefit of taking away some of the money the SOEs are currently squandering on inefficient investments.) But the government's problem is twofold: Its revenues from corporate taxation would drop sharply during a recession, so just when it may need the money it will have less of it; and it feels a clear need to build a more substantial social-security system, including health, pensions and education, which would add permanently to public financial obligations. Tax revenues of 20 percent of GDP are good compared with a decade ago, but are lower than in other developing countries of a similar level of wealth.

The title of Francesco Sisci's article in *La Stampa* from which the table was taken summarizes his rather interesting argument: "China's Inevitables: Death, Taxes and Democracy."[20] In other words, he suggests that the Communist Party faces a difficult choice during the next decade: It can keep tax revenues low and risk a rise in discontent over the state of public services, or it can broaden the tax base by increasing personal taxation and then risk hearing the time-honored slogan "No taxation without representation."

The party's record in controlling dissent and repressing revolts during the past two decades suggests that it could take the second option and brazen out the risk. But it would be quite a risk, of confrontation, of discontent, of disobedience. For China is not currently an orderly place, despite the party's control and willingness to use violent methods. By the government's own statistics, the number of what it calls mass incidents rose from 8,700 in 1993, to 58,000 in 2003 and 87,000 in 2005; since then the number of incidents seems to have declined. As the official definition of a "mass incident" is that it involves at least 100 people, these figures would mean that at least 8.7 million people took part in protests in 2005, but perhaps in fact double or triple that number. These incidents are of many kinds, including those concerning layoffs, nonpayment of wages or other benefits and (in rural areas) the levying of excessive taxes, but most notable in recent years have been three sorts of protest: those against land seizures by local officials or contractors for new development, generally in the countryside; those against compulsory evictions and house demolitions for new urban development; and those against environmental dangers or actual damage.

During 2007, two protests particularly caught the eye. In Chongqing in March and April a couple became nationally famous for their resistance against the demolition of their house. Like many evicted property owners, they felt that the compensation they were being offered was inadequate. Their house, left standing on a mound in the middle of the huge inner-city construction site, and known in Chinese as a "nail house" for the way it stuck up, became famous when photographs of it were published in the Chinese press all over the country. Rather as the image of a young man standing in front of a tank in Tiananmen Square in 1989 achieved iconic status around the world (but not in China, for it was banned from the media), the picture of the Chongqing nail house achieved iconic status inside China. The couple managed to secure what they wanted, more compensation. The episode has not prevented local governments and contractors from continuing to evict people, in cities all over the country. But it encouraged other protests and hold-outs. The spirit of resistance—and successful negotiation—shown by the Chongqing couple was evidently inspiring.

The other notable protest took place in the southern city of Xiamen in May, with further demonstrations in June. It was against the planned construction of a big chemicals plant in the city's suburbs, to be built by a company run by an exiled Taiwanese entrepreneur. Intriguingly, the initial protest was summoned to the streets by a text message sent anonymously to mobile phones. Thousands of people took part, in successive marches, despite clear disapproval from the city government. The protestors claimed the chemicals plant would be dangerous to life, limb and lungs, tantamount to "dropping an atom bomb" on the city. This protest was notable because it involved an urban middle class, because it was organized using new technology and because environmental problems are so rife all over China that protests about the environment have the potential for spreading from city to city.

What, in the end, does all this tell us about the chances of change in China during the next decade and about how that change might take place? It tells us that Chinese citizens are sufficiently motivated to protest even when the economy is booming. This shouldn't be surprising—after all, protest is their only means of expressing their views on controversial subjects, given the lack of a free media or democracy—but it contradicts the commonly heard notion that the Chinese are happy with their rising living standards and are not interested in politics or rights. The same used to be heard about Hong Kong, until in 2003 at least 500,000 people, out of a population of just 6.8 million, took part in a demonstration against a proposed antisubversion law.

It tells us also that the number of Chinese with property rights to protect and savings to worry about is currently small—for China remains a lot poorer than South Korea and Taiwan were when their middle classes began pressing for democracy—but is likely to rise quite sharply if the economy continues to grow. It tells us that the Chinese government faces a dilemma about how to raise more money to pay for the public services and social safety net that it has said are necessary if it is to retain public support. Taxation, including personal taxation, is going to have to rise.

Experience tells us also that the Communist Party is unlikely to relinquish control willingly. It has proven resilient in the face of challenges and pressures before. And although protests and discontent are on the rise, it would be wrong to think of China as being altogether lacking in safety valves or protest mechanisms by which such pressures can be released without posing a threat to the party. Internet blogging by disgruntled citizens, for example, seems to be tolerated by the authorities in order to provide an outlet for public opinion, as long as it does not turn into an effort to organize sedition. Protests against local officials seem almost to be welcomed by the central government: Blame the local officials, the center often appears to be saying, and we will step in and mediate whenever it becomes necessary.

The party is certainly going to face plenty of new pressures, however, chiefly arising from the economy: the need to change course, to suppress inflation, to force industry to adjust to a dearer currency. That change of economic course might prove to be orderly, to be well managed, but the larger the Chinese economy gets, the harder it becomes to manage change in a smooth way. A likelier assumption is that the economic change will be disorderly.

A disorderly economy will pose tougher political challenges than has the fast growth seen so far during this decade. It will pose the toughest political challenge seen since the late 1980s. The pressures coming from discontented urbanites are likely to grow and become increasingly difficult to deal with. Moreover, the pressure in China's "special administrative region," Hong Kong, for a move to elections by universal suffrage at some point in the next decade—the date for introducing direct elections for Hong Kong's chief executive has been delayed from 2012 to 2017—will also be strong, especially if economic times turn tough, and could set something of an example for the rest of China. There is a chance that this could lead to radical political change, even during the next five to ten years. But the battle against it will be fierce. The Communist Party's ability to control dissent and to deal with political pressures has been remarkable, although it is helped by its willingness to use the power coming from the barrel of a gun, as Mao put it. Unless there is a serious and protracted economic downturn that saps the party's confidence and provokes wider dissent, it would be foolish to bet against the party continuing to maintain its monopoly on power.

It may do so, conceivably, by introducing some of the trappings of democracy while ensuring that its substance remains suppressed. Mexico, where the Institutional Revolutionary Party remained in control from 1929 until 2000, with elections tightly rigged until 1993, offers one model. But there are models in its own neighborhood, too. The one most often noted is Singapore, where the People's Action Party has won all the elections held since 1959 by a landslide. But a city-state of just 4.4 million people can hardly be a model for a China of 1.3 billion people, and Lee Kuan Yew, the founding father both of Singapore and the PAP, also does not fit the Communist Party's current pattern: He has founded a family dynasty, with his son now as prime minister, which the Chinese Communist Party has shown no signs of doing.

The better model is probably to China's northeast, in the land of its traditional enemy: Japan. There, the essence of the prewar state managed to survive the American-inspired introduction of democracy during the occupation of 1945–51, and even remained staffed by many of the same people. After a few hiccups in the early 1950s, Japan was a one-party state from 1955 until 1993, when the Liberal Democratic Party briefly lost power. A decade and a half later, despite wrenching economic times, the LDP is still in power. It is quite impressive, really.

4. JAPAN: POWERFUL, VULNERABLE, AGING

ON THE FACE OF IT, Japan and China have little in common—apart from their eternal suspicion of each other, some shared cultural heritage and an ideographic writing system that originated in China but which the Japanese have adapted considerably since they imported it sixteen centuries ago. Under the new constitution bequeathed by the American occupation in 1945–51, Japan was turned into a democracy, with two elected houses of parliament (the Diet), elected provincial and municipal governments, a purely symbolic imperial household, an independent judiciary, and full freedoms of speech, association and the press. No wonder the government of Shinzo Abe, which was in office just for a year in 2006–07, made such a song and dance about how Japan hopes to build an "arc of freedom and prosperity" in Asia, and that in that effort India will be a prime associate. Japan and India are Asia's two oldest democracies. Japan and China are Asia's oldest enemies. The contrast could not be greater.

Well, sort of. Once you dig below the surface of Japan's free and democratic ways you find a system that has recently had quite a few features with which the Chinese might feel comfortable. For starters, it has had just one ruling party ever since 1955, the Liberal Democratic Party, which is almost as long as the Chinese Communist Party has had its monopoly of power. The LDP did lose power in

1993 but only for ten months. Following a devastating defeat in elections for the Upper House of the Diet in July 2007, the main opposition party, now called the Democratic Party of Japan, has a majority in that lesser house for the first time, and it even looks as if it might stand a chance of winning a general election and forming a government. Shinzo Abe was forced to resign two months after the election defeat—a delay that only added to the damage to his party. But such alternation of power, if it ever happens, might not change all that much: The DPJ is led by defectors from the LDP. Until the 1990s Japan's opposition consisted of socialists and communists who were genuinely different from the LDP but had no chance of gaining power. Now the opposition does have a chance but is much harder to distinguish from those it opposes.

In any case, politicians did not matter much at all in Japan until after the country suffered its huge financial crash in 1990. When I was based in Tokyo as a reporter for the *Economist* in the mid-1980s, we foreign correspondents used to debate whether it was really worth our while to devote much time to covering elections, or to making contacts in the political parties. Election results made no evident difference to government policy, and not only because the LDP always won. The factional maneuvering inside the LDP—intraparty democracy, as the Chinese might call it—was largely incomprehensible to foreign readers and to many Japanese, too, as it was about personality and position, not policy. That, it seemed to admirers, was the genius of the Japanese system. The politicians let the real experts—bureaucrats—run the country.

My first lesson in that point came as soon as I arrived in Tokyo in October 1983. The timing of my arrival was set to make sure I was there to cover the verdict in the trial of Kakuei Tanaka, the most powerful man in the LDP, on charges of bribery by the Lockheed Corporation. Tanaka had been Japan's prime minister in the early 1970s and was the man who normalized the country's relations with China once Nixon had shocked the world by visiting Beijing, but

Tanaka then had to resign in a scandal over a land deal. Revelations of bribes of the prime minister by Lockheed came later. The trial seemed terribly exciting and important. Tanaka was found guilty and was sentenced to four years in jail. I wrote a story saying what a watershed this could prove, which is just what it wasn't.[1] Tanaka remained Japan's most powerful politician and even refused to give up his seat in the Diet while he appealed against the verdict. He was reelected to his seat in the 1984 general election by a huge margin. He lost his power and status as the kingmaker of Japanese politics only when he suffered a stroke in 1985. His big faction inside the LDP, powerful because of its command over political donations, continued to dominate the party for a further decade. Corruption scandals continued to emerge periodically, providing the only real political stories, at least for the foreign press.

In those days, the true holders of power over policy were in the bureaucracy. Politics was essentially about money and the distribution of spoils. The bureaucrats were the people foreign reporters needed to get to know, and understand. Some of them might later move into politics in any event, and those who did were likely to emerge among the LDP's highflyers. Moreover, Japan's bureaucracy, especially the elite ministries of finance, international trade and industry, and foreign affairs, was (and to a large extent still is) something close to the ideal of a Confucian meritocracy that was described in chapter 3 as a possible future path for China. Trained in the best universities, most notably the law faculty of the University of Tokyo but also the universities of Kyoto, Doshisha, Waseda and Keio, they are chosen on the basis of merit through a set of rigorous examinations—just as Chinese mandarins were for centuries in the imperial system.

Rather as the Chinese Communist Party is seeking to do now, the ministries rotate staff between jobs as a matter of course, giving officials only two to three years in each post. This reduces the chance of corruption or of becoming too friendly with the outside organizations the official may be regulating—though it does not eliminate it.

On retirement in their mid to late fifties, top officials then often take jobs in the companies with which they have been dealing, a practice known revealingly as *ama-kudari,* or descent from heaven. This certainly can introduce a form of corruption, but only during the 1990s did it become controversial as in that time of economic stagnation the aura around the bureaucracy disappeared, leaving incompetence, deception and venality as popular targets for the media. Ever since the modern Japanese state was built after the Meiji imperial restoration in 1866, the direction of influence and power has been clear: The state is superior to all other centers of power, and it has always been assumed to be doing the influencing, not the other way around.

From 1866, when more than two centuries of rule by shoguns (the equivalent of generals) was replaced by government centered on the emperor, until 1945, the supremacy of the state was made plain by that imperial role. With Japan's defeat and occupation by the United States, the emperor renounced his claims to divinity as well as any constitutional role beyond a symbolic one. But the state remained supreme. Even in Japan's postwar democracy officials have done more to make the laws than the supposed lawmakers have, or at least they did until the bureaucracy became discredited by Japan's troubles in the 1990s and power shifted to the Diet and to politicians. A key Japanese phrase the foreign reporter had to learn in the 1970s or '80s was *gyosei shido,* or "administrative guidance." What this meant was that within the loose bounds set by laws that consisted of quite general principles, drafted of course by bureaucrats, the ministries had enormous amounts of discretion to decide how the law would actually be implemented—and could change their "guidance" at will, often without even announcing it. This was "rule by law" rather than "rule of law." Empowered by the law, officials had discretion to apply it, and the scope for challenging their decisions in the courts was limited. The judiciary, in turn, was nothing like as independent as it was supposed to be.

The task now in Beijing is one of working out who really holds power in the party and the ministries, and what really are the rules they are currently setting, and the same was true of Tokyo in the 1980s. Foreign businessmen troop to Beijing, have dinners or meetings with the party leadership and return both flattered and impressed, telling people how much cleverer those top Chinese politicians are than the equivalents back home. In the 1980s the same sort of thing happened in Tokyo except that it was the well-trained bureaucrats whom the visitors eulogized. Four decades of economic success produced an unsurprising feeling of self-confidence, even arrogance, among the bureaucrats, especially once the books and articles extolling their prowess and achievements began to stack up. While normally this arrogance was held within the confines of traditional Japanese politeness, it could occasionally burst through as rudeness or even intimidation.

Two small, personal examples spring to mind. One came from what was then a state-owned enterprise, as the Chinese would call it, the Japan Tobacco and Salt Public Corporation. In 1984 I wrote a short article about how foreign cigarette companies were in theory permitted full access to the Japanese market but were in practice being barred by rules such as one permitting advertising spending only in proportion to the previous year's sales, which was an ingenious way of protecting the incumbents.[2] I was summoned back to Japan Tobacco after my article was published and was confronted by a roomful of officials and a strange sort of presentation. They had taken my article, which was only about five-hundred words long, and had cut it up, sentence by sentence, and pasted the offending points on a large piece of card—alongside which was placed Japan Tobacco's rebuttal of each point. I was made to sit through a long lecture designed to convince me of the full nature of my "misunderstanding"—which essentially consisted of my not having understood how these rules were necessary to protect Japanese citizens and ensure an orderly market.

The other example involves the man in the Ministry of Foreign Affairs in 1983–85 who had the job of dealing with the foreign media. Usually that implies a desire or need to be friendly, or at least cooperative, with the media, but not in this man's case. On one occasion, when his minister gave a speech and responded to questions at a lunch at the Foreign Correspondents' Club in Tokyo, the official came over afterward to say hello to me and to a Canadian friend. "So," he said to my friend, "still asking your stupid questions, then?" He wasn't joking. On another occasion, I had asked him to fix up an interview for me with a foreign-ministry specialist, which I later canceled as the meeting was no longer needed. This proved to be a faux pas. The spokesman rang up, furious: "Is this the behavior of a gentleman?" he yelled, before slamming the phone down. He then refused to take calls from me for a week. He wasn't joking this time, either. He was just showing who was boss—in his view.

A media handler at the foreign ministry is not one of the more important examples of the species of arrogant officialdom, although he will have become one later when he was promoted to more senior posts. The prime examples were the top officials in the Ministry of Finance and the Ministry of International Trade and Industry. Typically, even at the height of Japan's powers they did not become offensive or aggressive. Rather, they became more impervious to argument or criticism, and more convinced—as Japanese businessmen were, too—that anything Japan touched would soon turn to gold. The 1990s destroyed that confidence. A breakfast with a senior finance-ministry official in the late 1990s offered the clearest and simplest sign that things had changed. His country's sovereign credit rating was declining, as worries grew about financial collapse and about the rising burden of public debt. "What I am not sure of," he said as he munched on his French toast, "is whether our rating will end up above, or below, Botswana's." His humility, mixed with a sense of humor, was refreshing. Neither quality is found in abundance in ministries in Beijing these days.

Japan's main resemblance to China in the decades before its troubles began lay in its resemblance to an idealized, socialist China rather than the real one. Lech Walesa, the hero of Poland's Solidarity trade union and later the country's president, visited Japan several times during the 1980s, while Poland remained under Soviet control. Japan, he commented, was the only truly successful example of socialism that had ever existed. He was directing a jibe at his own country's communist rulers, but he had a point. Incomes in Japan were so equal that 80 percent of the population told opinion pollsters that they considered themselves middle class. Unemployment was low. Industrial relations were excellent, with workers enjoying strong legal protections and a cooperative, consultative relationship with the managers. Banks kept a close eye on the companies to which they lent money, but in return did not force borrowers into bankruptcy nor impose penal lending terms. Financing conditions did not vary much between an industry's laggards and its leaders. This became known as the "convoy system," as all firms in an industry sailed together. Akio Mikuni, founder of Japan's first independent domestic credit-rating agency, coined a more critical term: "financial socialism."

Even during the twenty-first century's first decade, after more than ten painful years of stagnation, banking collapse and deflation, this "socialist" instinct lingered on. Cutting jobs was frowned on and rising inequality was considered highly controversial. In 2005, when I spent time in Japan researching a special article for the *Economist,* I was told a joke that was then circulating in Tokyo about young Chinese studying at a university there. The Chinese students are asked why they spend so much of their spare time with other Chinese rather than with the Japanese students. "Because we are afraid they might teach us communism," comes the answer.

Let us not exaggerate or mislead. Japan is not like Communist China. It really is a free country. There are no political prisoners. Public opinion, the media and the judiciary have all acted as checks on abuses of power by the monopolizing party, the LDP, by the bureaucracy and by big business. As in all countries, such abuses have occurred. But they have been restrained, kept within limits that have been considerably tighter than in China. When during the high point of bureaucratic domination of policy in the 1980s a Dutch journalist-scholar, Karel van Wolferen, wrote an eye-opening book on the country's politics, he did not conclude that there was some secret agenda behind Japanese behavior, nor a secret power structure, nor a hidden cabal pulling the strings—as an equivalent observer might conclude today if he were trying to unravel the mysteries of Chinese power and "the China threat."[3] He concluded that the problem with Japan was that there was no center of accountable power and no control room.

Subsequent events vindicated this analysis—though not quite in the way Mr. van Wolferen may have expected. His assumption was that because there was no center of power, Japan would continue careering along on its course of fast economic growth, rising exports and highly valued stock and property markets, while continuing to provoke disputes with America. Trying to bargain with Japanese politicians and even senior bureaucrats over those disputes would be fruitless, he said, because none of them was in charge; the course was set by the anonymous but pervasive interest in continual industrial growth. Yet starting virtually from the tolling in of the new year by the temple bells on January 1, 1990, when Japan's stock market crash began, the country took a different sort of course, one of economic stagnation, 75 percent falls in share prices and 70 percent falls in property prices, financial-system collapse and deflation. Japan moved from worldwide adulation in the 1980s to being dismissed as irrelevant, passé or even permanently dysfunctional in the 1990s. Since there was no center of power, and since the country's problems seemed so vast, there was no person, position or institution to take the lead in finding solutions.

Now Japan is back. Not that it ever went away exactly, but views of its economic prowess and political potential had been so positive during the 1980s that its prolonged stumble and at times near financial collapse during the following decade made it seem as if a giant had suddenly vanished. Since 2002 its economy has been recovering, with (by 2007) five years of continuous growth, which is the longest (though not the strongest) period of expansion since 1945. After April 2001, with the election of Junichiro Koizumi as leader of the LDP and hence prime minister, Japan again began to stand tall in the world and commenced a new period of assertiveness in its international relations, an assertiveness that saw it breaking old taboos by sending troops to help in the rebuilding of Iraq and ships to give logistical support for the war in Afghanistan, but also opening old wounds by arguing truculently with China over territory and history.

Mr. Koizumi did not invent all of these things; he was not a clean break with the political or policy past in the way that Margaret Thatcher was such a break in Britain during her time as prime minister in 1979–90. But he accentuated trends that were already underway, as well as ensuring that reforms were hard (though never impossible) to put in reverse. The Japan that he passed in 2006 to his ill-fated successor, Shinzo Abe, and to Mr. Abe's successor in 2007, Yasuo Fukuda, was a Japan with a stronger economy and with restructured companies; it was a Japan with more confidence about its stature and role in the world; but also it was a Japan acutely conscious that it faced two threats to its security and prosperity from among its closest neighbors: North Korea, with its missile tests (the first of which sent a missile sailing over the Japa-

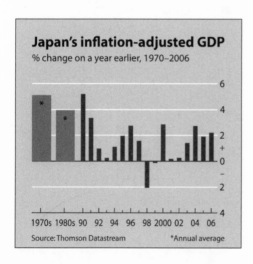

Japan's inflation-adjusted GDP
% change on a year earlier, 1970–2006

1970s 1980s 90 92 94 96 98 2000 02 04 06
Source: Thomson Datastream   *Annual average

nese archipelago in 1998) and its nuclear-weapons program; and of course China.

Since Japan's economic troubles began, the world has been changed by the rise of China. Its economy is now almost five times bigger than it was in 1990; its share of world exports has risen from 1.9 percent to 8.1 percent, overtaking Japan's (which was 8.5 percent in 1990, 5.4 percent in 2006); and, crucially for the region, China's share of imports from other Asian countries has risen from 4.3 percent to 10.5 percent. China's official military spending is now slightly higher than Japan's, at $45 billion in 2007. For the better part of a century, Japan was alone in Asia as a modernized, industrial country; for a further half century, Japan was well ahead of Asia's other modernizers. Now, politically, Japan risks being overshadowed in its own neighborhood, or even physically endangered.

Japan's military forces are currently a fair match for China's, except for Japan's lack of nuclear weapons. There has anyway been no direct confrontation between the Chinese and Japanese forces for more than half a century. Nevertheless, Japanese strategists have noted the increasingly daring operations of China's submarine fleet in the international waters around Japan. Most alarmingly, a nuclear-powered Chinese submarine entered Japanese waters (near its southernmost islands) in November 2004 in a journey that seemed designed to test the Japanese and American navies' detection technology. In recent years, Chinese exploration vessels have also made increasingly provocative forays into an oil and gas field in the East China Sea, the rights to which are disputed between Japan and China.[4]

After October 2001, when the newly elected Mr. Koizumi paid an apologetic visit to the museum of the Sino-Japanese War at Marco Polo Bridge, just outside Beijing, the place from which all-out war between Japan and China is said to have begun in 1937, the Japanese prime minister exchanged no further official visits with his Chinese counterparts until the newly elected Shinzo Abe visited in October

2006.[5] Instead, Mr. Koizumi's long prime ministership was a period of Sino-Japanese rancour, during which anti-Japanese demonstrations were held in Beijing and other cities, and Chinese football fans attacked Japanese fans at the final of the Asian Cup in Beijing in 2004. Some of these protests were provoked by Mr. Koizumi's annual visits to pay homage at the Yasukuni war shrine in Tokyo, protests that only made the proud prime minister even more determined to visit the shrine. During this period, I asked Taro Aso, who was later Japan's foreign minister under both Mr. Koizumi and Shinzo Abe, what interpretation should be put on the recurrent tensions between China and Japan. His reply was typically blunt, and unfortunately accurate: "China and Japan have hated each other for a thousand years," he said; "Why should things be any different now?"

Why indeed? Mr. Aso, Mr. Abe and Mr. Koizumi are all among the more nationalistic Japanese politicians. But standing up to China is also advocated by senior politicians in the opposition Democratic Party of Japan, notably by a former leader, Seiji Maehara. The DPJ's current leader, Ichiro Ozawa, is also a nationalist, even if (unlike Mr. Koizumi) he wants all Japan's military involvement overseas to take place under United Nations mandates. "Standing up" does not necessitate confrontation, which is why both Mr. Abe and, since September 2007, Mr. Fukuda have used their prime ministerships to try to soothe the rancour between Japan and China, to prevent it from getting out of hand. Japanese public opinion appears to favor a soft sort of nationalism rather than a hard, militaristic sort. But there is no strong group in mainstream politics that advocates an actively conciliatory approach to China. The debate is about degrees of firmness, rather than about, for example, whether to snuggle closer to China as an alternative to the alliance with the United States.

Concern about China is now a central feature of Japanese politics and policy. Since the concern is only likely to grow as China's strength and regional interests grow, too, more and more of Japanese policy will be shaped by it. That has already been true of efforts to reform and reinforce the terms of the U.S.–Japan alliance; it explains Japan's investment in surveillance technology, satellites and a space program; it explains Japan's eagerness to involve India in regional affairs through the East Asia Summit launched in 2005; it is likely to shape further Japanese initiatives to develop and deepen pan-Asian regional institutions; and it will be the spur that will keep all Japanese governments, regardless of which party leads them, forever seeking ways to bolster economic growth, introduce more market-based reform, and encourage Japanese industry to maintain a clear technological lead.

That economic effort will, however, have to overcome another obstacle: aging. In 2005 Japan's population started to decline, albeit by just .02 percent per year, as did its labor force.[6] The birth rate has slumped, to 1.3 per woman (the replacement rate is 2.1); life expectancy is the world's highest, and the eight-million-strong baby-boom generation of 1947–49 is starting to retire. By 2015, more than 25 percent of the Japanese people will be age sixty-five or older and by 2025 the figure will be almost 30 percent, compared with 12 percent in 1990. The proportion of the population who are of working age, defined as fifteen to sixty-four years old, is slipping, from nearly 70 percent in 1990 to 65 percent now and 60 percent in 2020, but the most dramatic drop has been in the number of children: 35 percent of the population in 1950, 18.2 percent in 1990 and 13.5 percent now.

The result is that both population decline and a rise in the average age are inevitable, at least for the next thirty to forty years: Even if fertility were to increase dramatically, there are too few children today to be able to generate a big increase in the total number of children any time soon. Demographic projections that go further ahead than that depend on assumptions about highly variable factors such as marriages, births and deaths, and so should be considered to be guesses rather than destiny, but the range of guesses for the Japanese population in 2050 are that it will have shrunk from about 128 million now to somewhere between 85 million and a little over 100 million. Whether or not those longer-term guesses turn out to be correct, it is clear that during the next decade or two Japan is going to be carrying extra economic burdens: The public finances will be stretched by increasing medical and pensions costs; and companies will find that the Japanese citizens available to work for them decline in number and increase in age, both of which mean that labor costs are likely to rise.

The superachieving Japan of the 1980s would have been expected to take those extra burdens in stride. The underachieving Japan of the 1990s might be expected to be flattened by them. The key questions are essentially two: How might Japan's economy now cope with its new burdens and with this new environment; and how might Japan react, in political terms, to the new challenges that it faces?

To come to a view of the potential strength of Japan's economy during the next ten to fifteen years, we must try to decide how much of the weakness that it has shown during the past fifteen years was caused by the exceptional conditions of that period rather than by underlying problems; to try to decide how much has been done to deal with any underlying problems that did play a significant part in shaping Japan's poor performance; and, finally, to try to decide how much difference the burden of demography will make.

There can be no doubt that Japan did suffer conditions during the 1990s that were exceptional and are extremely unlikely to be repeated. The best, if perhaps overdramatic, analogy is with America during the Great Depression of the 1930s. The Wall Street crash of 1929 and the monetary contraction that followed caused huge direct losses to those who had invested in shares that lost 89 percent of their value between their peak in September 1929 and their trough in July 1932; more important, it caused a cascade of bank collapses and financial insolvency that led to foreclosures on loans, personal and corporate bankruptcies, and a vast contraction in credit. Falling prices led to falling wages and a spiral of deflation, with consumption dropping all the while. Even Franklin Roosevelt's New Deal reforms and expanded public spending found it hard to lift the American economy out of its trough. But America's dismal performance during the 1930s was not a good indication of the country's underlying strengths in wartime, nor of its postwar economic and political status.

Some of the same things can be said of Japan during the 1990s and now in its poststagnation decade.[7] When a financial bubble as large as Japan's of the 1980s finally bursts—and pretty much everyone now agrees that it was a bubble, though few thought so while it was inflating—the consequences are bound to be disastrous. The 55 percent fall in the broad TOPIX (Tokyo Stock Price Index) of share prices between January 1, 1990, and the end of 1992 caused big losses for retail investors and for the many companies that had taken to boosting their profits by *zaiteku,* financial engineering, and an even worse situation for the banks that had relied on their own holdings of shares as part of the capital cushion they were obliged to maintain under international agreements. Share prices did not reach their trough until March 2003, by which time the TOPIX was down 73 percent (and the narrower but more widely cited index, the Nikkei, was down 80 percent). Property prices in Japan's six biggest cities peaked in September 1990 and fell 76 percent to their trough in early 2005; residential prices fell 66 percent in the same period. That property collapse played havoc with the other side of the banks' balance sheets as borrowers defaulted on their debts and collateral was wiped out. Depositors withdrew their cash, and some banks went bust themselves. Lending growth slowed and then went into reverse. Falling consumption and the credit contraction put thousands of conventional companies into trouble, too, unable to service their debts. "Nonperforming" loans on the banks' books kept on climbing, reaching their peak (of ¥4 trillion, or $328 billion at the then exchange rate) only in 2001, eleven years after the bubble had initially burst.

Compared with America in the 1930s, Japan had a much more favorable international economic climate in which to have its financial crash. Trade was growing, not contracting as it had during the 1930s. Capital flowed freely between countries. International politics were benign—in fact, given that the cold war was just ending, they were more benign than at any point since 1945. Japan also had a very favorable situation in its own public finances: As the 1980s ended, the government was running a budget surplus. This made it easy to expand spending and borrowing in an effort to support domestic demand and prevent stagnation from turning into a full-blown slump—which the government did, sending the budget deficit to a peak of 8.2 percent of GDP in 2002. The formula recommended by John Maynard Keynes as a solution to the deflation of the 1930s—borrow and spend as much as you can, even on wasteful activities, just to inject cash into the economy—was adopted wholesale by Japan in the 1990s. That expansion in public spending also helped delay the process of political change, for it provided a huge flow of cash for the traditional, pork-barrel tendency of the LDP to exploit. But it helped prevent an economic drama from becoming a disaster.

The boom in share and property prices in the latter half of the 1980s had made an already strong Japanese economy look far more powerful than it was, rather like an Olympic athlete using steroids. Ultracheap, abundant capital inflated growth artificially, stimulating a lot of investment that later turned out to be wasteful. Similarly, the postbust financial conditions of the 1990s depressed the economy in an artificial—or, at least, temporary and exceptional—way. The Olympic athlete now looked like a wimp.

The banking system ceased to function under the weight of nonperforming loans and of fear of collapse. The excessive, wasteful investments of the late 1980s burdened business with a huge amount of unused and uneconomic production capacity. Mass unemployment was avoided as banks kept bankrupt companies afloat by not withdrawing their credit lines, and as larger companies dealt with overcapacity by cutting pay and freezing recruitment rather than by lay-offs. That meant, however, that prices and profits in many sectors were depressed by the continued presence of thousands of "zombie" companies being kept alive by the banks. It also meant that a generation of young school-leavers and university graduates ended up unemployed or, more usually, underemployed in low-skill part-time jobs.

Cheap capital had led to waste and misallocation of resources during the 1980s, as companies, small and large, diversified recklessly and built unneeded factories and buildings. But the waste and misallocation took a new and equally damaging form in the 1990s as capital was channelled to inefficient zombie firms rather than efficient ones, and to vast public works schemes in a country that already had all the bridges, roads and flood defenses that it really needed. The result, from 1998 onward, was deflation, a spiral of falling prices and wages that deterred consumption (because things would get cheaper if you waited) and kept the economy weak and vulnerable to further shocks.[8]

These exceptional, postcrash conditions can be summarized as consisting of three sorts of excess: excess debt, excess capacity and excess labor. Analytically, excess labor is slightly different from the other two, for it is more an effect than a cause of problems, though it has, as we shall see, prolonged the period of deflation and has depressed consumption. By 2007, it was the only one of the three excesses that had still not disappeared.

Excess debt, in corporate balance sheets and as nonperforming loans weighing down on the banks, lasted until 2002–04. The initial reaction to the financial crash in the banks and their then supervisory agency, the Ministry of Finance, in the early 1990s was to deny that any excess existed in the hope that conditions would improve and allow lenders and borrowers to work their way out of their problems; accounts were falsified and official reports on the level of bad loans were deliberately understated. By 1997–98, when the East Asian financial crisis dealt another blow to Japanese banks, the problem had become too large to deny or ignore. Big Japanese lending institutions were in danger of collapse. The government of Ryutaro Hashimoto (an LDP prime minister, of course) became Japan's first big reforming government of the decade. His administration set up a new agency to take over the task of financial regulation, the Financial Services Agency; injected ¥30 trillion (then $263 billion) into the banks, taking several into public ownership; and laid down new rules for how banks needed to account for and write off bad loans. The Hashimoto administration also brought the public spending boom to an end, as a ballooning budget deficit threatened to send the public finances out of control.

The final years of the 1990s were Japan's time of awakening, when civil servants and politicians alike came to recognize that action to reform the financial system was unavoidable. It was not quite a watershed, however, as resistance to tougher financial regulation from the banks and their LDP backers remained fierce, as was the backlash against public spending curbs. The new agency, the FSA, struggled to establish itself; its new rules on banks' bad-loan accounting were applied only limply. No center of power proved strong enough to push through reform against the interest-group resistance.

It took a political drama to change things: the election to the LDP leadership in April 2001 of a maverick, Junichiro Koizumi, who was prepared to flout party conventions, to challenge party interest groups and to appeal directly to the public for support. Mr. Koizumi did not invent the financial reforms that eventually cleaned up the country's excess debt and restored its banking system to health; but it was he, through the use of a stubborn, market-minded economics professor from Keio University, Heizo Takenaka, as his financial-reform supremo, who actually implemented them. Between their peak in 2002 and Mr. Koizumi's retirement from office in 2006, the vast pile of nonperforming loans was cut by three-quarters. The banking system was at last cleaned up.

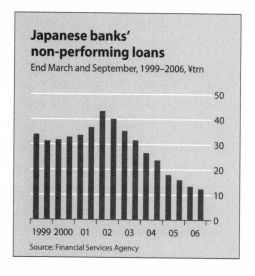

Japanese banks' non-performing loans
End March and September, 1999–2006, ¥trn

Source: Financial Services Agency

The removal of this excess debt was helped, ironically given Mr. Koizumi's frequent arguments with the Chinese leadership, by a strong rise in Japanese exports to China in 2002–04, which raised the profits of companies in a wide range of industries, enabling them to pay down some of their debts. The ratio of debt to operating profits for large and medium-sized firms halved from 15–20 percent at its peak in 1999 to well below 10 percent by 2005; smaller firms also reduced their debt ratios, though only by about a quarter.

The removal of excess capacity was a matter of attrition and time rather than of new laws or government policies. It was a process that depended on the state of domestic and export demand as well as on companies' decisions to mothball or close unwanted factories. The weakness of demand until 2002 delayed this process. By 2005, however, the capacity-utilization rate reported by the Ministry of Economy, Trade and Industry (the restructured Ministry of International Trade and Industry) was back at 1992 levels. Excess labor, however, has taken even longer to absorb, with the result that wages were still rising only modestly in 2007 despite five years of economic recovery and despite widespread predictions by demographers and economists of a looming labor shortage. Those modest rises in wages explain why economic growth during those five years has also been only modest (if a lot better than during the previous five), for without higher incomes, consumer spending cannot be higher either, in the medium term.

The labor market has been Japan's greatest area of legal and social change—and is probably the single most important part of the economy to watch to find indications of whether the current recovery is likely to be sustained and even gather strength.[9] During the 1960s, '70s and '80s, workers were given a great deal of protection and security in return for cooperative behavior. Strikes were few and far between and incomes rose steadily but never spectacularly. Workers at smaller companies were protected chiefly by the law; at bigger companies legal protection was supplemented by corporate promises of lifetime employment, pay rising with seniority and comfortable pensions. Part-time workers had a less cushy time, but most of them were women whose husbands' jobs were protected.

In 1990, part-timers and workers on temporary contracts accounted for 18.8 percent of the labor force. The use of part-time workers expanded during the 1990s, though legal restrictions prevented companies from replacing whole swathes of their workforces with such cheaper "nonregular" workers. But changes to the labor laws in 2001–03 then opened the floodgates for such restructuring of workforces, especially in manufacturing. Firms were allowed to treat workers as temporary for up to three years, and permission to use nonregular workers was extended to virtually the whole of the economy. As a result, by 2005 such workers made up 30 percent of the workforce and companies had boosted their profits spectacularly by cutting their labor costs. Full-time, regular employment continued to fall until that year; part-time and nonregular employment was growing by 6–8 percent a year, as the chart shows, saving employers huge sums in wages. Many big employers have continued to voice their commitment to the old lifetime employment system. Prominent among them has been Fujio Mitarai, president of the Canon camera and printing company until 2006 and since then the firm's chairman and the head of the Nippon Keidanren, the country's biggest employers' federation. He says Canon will continue its lifetime commitment for its "core" workers—but that now means those in sales and R&D. In Canon's Japanese factories fully 70 percent of the workers are on nonregular terms, up from 50 percent in 2000 and only 10 percent in 1995.

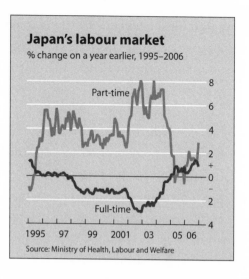

Japan's labour market
% change on a year earlier, 1995–2006

Source: Ministry of Health, Labour and Welfare

In the spring of 2005, the lines in the chart finally crossed: Full-time jobs were being created again, and the rate of growth of part-time employment dropped sharply. It looked as if companies were becoming sufficiently confident again to take on costlier full-timers, and that the supply of potential part-timers might anyway be drying up. The second of those impressions proved to be false. In 2005–07, part-time jobs resumed their growth. Labor turned out not to be scarce after all. The reason was that there were more people available and willing to do part-time jobs than had been expected: women, who had been discouraged from looking for work when the economy stagnated in the 1990s; recent retirees, whose number is already being boosted as the first members of the postwar baby-boom generation reach the age of sixty; and young unskilled people who lack the training to take full-time jobs. Instead of contracting, the labor force expanded.

The result, in 2007–08, was that the much-forecast labor shortage still seemed only a remote possibility; wages and incomes remained flat; and a new political issue emerged, of inequality. The gap between the top 10 percent of Japanese incomes and the bottom 10 percent had widened, not quite to American levels of inequality but close to the British level. This took Japan's income inequality to a point just above the OECD average, where Japan had always previously been below average.[10] Furthermore, Japan was the only member country in the OECD in which the level of absolute poverty rose between the mid-1980s and 2000. Unlike America, the cause of rising inequality was not principally a rise in top incomes, but the stagnation or even fall in the lowest incomes, under pressure from cheap global competition—i.e., China—but also because of the creation in the 2001–03 labor reforms of a two-tier labor market. The main opposition party, the Democratic Party of Japan, has begun to use the issue of inequality as its main means of differentiation from the ruling LDP.

With no fresh impetus from rising household consumption, economic growth has looked respectable but unexciting: Average annual growth in real terms of 2.1 percent in 2002–06 was not to be sniffed at, especially in comparison with the 1990s, but was hardly a renaissance. Deflation continued to cast a shadow over Japan's future. Although price-adjusted GDP growth ("real" GDP) was positive throughout that period, the nominal value of Japan's GDP remained below its 1997 peak until 2007, as the chart shows.

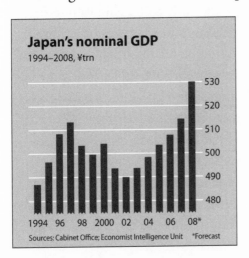

Japan's nominal GDP
1994–2008, ¥trn

530
520
510
500
490
480

1994   96   98   2000   02   04   06   08*
Sources: Cabinet Office; Economist Intelligence Unit   *Forecast

Hence, after much excitement during the Koizumi years at the fact that Japan was recovering at all, and at the sense that change was occurring both in politics and in economic policies, questions began legitimately to be raised about how healthy Japan's economy really promised to be in the future. The OECD regularly publishes estimates of the future potential growth rate for its member countries, based on trends in their labor forces and in productivity growth. For Japan, its forecast for 2008–12 is bleak: a mere 1.4 percent annual average growth in real GDP. That is better than for Italy (1.1 percent) but compares with forecasts of 2.4 percent for Britain and 3.1 percent for the United States. After all, the Japanese labor force is due to shrink, and productivity growth in the past decade has been meagre. Productivity growth has accelerated a little since 2002, from just 1.5 percent a year in 1991–2001 to about 2 percent a year, but faster productivity growth is a normal feature of economic recoveries as firms are able to expand output without hiring more workers. An uptick from 1.5 percent to 2 percent during that part of the economic cycle is not an indication that anything fundamental has changed. What is needed is something more dramatic. Japan in the next decade needs to emulate America in the 1990s, when the "new economy" brought a sharp and unexpected jump in U.S. productivity.

If the OECD's forecast turns out to be accurate, then Japan will have little chance of standing tall and strong alongside Asia's new rising power, China. In that case, the task in Japan would be one of managing the country's relative decline, and of preventing China from exploiting that decline or America from becoming disenchanted with its main ally in the Pacific.

The political trends in 2007 seemed to confirm this poor prognosis. Mr. Koizumi's survival as prime minister for five years in 2001–06 had brought to an end a period of revolving-door politics, under which Japan had had ten short-lived and forgettable prime ministers in little more than a decade. His successor, Shinzo Abe, was, at fifty-two, the youngest prime minister since 1945. But then in July 2007, elections were held for half the seats in the Upper House of the Diet, and Mr. Abe's LDP suffered its worst result in half a century. As has already been noted, Mr. Abe had to resign two months later, to be replaced by an older and safer pair of hands, those of Yasuo Fukuda, a seventy-two-year-old former cabinet secretary whose father was prime minister during the 1970s. The main reasons for the 2007 defeat, according to opinion polls in the *Yomiuri*, Japan's largest-selling newspaper, were depressingly familiar ones: outrage at bureaucratic mismanagement, this time by the state pensions body, the Social Insurance Agency, which turned out to have lost 50 million pension records; political corruption scandals, which had forced three of Mr. Abe's cabinet ministers to resign and one to commit suicide in a nine-month period in office; and, above all, worries about the economy.

So has nothing changed? Plainly, not enough. But contrary to appearances much has in fact changed, and there are several good arguments for greater optimism both about the evolution of Japanese politics and about the prospects for faster economic growth. Admittedly, the task of assessing how much reform has really taken place, and with what future effect, is hard. Japan is not a society that favors sudden, revolutionary, highly visible change: The only example in the past several centuries came with the Meiji Restoration in the 1860s. In 1945, dramatic change was forced on Japan by wartime defeat and occupation, but in that situation Japan had no choice.

Since 1990, despite calls by many pundits for Japan to find its own Margaret Thatcher or to emulate the "shock therapy" used to jolt Poland from communism to capitalism, there has been no such revolution. The analyst of Japan instead has to add up the many small, incremental reforms that have taken place and decide whether the cumulative effect has been, or will prove to be, transformational. The incremental changes that are now bearing down upon politics, the bureaucracy and the economy began to be introduced in the early 1990s and have been added to, bit by bit, ever since. And they do appear to add up to a transformation: a revolution by stealth.

Let us start with politics.[11] In 1993, the LDP lost power for the first time since 1955. It regained it swiftly when the new government, led by Morihiro Hosokawa, an LDP defector, and consisting of a motley collection of new parties, collapsed nine months later. But politics really had changed, for to recapture power the LDP had to form a strange coalition with its main, longtime opponent, the Japan Socialist Party. It was a time of great political flux, with new parties forming and mutating with bewildering speed. It was also a time when political reform was the one issue on which this mutating set of political parties could agree. So in 1994 the electoral system was reformed to replace the old multiseat constituency system with one based on single-member constituencies. And in the same year public financing of political parties was introduced, along with a political ethics law that made candidates legally responsible for illegal actions by their campaign supporters even if they have no direct knowledge of them.

These changes reduced—though of course did not eliminate—the role of political donations and corruption. They made election campaigns a bit cheaper, but also funneled money through the party secretaries-general rather than through internal party factions, making the raising and use of it easier to police. The new ethics law removed what had been a common defense against corruption charges, namely that candidates claimed not to know what their staff had been doing in their name.

A second important area of change lay in the relationship between the Diet and the bureaucracy.[12] Decades of domination of the Diet by the LDP had meant that parliamentary committees counted for little, and the LDP itself got involved with policy chiefly when public-works spending was involved. As we have seen, the civil service's role was paramount. But economic failure, combined with corruption scandals that even involved civil servants at the elite ministries of Finance and Foreign Affairs, served to undermine the bureaucracy's credibility and to subject it to much greater public scrutiny than before. And a more evenly balanced electoral situation, with new parties and LDP defections challenging the old ruling party's hegemony, made parliamentary politics more active and increased the role of the parties' policy committees and of the Diet committees themselves. Much more legislation came to be written or amended in the Diet, and less was simply passed on by the bureaucracy.

A third set of changes, supplementing this alteration of the balance between civil servants and politicians, increased the role of public pressure. Until a new law was introduced in 1998, individuals could not easily form associations or lobby groups to promote their ideas or favorite issues because such nonprofit organizations had no legal basis. Since then, well over 30,000 nonprofits have been registered, and there are thought to be a further 50,000 such civil society organizations that have not registered. That opportunity to influence policy debates has so far mainly had an impact at a local level, especially on environmental disputes. In addition, a freedom-of-information law was passed in 2001. The way has also been laid for courts of law to play a bigger role in reviewing public policy, with sixty-eight new professional law schools being established with the intent of doubling the number of qualified lawyers during the next decade. A new intellectual-property court has been established; a two-year time limit has been imposed on all first-instance trials of criminal and civil cases in order to speed up the judicial process; and citizen juries are to be introduced for some civil cases.

Jeff Kingston, professor of Asian studies at Temple University in Tokyo, describes this process in a book titled *Japan's Quiet Transformation,* as one by which the old system of "rule by law," with wide administrative discretion and limited legal redress, is gradually being replaced by something more akin to rule of law, in which citizens have the ability to gain information about the activities of those who govern them and to challenge the government in the courts.[13]

The practice of *gyosei shido,* administrative guidance, has now for-mally been banned. The media are now just as keen to expose bu-reaucratic malpractice as political corruption, and the information law makes it easier to do so. The fact that in 2007 the Social Insur-ance Agency had lost 50 million pension records (each person may have several, for different sorts of pension) was discovered by a for-mer journalist from the *Nikkei* financial daily who is now a Diet member for the opposition DPJ. That is why this became a decisive issue in the Upper House election of that year. Bureaucrats remain powerful, but their power is in decline and they are no longer im-mune from criticism and attack.

Politicians remain money-obsessed and are organized in parties that are pretty dysfunctional. The parties have also changed, how-ever. Mr. Koizumi reformed the LDP by weakening the power of its factions; the new political funding law of 1994 had already weakened them by transferring control of money to party headquarters, and Mr. Koizumi added to that process by disregarding the factions when choosing his cabinets, flouting previous practice. Frailer prime ministers may well revert to old practices, but Mr. Koizumi showed that it was possible to make loyalty to the leadership matter more than loyalty to the factions. He reinforced that point by strength-ening the prime minister's office itself, giving it more money and staff, and establishing a new Council of Economic and Fiscal Pol-icy to act, at least in theory, as an overlord, under the prime minis-ter's control, of all economic policy.

Mr. Koizumi's biggest contribution to politics lay in his demon-stration that personal popularity, enhanced by clever marketing techniques and his strikingly photogenic appearance, could be a new source of political power. He used it to spectacular effect in 2005 when he called a snap general election after being defeated in the Diet over his trademark policy proposal, the privatization of Japan's Post Office. That measure was more important than it sounds, for as well as delivering mail Japan Post also runs the country's (and by some measures, the world's) biggest savings bank and had in effect financed most of the government's public works schemes. Mr. Koizumi kicked out of his party thirty-seven Lower House members who had opposed postal privatization, and succeeded in winning the general election by a landslide, gaining the LDP its biggest Lower House majority since 1986.

It is, you might well think, peculiar that a political party that presided over Japan's equivalent of the 1929 Wall Street crash and that failed to cure the country's ensuing economic stagnation should be reelected at all, let alone by a landslide. As long ago as 1998 I put a headline on the cover of the *Economist* that drew a rather petulant protest from the Japanese embassy in London: Commenting on the government's bungling of a bank-rescue plan, my headline was JAPAN'S AMAZING ABILITY TO DISAPPOINT.[14] A veteran Diet member with a wry sense of humor, Motoo Shiina, who was chairman of an annual UK-Japan conference in which I often took part, offered a different sort of dissent when that cover was discussed at the 1999 conference. The correct headline, he said, would have been THE JAPANESE PEOPLE'S AMAZING ABILITY NOT TO BE DISAPPOINTED. He was right, even if his headline was not as snappy as the original.

During the 1990s, Japanese voters frequently showed their displeasure with conventional politics by electing outsiders such as comedians, actors and novelists as city mayors and prefectural governors, but they never plucked up the courage to kick out the LDP altogether and give the opposition enough seats to form a government. That is because the opposition parties looked incoherent and were forever changing their names and memberships. Now, though, the main opposition party, the DPJ, has existed for ten years and is gaining credibility. It made the mistake in 2005 of opposing Mr. Koizumi's postal privatization, which lost it a lot of ground in the general election of that year. But it is now strong in the Upper House since the 2007 elections and even stands a fair chance of being able to do well enough to form a government after the next Lower House election. Of course, that doesn't guarantee that it will. But even to contemplate an alternative government feels quite radical, for Japan.

Just as political reform laws were creeping stealthily on to the statute book during the 1990s, so were economic reforms. Important sectors such as telecommunications, transport, energy, financial services, food and drink, and retailing were all opened up through deregulation to new competition. The Cabinet Office, no doubt self-servingly, claimed in 2004 that reforms in those industries since 1992 had added 4.6 percent to national income. But a lot more needs to be done if the rate of productivity growth is to accelerate.[15]

Japan's economy is not as open to trade, and thus international competition, as are other rich, developed economies. Formal trade barriers are low, but informal barriers still restrict imports as well as foreign direct investment, according to the OECD. Nevertheless, capital market reforms could eventually break open some of the barriers to competition, efficiency and even foreign investment. Their effects can be subtle, but also slow to emerge.

For example, accounting rules have been changed to force companies to report full, consolidated results taking in all their subsidiaries, and to permit them to organize their subsidiaries under a single holding company, a practice that had been banned by the American occupation after 1945 in order to weaken the Japanese conglomerates, known as *zaibatsu,* that had supported the prewar military regime. The whole of Japan's commercial code has been rewritten, making it easier (among other things) for companies to dispose of unwanted divisions and clarifying the rights and responsibilities of shareholders. Industries that were highly fragmented before the 1990s have undergone consolidation: James Abegglen, a veteran consultant in Tokyo whose book *Kaisha,* cowritten with George Stalk of the Boston Consulting Group, helped build global admiration for the Japanese corporations in the 1980s, wrote in his 2006 sequel of how fourteen oil companies became just four; how seven big cement firms merged into three; how fourteen pulp and paper firms became three; how five big steel firms became four; how fifteen big banks became just three; and so on.[16]

In broad terms, the reason why things went wrong in the 1980s is that firms that had previously shown great discipline, flexibility and strategic clarity lost those virtuous characteristics. In part, some may simply have become overconfident: Nemesis followed hubris. But also, rather as in China now, the availability of abundant and seemingly costless capital took away the incentives to choose and manage investments rigorously. That happened because of a monetary policy that was directed at managing the exchange rate of the yen against the dollar, rather than at preventing an asset-price bubble, but also because there was little deregulation during the 1980s and thus little stimulus from fresh domestic competition and innovation. Cheap and abundant capital meant that banks lost their grip over companies that had previously been under their supervision, but capital markets—i.e., shareholders and bond investors— did not provide a substitute for that lack of discipline.

It follows from that analysis that an important sort of change to look for now is the emergence of new discipline, better incentives, fresh sources of competition. And the best evidence for that can be found in the capital markets, where a land that had been unremittingly hostile to the very idea of hostile-takeover bids has seen a string of attempts in the past three years. A then thirty-two-year-old Internet entrepreneur, Takafumi Horie, set the ball rolling with efforts to buy the Osaka Kintetsu Buffaloes baseball team and then a huge media group, Fujisankei Communications, through his Internet vehicle, Livedoor, in 2004 and 2005 respectively.[17] Both failed, and although Mr. Horie became a household name for his tilt against the establishment, he was rewarded by being prosecuted for accounting fraud.

Other firms, operating on the right side of the law, have since followed his example, however. Almost all have also failed, but the efforts have often brought rich rewards in terms of share-price rises and compensation for the losing bidder, which have in turn stimulated others to have a try. The one semihostile bid that has succeeded occurred in 2007, when the Pentax camera company was bought by Hoya Corporation, against the will of the Pentax board. Yet even that bid began as a friendly merger about which Pentax changed its mind, only to be forced back to the merger by its shareholders. Such efforts have brought about a defensive response, too, with hundreds of companies introducing antitakeover measures such as "poison pills" that automatically weaken the company in the event of it being purchased, or the issuance of new shares to dilute the holding of a hostile bidder. But the fact that battle has been commenced is itself having a disciplinary, mind-focusing effect: Dividend payouts have risen sharply, albeit from a low base, and managements have been forced to justify their actions in new and more frequent ways. Even the Japanese government, usually a bastion of conservatism and tradition, has weighed in on the side of mergers and acquisitions: It warned, in a new "white paper" on the economy in August 2007, that defenses against takeovers such as poison pills could harm productivity and efficiency.

Although hostile takeovers have mostly failed, there has been plenty of friendly trading in companies and divisions of companies. During the 1980s, big firms diversified widely, setting up thousands of subsidiaries. Now they are trimming themselves down by selling their unwanted babies. During 2006 there were 2,882 mergers-and-acquisitions deals completed, worth $182 billion in all; that was a similar number to 2005 but with a lower value. Nevertheless, in 2000 there had been just 979 deals, worth $91 billion.[18] This whole process has been pushed along by a rise in the proportion of shares owned by foreign institutions: As of March 2007, 28 percent of all listed shares by value were held by foreigners, compared with just 4 percent in 1990 and 18 percent in 2000. During the current economic recovery, which began in 2002, Japanese companies have been repaying debts and building up large hoards of cash, which makes them more attractive to bidders and to activist shareholders, who want to get their hands on that cash, but also makes them less beholden to shareholders and to banks, because they are not short of capital. That may be why managements have been able to resist bidders and activist shareholders quite successfully. But it will not last forever. Once cash becomes scarcer, shareholders' grip will increase.

Another source of better incentives and discipline is government, through the enforcement of existing laws and the enactment of new, clearer, more justiciable laws. That has been a particular feature of the financial-services business, where the FSA has brought in tougher enforcement, along with the Tokyo prosecutors office, but it has also been a feature of antitrust policy. Japan's trustbuster is called the Fair Trade Commission, which until 2002 was a small agency with low status and a budget to match, firmly under the thumb of the Ministry of Economy, Trade and Industry. Mr. Koizumi, however, moved the FTC so that it reports directly to the Cabinet Office, gave it a new boss and more money. Whereas in 1995 it had 220 investigators, by 2004 it had 331 and had begun much more vigorous and effective raids, helped by a new antimonopoly law, on companies for price-fixing, bid-rigging and other restrictive practices.

There is now more competitive pressure on Japanese companies, and their shareholders are getting more demanding. The state is playing a smaller and smaller role in the economy, and so is now much less likely to distort competition itself or to direct resources to unproductive uses. Mr. Koizumi succeeded in privatizing Japan Post, albeit in a typically slow process that will last until 2017; he withdrew the state from housing finance and trimmed back other remaining state lending institutions; and he broke up the biggest source of public corruption, bid-rigging and pork-barrel politics, by splitting the Japan Public Highway Corporation, the agency in charge of building roads and bridges, into six bodies with responsibility for servicing and repaying their own debts, which should force them to act in a more businesslike fashion.

Such policy measures could be reversed by future governments, but there is one huge constraint on such recidivism: The state has run out of money. A budget deficit of 8.2 percent of GDP at its peak in 2002 was enough to convince even LDP governments that enough was enough and that in the future spending had better be cut; by 2006 it was down to 5.5 percent of GDP, but that was still more than double George Bush's notorious budget deficit in America. Public debts totaling about 170 percent of GDP are enough to ensure that the deficit will have to be cut further, since interest rates on the debt are bound to rise, and that this process will be hard or perhaps impossible to reverse. The DPJ talks about increasing public spending in rural areas, and helping the country's poorest, but it will have to get the money from somewhere. An aging society will put even greater pressure on public spending on health and pensions in the future. So politicians, of whichever party, face a simple choice: spend less, or tax more, or some combination of the two.

Japan has had no revolution. It has not had mass unemployment as Britain had during the Thatcher years of the 1980s, nor a massive bout of corporate restructuring as America has had on several occasions during the past three decades. It has, however, had a stealth revolution, in corporate law, in politics, in its labor markets, in capital markets, in its banking system, in the role of the state, the effects of which will become clear only during the next decade or so. Those effects were suppressed by the exceptional conditions of the post-crash era. Now the effects are proving slow to manifest themselves. But that does not mean that they are an illusion.

The chief reason to expect that positive effects will be seen and that reform will continue is necessity. The main force for that necessity is demographic, the gradual shrinkage of the Japanese labor force. That shrinkage will reduce economic output and add to labor costs unless Japanese companies manage to neutralize it by increasing their productivity. Some will be able to do so simply by expanding abroad rather than at home. But that does not apply to most companies, which do not have that option. Rising labor costs will reduce corporate profits and deprive companies of some of the funds for investment, unless they seek other ways to become more efficient and profitable. Apart from overseas investment, the choice is simple: raise productivity through capital investment in better machinery; restrain labor costs by luring more women and retired people into the labor force; or use mergers and acquisitions to cut costs and seek new economies of scale. In effect, scarce labor will provide a new source of discipline.

Japanese companies have plenty of scope to do all these things. Their poor productivity performance in the 1990s means they have a chance to catch up with foreign rivals by copying techniques pioneered elsewhere; their high level of spending on research and development, totaling 3.2 percent of GDP, one of the highest in the OECD area, gives them a lot of scope for innovation; their lack of mergers and acquisitions in the past means there is a lot of potential in new combinations and strategies in the future.[19] The question is whether Japanese managements will want to take these chances.

The same question can, and should, be asked about Japanese politicians, Japanese bureaucrats and Japanese public opinion: Do they want to do what it takes to stimulate fast enough growth to overcome the burden of their aging and shrinking population, and to reverse the adverse trends in absolute and relative poverty that Japan has seen during the past decade?

When Japanese exports thudded into European and American consciousness during the 1960s, '70s and '80s, with motorcycles,

machine tools, cars, consumer electronics and other products pushing aside local producers, Japan seemed to be the epitome of globalization. Its companies indeed treated the globe as their market,
and were exploiting the much freer trading conditions presented to
them by the General Agreement on Tariffs and Trade from the 1940s
onward. The word *globalization* was not in common use, but if it
had been, Japan would have been the country in the user's mind.

Yet the odd thing is that Japan is not a very globalized country
at all. For an island economy to be engaged in trade (imports plus
exports) equivalent to only 28 percent of GDP in 2006 is surprising:
that is higher than America (22 percent) but far lower than China
(67 percent). English, the language of globalization, is taught in all
Japanese schools. But just as few Britons emerge from their schools
able to converse in French despite years of supposed study, so few
Japanese emerge confident in English. While more than 130,000
Chinese students are at school or university abroad every year, the
equivalent figure for Japanese is about 80,000. Japan has a far
smaller population (120 million compared with China's 1.3 billion)
so as a percentage its number is higher. But it is nowhere near as
high as might be expected, given its affluence and thus its ability to
afford foreign tuition fees and living costs.

Part of the explanation is that Japan has a large economy and a
large population, both of which reduces the need to look outside,
or to lure the world inside. This is the way Japan has been for centuries: highly protective of its autonomy, resistant to China's tribute
system, willing to close itself to foreign trade for 200 years until 1853
in order to prevent Jesuit missionaries from subverting the nation.
Historically, Japan's engagement with the world has been highly selective and pragmatic: done when necessary, but not to be done
simply for its own sake.

The new source of necessity is competition, both political and
economic. The new competitor is also Japan's oldest rival: China. Ex-
plicit acknowledgement of that fact is quite a recent phenomenon.

Only in December 2004 did the Japanese government for the first time mention China and North Korea as the main potential threats to Japanese security.[20] In 2005 Japan drew protests from China by including the peaceful resolution of the status of Taiwan as a common strategic objective between Japan and the United States in a joint ministerial statement about their security relationship. As with all outsiders, China responded that Taiwan is none of Japan's business. But what was striking is that the Japanese government felt a need, or a desire, to state publicly that it did indeed consider Taiwan its business.

The adoption of this new military doctrine has coincided with a change in Japan's domestic politics and in its overall foreign policy. Ever since 1945, and especially since the dropping of the atom bombs on Hiroshima and Nagasaki in August of that year, Japan has been divided between those believing strongly in pacifism and the preservation of Japan's pacifist constitution, and those of a more right-wing bent who have argued that if Japan is to be a normal, sovereign country, able to shed the burdens of the past, it must revise that constitution and regain all the conventional attributes of a state including an armed force restrained only by international law and by civilian control. For almost fifty years the pacifists were dominant, in a subconscious coalition of sorts with a conservative foreign-policy doctrine established by Japan's first elected postwar prime minister, Shigeru Yoshida. This stipulated, in effect, the same as Deng Xiaoping later said for China in the early 1990s: that Japan should keep its head down and concentrate on economic growth.

The rise of China during the 1990s began to tilt the balance of that debate, as more and more Japanese politicians and pundits came to worry that Japan might in the future become vulnerable to Chinese strength or simply Chinese bullying. The North Korean missile test of 1998, followed as it was by a revived nuclear-weapons program and by revelations of the abduction by North Korean agents of Japanese citizens during the 1970s and '80s, shifted the balance decisively. During the cold war, despite the constant confrontation between the West and the Soviet Union, Japan's immediate security environment had been fairly predictable and probably safe: America could be relied on in the event of conflict on the Korean peninsula, next door to Japan; China was economically and militarily weak; and following Nixon's opening to China in 1972 the Japanese, too, achieved a rapprochement with the Chinese leadership.

Now all that has changed. America's relationship with South Korea has grown more fragile. North Korea has developed long-range missiles and tested a crude nuclear weapon in October 2006. South Korea has drifted somewhat in China's direction, especially under the populist president Roh Moo-hyun in 2003–08. And, as we have already seen, violent anti-Japanese street protests took place in Chinese cities, including Beijing, in 2004–05, putting pressure on the Chinese government to be tough on Japan—or, depending on your interpretation of Chinese politics, as a deliberately engineered part of China's tough policy toward Japan. The Yoshida Doctrine has faded, probably to disappear altogether.

In 2006–07, efforts were made both by Japan and China to mend their tattered relationship. But while the style of relations improved under Shinzo Abe and Yasuo Fukuda, the substance was unchanged. The improvement in relations may in fact last only until the 2008 Summer Olympics in Beijing are safely out of the way. That, at least, is what Japanese Foreign-ministry officials say privately. They assume that China's main objective in being friendlier to Japan is to avoid the Olympics being disrupted by anti-Japanese protests, as happened at the Asian Cup for soccer when it was held in Beijing in 2004 and when Japan defeated China in the final. There was a bad omen for the Olympics in September 2007 when the women's soccer World Cup was held in China: The Japanese team was greeted with booing, even when they held up a banner, in Chinese and English, saying "Thank you China." Whatever the politicians may hope, public opinion in China can be hostile and nationalist toward Japan.

We have already noted that Japanese politics have become more nationalist, in the face of China's rise and of the North Korean threat, and that there is a crossparty consensus in favor of a stronger defense posture, of a tough line on North Korea and of firmness in any negotiations with China. The status of what was simply a government agency handling the Self-Defense Forces was upgraded in 2006 to become a full-fledged Defense ministry, represented in the cabinet. This consensus has not yet extended itself to an agreement that the constitution should be revised to remove its restrictive pacifist clauses, although in his short time in office Mr. Abe proposed that it should be. His resignation in September 2007 means that the chances of revision have declined. But the issue is bound to recur.

Consensus has, nevertheless, been reached about the strategic importance to Japan of new or stronger friendships in the Asia-Pacific region. In March 2007 Japan signed a new security declaration with Australia that, while falling short of a formal alliance, was the first such agreement signed with any country since the U.S.–Japan Security Treaty was signed in 1952. The joint declaration with Australia included provisions for intelligence sharing and joint military exercises. John Howard, Australia's prime minister at the time, said that the military relationship with Japan would be "closer than with any other country with the exception of the United States." An even bigger target for Japan, however, lies on the other side of Asia: India.

The first overtures were made to India by a prime minister with a very brief term of office in 2000–01, Yoshiro Mori, a man who nevertheless remains influential in Japan's ruling Liberal Democratic Party; those approaches were extended by his popular successor, Mr. Koizumi, and then followed up by Mr. Abe. Japan and India have had very little contact in the past; their current efforts to expand that contact are starting from a low base. Trade between the two countries remains only about one-twentieth as large as trade between Japan and China; in December 2006 there were only eleven weekly direct flights between Japanese and Indian cities compared with 676 between Japanese and Chinese cities.

Yet this is beginning to change, with energetic official encouragement. India seems to welcome the attention it is getting from Japan, even if its officials and politicians remain puzzled about where it is going to lead. The Indian government designated 2007 as "the year of Japan," which brought conferences and cultural events galore. There were lectures on the influence of Hindu gods and goddesses in historic Japanese temples; a tour of India by Japan's celebrated all-female acting troupe, the Takarazuka Revue; kite festivals, pottery exhibitions and concert tours by Japanese drummers and singers. The Japanese government is flying planeloads of businessmen in either direction to encourage trade and investment. The number of weekly direct flights between the two countries is being expanded, at last.

An "economic partnership agreement" is being worked out between the two sides. Japan has been India's biggest bilateral aid donor, mainly in the form of soft loans, ever since 1986, but India has now superseded China as the biggest recipient of such Japanese aid. The new Delhi underground railway system (the Delhi Metro), opened in 2002, was largely financed by Japan; a massive new project to connect together Delhi and Mumbai with a new route for freight transport and an "industrial corridor" of factories and business parks will commence in 2008 at a cost of at least $90 billion, of which as much as one-third may eventually come from Japan. Military exchanges between the two countries' navies have begun, to be followed by joint exercises; a joint naval exercise was conducted by Japan, India, Australia, Singapore and the United States in September 2007.

It is all a sensible precaution. In principle, economic growth in China and the rest of Asia offers a fine opportunity, a warm benevolent wind, for Japanese business. It is a good neighborhood to find yourself in. But the resulting competition also sends a chill down political and corporate spines. That chill could be the making of Japan during the next decade, forcing it to continue to reform itself and to continue to play a bigger regional and global role. If there were a choice, Japan would probably prefer to isolate itself, to stay within its shell. But such a choice is not available. The same can be said of Japan's new friend, the budding economic giant, another traditionally inward-looking place far away on the other side of Asia.

5. INDIA: MULTITUDES, MUDDLE, MOMENTUM

TARUN TEJPAL, the editor in chief of *Tehelka,* a campaigning weekly newspaper, is fond of telling foreigners that "everything you think you know about India is correct. But the opposite is also true." With countries on the scale of India and China, and with the cultural and ethnic diversity of India, that is only to be expected. It brings to mind the best-known lines by one of America's greatest poets, Walt Whitman:

> *Do I contradict myself?*
> *Very well then I contradict myself,*
> *(I am large, I contain multitudes.)*

No Indian, nor anyone who visits India, can be in any doubt that it contains multitudes. It is also the source of enormous frustration and even bafflement. It seems to be full of intelligent, worldly people who know what needs to be done to reduce poverty for the destitute multitudes and to turn India into a great global power and yet can't persuade the world's biggest democracy to do it. It is ironic that those who sympathize with India and would like to think that it might in the long run do better than China, despite its past failures, invariably include among its advantages the fact that it has democracy, the rule of law, an independent judiciary and a free press. The argument is that although democracy and a free press may slow down decision making, in the end they contribute to greater social and political stability and provide a more secure environment for investors. It is surely correct that democracy has acted as a safety valve during India's sixty years of independence and that justice and a free press are also valuable Indian assets. But, as *Tehelka*'s own story shows, the opposite is also true: Indian government can be unjust, undemocratic and unfriendly to the freedom of the press, and can get away with it.

Tehelka, whose name means "sensation," was founded in 2000 as an online site for news and opinion. It leapt to fame, or notoriety depending on your view, the following year when it used a sting operation to expose corruption among military officers buying defense equipment and among politicians in the then-ruling party, the Bharatiya Janata Party (BJP) and a small coalition partner, the Samata Party.[1] With hidden cameras, it filmed cash being handed over and stuffed into pockets. The ensuing scandal forced the defense minister, George Fernandes of the Samata Party, to resign. But it also forced *Tehelka* itself out of business. The government retaliated against the *Tehelka* exposure by launching an assault against the Web site's largest investor, a stockbroker called First Global, and its founding partners, Shankar Sharma and Devina Mehra. First Global's license to trade was suspended, Mr. Sharma was arrested under a law that turned out already to have been repealed, the founders' bank accounts and property were frozen, and Mr. Sharma spent more than two months in jail before he was able to get bail. Although he was alleged to have committed tax offenses, in the end, after eighteen months of investigation, no charges were brought. But by then the business was bankrupt.

Tehelka itself was bankrupt, too. It was assaulted both through the intimidation of actual and potential investors and other commercial partners, and through the launching of a commission of inquiry into the defense deals that *Tehelka* had exposed as involving corruption. Rather than being an investigation into allegations of corruption, the commission was set up as an investigation into First Global and *Tehelka,* amid allegations that they had been using the stories to manipulate the stock market in some way. While the commission was still under way, George Fernandes returned to the government as defense minister.

The Indian establishment had shown that it was prepared to be ruthless, to abuse the law to punish its critics, to subvert the truth and to ignore clear evidence of corruption. So much for the "advantage" of democracy and the rule of law. Yet there is a happier side to this sorry tale as well. The commission of inquiry eventually collapsed in ignominy after *Tehelka's* lawyers fought off the first commission and then boycotted the second, refusing, as the publication's Shoma Chaudhury wrote, "to be a part of our own witchhunt."[2] India's Central Bureau of Investigation did eventually look into the allegations of corruption. Five years after the exposé, R. K. Jain, the former national treasurer of the Samata Party who had been featured in the *Tehelka* films naming his prices and boasting of his influence, was finally arrested, as were seven others. In 2004, three years after its closure, *Tehelka* managed to raise enough money to relaunch itself, this time as a weekly newspaper with a Web site attached. India's freedom of speech and rule of law did exist, after all. Pluralism lived on, albeit fitfully and painfully.

The city of Kolkata, known previously as Calcutta, offers a fine window on India's paradoxes, but also on its imperial history, since it was the British capital until that honor was given to New Delhi in 1911. On a visit there in 1999, as part of a trip to open the *Economist's* first full editorial office in Delhi, I thought it might be appropriate to engage in a little ancestor worship. The man who founded the *Economist* in 1843, a Scottish businessman turned free-trade campaigner named James Wilson, later entered politics and was sent to India as finance minister to the viceroy, Lord Canning. He died in

Calcutta in August 1860 after barely ten months in his post. Yet having been responsible for the restoration of public finances following the Indian Mutiny of 1857–59 and previously for the founding in London in 1853 of the Chartered Bank of India, Australia and China, the precursor of today's Standard Chartered Bank, he was a respected figure in the British community there. His funeral drew the largest crowd said to have attended a Western funeral up to that date, and a statue was raised to him in Calcutta that now in fact provides a spectral presence in the lobby of the *Economist* building in London.

I had a little spare time between meetings, so along with my two colleagues I decided to hunt down Wilson's grave in what is known as the "Scottish cemetery" in Kolkata. At the entrance gate there is a small office. Taped to the glass door was a sign bearing the following inscription:

**IF YOU HAVE
TIME TO WASTE,
DON'T WASTE IT HERE**

Not quite Walt Whitman, perhaps, but there is a certain poetry in those lines as well as a typically Indian elegance in the use of the English language. Nevertheless, the manager allowed us to while away our spare time in his office while he searched his set of ancient, dusty ledgers for a clue as to the exact location of Wilson's grave. After much thumbing through he found the entry, written in beautiful copperplate handwriting more than 130 years earlier, and which said rather pleasingly: "Wilson, the Right Hon'ble James, who was expressly sent from England to restore order in the finances of India." The cemetery itself was a lot less well ordered than the office, with overgrown paths and fallen headstones, but we did eventually find Wilson's memorial. It, too, was in rather tumbledown condition, suffering, as its inscription said Wilson had, from "climate, anxiety and labor," but we were still able to pay our respects.

Our next appointment, appropriately, was with the state of West Bengal's then finance minister, Asim Dasgupta—in effect, one of Wilson's successors—and his veteran boss, the state's chief minister, Jyoti Basu. But I am not sure that James Wilson, a rather austere man, would have approved.[3]

A very generous and hospitable local businessman had laid out a dinner for us at his home, and had kindly invited the two politicians. In Kolkata, poverty is highly visible right on the streets, and so the contrast of gliding past beggars and street dwellers to visit a comfortable home is always disconcerting, at least for an outsider. The politicians underlined the contradictions even more. For since 1977, West Bengal politics have been dominated by none other than the Communist Party of India (Marxist), and Mr. Basu was the chief minister for twenty-three years from then until his retirement in 2000. Our host's table was excellent: The first course essentially consisted of caviar, accompanied by a fine Puligny Montrachet wine. The Communist politicians were not disconcerted at all. They seemed to enjoy the hospitality hugely, especially the caviar.

Yes, it is a cheap point. Communist politicians everywhere have occasion to sup with capitalists, and *champagne socialist* is a term familiar in London, too. But the CPI (M) in general, and the government in West Bengal in particular, is a rich source of paradox. At the national level, the CPI (M) currently supports the governing coalition that has been led by the Congress Party since 2004, with Dr. Manmohan Singh, the architect of India's economic reform program, as prime minister; it hasn't joined the coalition, but supports it "from the outside." Nevertheless, along with other left-wing "supporters" of Dr. Singh, the CPI (M) has used its influence to slow the reform process down, blocking the sort of changes that in China have given the economy much of its vigor, notably privatization (known euphemistically in India as "disinvestment") and changes to the labor laws. It also walked out of the national parliament in August 2007 in protest at the civil nuclear pact that Dr. Singh and his government have signed with the United States—before, in an equally baffling move, backing down.

Yet in its own stronghold of West Bengal, a state it has now run for three decades (the other state it dominates is Kerala in India's southwest), the CPI (M) has been in the forefront of reform and of encouraging industrialization, permitting private participation in the management of ports long controlled by the state, allowing the redevelopment of suburbs of Kolkata and, most recently, enthusiastically implementing the national government's policy of permitting Special Economic Zones (SEZs) to be set up for new factories and industrial parks and granting tax breaks to companies that invest there.[4] Mr. Basu's successor as chief minister, Buddhadeb Bhattacharya, is considered a pioneer of industrial development, so much so that he has gotten into trouble for it, with two land deals in West Bengal causing protests by local villagers in 2007: an SEZ planned at Nandigram for a chemicals plant that was to be built by an Indonesian conglomerate, the Salim Group, and a new car factory at Singur (though not an SEZ) for Tata Motors, India's biggest car maker. At Nandigram, efforts by the West Bengal police and by members of the CPI (M) itself to clear the protesters away led to at least fourteen deaths.

There, in brief, is the confused essence of India as a contemporary political economy: The central government of the world's largest democracy, one of its fastest-growing economies, depends on the support of Communist parties who oppose reform at national level but encourage it in states where they govern, and who have themselves been directly involved in one of the most violent antidevelopment protests of recent years—but on the side of development, not of the protestors. It is no wonder that even a government led by a wise, gentle, proreform economist, Dr. Manmohan Singh, and steered from the shadows by the head of India's most famous and powerful political family, Sonia Gandhi, has been unable to achieve very much since it entered office in

2004. Its most high-profile achievement, the civil nuclear deal with the United States, has been held hostage by its Communist supporters and opposed by the party whose government ordered India's nuclear-weapons tests in 1998, the Hindu nationalist Bharatiya Janata Party—even though the BJP itself began India's rapprochement with the United States and has been more vociferously critical of China, the presumed target of any U.S.–India pact, than has the governing Congress party.

It is a muddle on multifarious levels. Progress is impossible. Or is it? The curious thing about Indian public policy, whether in foreign affairs or economics, is how consistent it has actually been for at least the past fifteen years, regardless of which party has been in power. Governments led by the BJP, by the Congress Party or by smaller parties have all moved steadily closer to the United States, and all have sought to deepen India's engagement with the countries of East and Southeast Asia, in a process called "Look East" and begun in 1994 by Narasimha Rao, who was the Congress Party's prime minister in 1991–96.[5] Mr. Rao also launched India's main round of economic reforms, beginning a process that has been continued by every subsequent government. The speed of economic reforms has varied, depending on the fragility of the governing coalition, between slow and moderate rather than fast, but the direction has never changed.

The result is that for all the muddle India has built up quite a momentum. Its foreign policy has become steadily more outward looking, in sharp contrast to the very inward looking, rather isolationist policy of the country's early postindependence decades, and has become more and more defined by a sense of the national interest, especially economic interest, rather than any moral considerations. The trend in India's economy is at last one of accelerating growth and, as chapter 1 argued, of sharply rising private investment. The chart shows how volatile India's growth was until the current decade, but also how low the rate of investment was, by comparison with the levels of 35–45 percent of GDP seen in the East Asian success stories and recently in China. Now the rate of investment has shot up to 34 percent of GDP.

This is a truly dramatic change. During the three decades that followed independence in 1947, India's annual average rate of real GDP growth was a mere 3.5 percent a year. With population growth in the 1960s and '70s of more than 2 percent a year, this meant that growth in GDP per head, or average incomes, was meagre. A throttling system of government licensing and quotas, which was set up in the 1950s under Nehru, was refined by his daughter, Indira Gandhi, in the 1970s to the point where it became virtually impossible for companies to produce anything. Liberalization of this system, known as "the license raj," began in the 1980s, helping real GDP growth to accelerate to an annual average of 6 percent per year in that decade. As population growth was by then slowing, incomes per head began to improve substantially. But although better, the economy's performance was still disappointing by East Asian standards.

After a financial crisis in 1991, India's second spate of liberalization took place when Dr. Singh was finance minister in the government led by Narasimha Rao. This liberalization was quite radical, with cuts in taxes and tariffs and the virtual abandonment of licensing and quotas. However India was still unable to achieve the sort of growth rates being seen on the other side of the Himalayas, in China: It remained stuck at annual average growth of about 6 percent. But now some sort of breakthrough has occurred. In the four fiscal years from 2003–04 until 2006–07, the average real GDP growth rate reached 8.6 percent. In 2005–06 it was 9 percent; in 2006–07 it was 9.4 percent.

If that speed is sustained India will double its GDP roughly every eight years. Its consumer market, while still small given the country's overall poverty, will grow substantially: A study by the McKinsey management consultancy in 2007 forecast that by 2025 India will have the fifth largest consumer market in the world, with

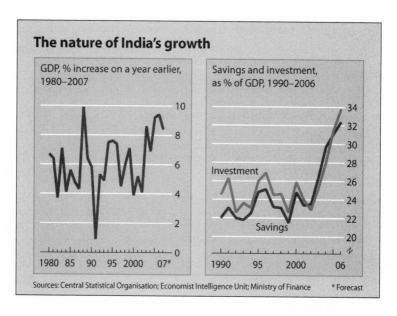

The nature of India's growth

GDP, % increase on a year earlier, 1980–2007

Savings and investment, as % of GDP, 1990–2006

Investment

Savings

Sources: Central Statistical Organisation; Economist Intelligence Unit; Ministry of Finance   * Forecast

consumption quadrupling.[6] Meanwhile the biggest Indian companies such as Tata, Mahindra and Mahindra, Reliance, Infosys, Wipro, Ranbaxy and others are becoming forces to be reckoned with in international markets. India's trade is expanding, and with it the country's contacts with suppliers and markets all over the world, but especially in Asia, the Middle East and Africa. At last India has been achieving economic growth that is not just good by Indian standards: It is good by global, even Chinese standards—especially given that Indian GDP statistics are thought to be more reliable than Chinese ones. If it can be sustained, such growth stands a real chance of turning India from just a big important country into one of Asia's, and the world's, leading powers. In the past, India has been overlooked by its Asian neighbors or even, in China's case, treated with some contempt. That is no longer going to be possible. Or, at least, it is no longer going to be wise.

The debate within—and about—India has changed. It has ceased to be an argument about whether India can or will grow slower or faster than the "Hindu rate of growth" of 3–6 percent a year, as it was in the 1980s and early '90s. It is now about whether India can or will grow at 8 percent a year or whether it might in fact be able to sustain growth rates of 10 percent or more. A comprehensive study by economists at Lehman Brothers in 2007 concluded that with the right reforms, India could achieve growth of more than 10 percent for at least a decade.[7] The OECD, in its first ever study on India, concurred with that view, calculating that the potential rate of growth of GDP per capita—the more crucial measure of living standards and thus poverty reduction—is already more than 7 percent a year, which is almost five times higher than was achieved in 1950–80.[8] Yet even as that debate has changed, another debate persists. India is an argumentative place, after all.[9] This other debate is about inequality, and the effect of capitalism on that gap between the rich and the poor.

Communism, whether fed by caviar or by dispossessing poor Bengali farmers, is rife with ironies. But it is not hard to understand why it has survived and even thrived in India, a country where the rich look very rich and the poor look abject. Mukesh Ambani, one of the two feuding heirs to the vast Reliance conglomerate, has just stirred up feelings about that very issue by virtue of his plan to construct in his home city of Mumbai, formerly Bombay, a new building for his family that will be strikingly opulent, even by Indian standards. The new family home—it is common for extended Indian families to share a building or live adjacent to one another—will have twenty-seven floors but will be as high as a normal sixty-story building, and will include six levels of parking, a swimming pool and a helipad, all at a cost variously estimated at somewhere between $500 million and $1 billion. As if to rub in the point in a city half of whose population lives in slums, the site was bought from an orphanage trust controlled by a Muslim religious board. Even though construction is already underway, the government of Maharashtra, the state in which Mumbai is the capital city, claimed in mid-2007 that the sale of the site was illegal and has ordered the land to be confiscated. Land acquisition disputes can hit capitalists as well as communists.

No doubt the legal and political battle will run on for years, and perhaps Mr. Ambani may be inclined to increase his philanthropic donations as a result. But it is not as if many parts of India's business capital do not need redeveloping. Mr. Ambani's own head office is a case in point. A visitor to the building in downtown Mumbai where the office is located, Makers Chambers IV, is inclined to decide he has come to the wrong place, so tatty is the structure's appearance. There are no parking levels on view here, nor helipads: You take your chance in the melée outside. The lifts barely seem to work, take ages to arrive and are packed with people. Entering the Reliance headquarters floor, however, is like being transported to another planet: humming air-conditioning; thick and heavy wooden doors; crisp white-painted walls; an air of calm, wealth and efficiency. While the building is decrepit, the Reliance interiors are world class.

Mr. Ambani himself, said by *Forbes* magazine to be the world's fourteenth richest man, is engagingly informal, seated for our interview on a sofa in his vast office under a garland-clad painting of his father, Dhirubhai, who founded the company and made its first fortune. Now Mukesh's side of the firm makes its main income in oil and petrochemicals, but is also heavily involved in textiles, real estate and a new venture, retailing. Reliance was split into two in 2006 after the family feud, and Mukesh's brother Anil runs the other half, in power, telecommunications and other industries.

Mukesh Ambani and his side of Reliance are also engaged in what is India's most ambitious urban development project yet. Across the bay from the crowded peninsula on which the country's business capital sits, a new city, known as Navi (new) Mumbai, has been planned since the early 1970s and is at last under construction. Within Navi Mumbai, Reliance is taking the lead in developing a 150-square-kilometer (15,000 hectares, 37,000 acres) area that has been designated as two Special Economic Zones. Reliance's share of the area will be the largest SEZ developed so far in India and the first to take shape on a scale similar to the special zones and new cities in China, such as Shenzhen near Hong Kong, with a mixture of housing, offices and factories. Not that any such development is ever smooth: Following controversy over SEZs (see later in this chapter), Reliance had to lop 5,000 hectares off the SEZ and lost all government help with land acquisition. Although the zone will be developed using private money, the state government of Maharashtra is chipping in $2 billion for a transharbor road bridge to connect the new city with old Mumbai.[10] Reliance also has another, similar project in the state of Haryana, not far from Delhi, where its new city will cover 100 square kilometers.

The Ambanis now symbolize the opposite end of India's elite from the CPI (M): its energetic, hugely wealthy and highly successful private sector, full of the ambition and capital that India needs if it is to develop, but also perfectly comfortable with conspicuous consumption. The gap between the tycoons and the slumdwellers could not be larger. Yet the paradox here is that while, as with the tale about Jyoti Basu and the caviar, such an emphasis on the superrich and their opulent family homes provides an easy point, it is also misleading. You may think that India is grossly unequal, and in some ways it is, but the opposite is also true. If you look at the data rather than at the silks, the gold and the palatial homes, the idea melts away. Try this, from the World Bank: "Compared with other countries, India remains a society of low inequality of income."[11]

What? But it is true, if measured properly. The superrich such as Mr. Ambani make up only a tiny proportion of the population. The dispersion of incomes and consumption patterns among the people as a whole is quite narrow: India's Gini coefficient, which is the standard way in which the distribution of incomes is measured by economists, is about the same as in Britain, a bit lower than in the United States, and a lot lower than in China. On the Gini measure, a score of one signifies perfect equality, and 100 perfect inequality. According to the World Bank, the Gini coefficient in India in 2004–05 was 36.8, while Thailand's was 42, Singapore's 42.5, China's 46.9 and Malaysia's 49.2.[12] By comparison, in 2000 Japan's was 31.4, Britain's was 32.6 and America's 35.7.[13] Levels of inequality in Latin American and African countries are typically far higher: For example, Brazil and South Africa both have Gini scores of about 57. India is more unequal on other measures, such as health and literacy, than it is on income. This suggests that privilege is not based simply on money, and that being better educated has not brought substantially higher incomes, either.

The socialists who dominated Indian politics and economic thinking for the first four decades after independence would consider India's relative equality to be a sign of success, as probably do many members of the CPI (M). Yet it is also a measure of India's past failure. In India the poor are very poor: According to the World Bank again, in 2004–05, 33.6 percent of the population (i.e., about 370 million people) had incomes of less than $1 a day. What the inequality measure also means, however, is that even well-educated Indians, who would consider themselves middle class, have not been engaged in activities with high productivity or generating high value.

Among East Asia's economic success stories, the latest of which is China, rapid economic development brought with it an increase in income inequality. Millions of people moved from low-productivity jobs, in agriculture and services, into higher productivity ones, generally in industry, which command higher wages, but not everyone could move simultaneously, so the income gap widened. Until recently, that hadn't happened very much in India. Any foreigner who has visited India as a tourist and has found that the guide showing them around a historic site has a PhD in engineering should recognize this problem.

Rising inequality can generate its own problems, as China has found, when those left behind start to complain and to fight. India has that sort of trouble, too, especially in the poorest rural areas.

The violence at Nandigram was one example, but even more worrying are the activities of Naxalite guerrillas connected to a different Communist Party of India (M), where the *M* stands for Maoist rather than Marxist. The Naxalites exploit grievances and pursue a violent insurgency: named after Naxalbari in West Bengal, where they staged their first uprising in 1967, the Naxalites were responsible for about 1,600 incidents in 2005 in which 669 people died, and are active in a big swathe of central and eastern India. Such problems have to be managed and rural grievances responded to, by improving health clinics, schools and infrastructure as well as by fighting the guerrillas.

Manmohan Singh, the prime minister, has described the Naxalites as "the single biggest internal-security challenge ever faced by our country." As inequality rises, so the Naxalites may well be able to recruit more supporters. In his speech to mark the sixtieth anniversary of India's independence from Britain, on August 15, 2007, Dr. Singh underlined the importance of the issue:

> Even after years of development and rising growth rates, why have we not been able to banish mass poverty and provide employment to all? Why do some regions of the country continue to lag behind? . . . India cannot become a nation with islands of high growth and vast areas untouched by development. Where the benefits of growth accrue only to a few.

But as Dr. Singh, a fine economist, also knows, India's situation is unlikely to improve unless inequality does rise. It is a question of how much it rises, and in what way.

People who study or write about both China and India are often asked, "Which one do you think will win?" Quite apart from the fact that economic growth is not a sport in which one side "wins" or the other "loses," the question is futile if by it the interrogator wishes to ask which country will be bigger and richer in ten, twenty or even thirty years' time. The answer is plainly China. Its GDP, at $3.1 trillion in 2007 give or take some statistical uncertainties, is already more than three times as large as India's ($1 trillion); so therefore is its GDP per head. The only way in which India could take the lead within those sorts of time frames would be if China suffered an economic collapse that lasted for a decade or more, during which India continued to grow rapidly. In other words, it is feasible only in the event of an extreme form of Chinese failure, not of Indian success. Japan has shown that prolonged failure is not impossible. But that does not make it probable.

It is more relevant, and realistic, to look at India on its own terms. On that basis, there are three important questions: Can the country really overcome enough of the obstacles that impede its economic development to maintain or even accelerate its growth during the next decade? If that happens, how will it change India's behavior in world and regional affairs? And how will India's growth affect the other great Asian powers, namely China and Japan?

The arithmetic of India's potential growth is fairly straightforward. If India were to achieve the annual average growth rate for real GDP of 9 percent that is envisaged by its Planning Commission (an economic coordination agency chaired by the prime minister) in its 11th Five-Year Plan, covering 2007–12, accelerating to 10 percent for the following five years, its economy would double in size after about seven-and-a-half years; its incomes, measured by GDP per capita, would double in nine years since its population is growing by 1.3 percent per year.[14] The long-term forecasters at Goldman Sachs, famous for their views on the possible growth of what they call the BRICs (Brazil, Russia, India and China), base their projections on an average annual growth rate for India of just 8 percent over the next two decades.[15] But on that assumption India's GDP would still overtake those of Italy, France and Britain in 2015–20, and both Germany and Japan during the subsequent decade. By 2020, reckons Goldman Sachs, Indians would then be buying five times more cars than today and three times more crude oil.

This improvement remains too new to have fully convinced everyone that it can be sustained. Previous shorter spurts of growth have ended in balance-of-payments crises and inflation. Sure enough, in early 2007, consumer-price inflation rose worryingly above 5 percent a year, forcing the central bank, the Reserve Bank of India, to raise its interest rates and tighten monetary controls sharply, which in turn led to a rise in the value of India's currency, the rupee: Both of those measures could lead to a slowing of India's growth rate during 2008, tarnishing the hopes of those who believe that the country's natural pace of expansion might now be a Chinese-style 9–10 percent a year. Nevertheless, the acceleration that was seen in 2003–07 contained four elements that do suggest that something fundamental has changed in India, and which promise to have a long-lasting effect.

The first is the one shown in the chart earlier in this chapter: that growth since 2003 has been led by a sharp rise in investment, to a level of 34 percent of GDP in 2006–07, up from the 25 percent typical during the previous decade. The main feature of that rise has been a boom in private investment, as existing businesses and new entrepreneurs have felt confident enough to risk their money in new Indian factories, offices, real-estate developments, hotels, infrastructure and more. A buoyant world economy undoubtedly helped encourage this by providing strong markets for exports, as did a fall in interest rates. This investment-led boom has nevertheless laid a firm foundation for future progress. Most of the investment is Indian, but there has also been an increase in foreign direct investment into India by foreign companies: Foreign direct investment (FDI) into India totaled $19.5 billion in 2006, which is far below China's annual FDI inflows of $60 billion–$80 billion in recent years but was still a jump of more than $12 billion over 2005.

The second new element is inflation, or rather anti-inflationary policies. The speed with which the jump in inflation in 2007 was brought under control suggests that India can now expect a more stable macroeconomic climate and government policy, which is good for investment. Inflation ruins investment plans by eroding the value of future profits, as well as introducing the risk of draconian policy measures, economic recession and perhaps collapses of banks and other financial firms. A cycle of boom and bust, in which fast growth leads to rapid inflation and then a monetary crackdown, would make it probable that the higher rate of private investment would prove temporary.

The reason why inflation was dealt with swiftly in 2007 was partly political: Rising food prices threatened to overshadow some important state elections. That is a good sign: Political pressures in a democracy often lean the other way, toward the tolerance of inflation. The firm policy response may also have reflected a healthy evolution of thinking in the Reserve Bank of India and in the government itself, away from seeing inflation as an acceptable by-product of growth and toward seeing it as a threat to growth's very sustainability.

As well as hurting investment, high or volatile inflation rates would also deter households and companies from accumulating savings. Inflation erodes the value of savings. A crucial part of the optimistic case for India is that the sharp rise in investment to 34 percent of GDP in 2006–07 was matched by a rise in domestic savings, limiting the extent to which investment needed to be financed by borrowing and other capital inflows from abroad. That rise in savings is the third new element in India's growth. Unlike China with its huge surplus, India has a deficit on the current account of its balance of payments. But the deficit has stayed small—about 2 percent of GDP—and the central bank's foreign exchange reserves have climbed to $220 billion as of August 2007, providing a far more comfortable cushion against financial difficulties than was the case during the 1980s and '90s. Moreover, India's demographic structure is moving into a phase that during the next decade should favor a further increase in domestic savings: With fewer children being born and an increasing proportion of the population in the working age of fifteen to sixty-four, the dependency ratio is falling. In other words, Indian workers will have fewer young and old people to look after, and more money to spare for their own savings.

The fourth new element is that India's growth has become more broadly based. Investment and output growth alike have spread in the past four years from services into manufacturing and other industrial activities, too. As the twenty-first century began, India became famous as a services economy, and rightly so: Services account for more than half of GDP, and the snazziest of those services, information technology and the use of IT to provide the business services known collectively as outsourcing, grew especially rapidly in the early years of this decade. Now this services growth is being matched—and as the chart shows, recently even outpaced—by manufacturing.

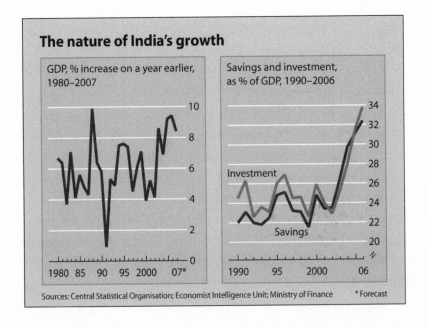

The nature of India's growth

GDP, % increase on a year earlier, 1980–2007

Savings and investment, as % of GDP, 1990–2006

Investment

Savings

1980 85 90 95 2000 07*

1990 95 2000 06

Sources: Central Statistical Organisation; Economist Intelligence Unit; Ministry of Finance   * Forecast

Tom Friedman of the *New York Times* heard the famous phrase that became the title of his bestseller on globalization, *The World Is Flat*, when he visited one of India's biggest outsourcing companies, Infosys, in Bangalore. The phrase, spoken by Infosys's eloquent chief executive, Nandan Nilekani, is apt for IT and outsourcing, since high-bandwidth telecommunications and cheap computing power make it possible to offer such services from anywhere on the planet, to anywhere and anyone.[16] But a visit to Infosys's headquarters confirms that it is not at all apt for India in general. The company has a beautifully groomed campus, around which visitors purr along on golf carts and can even play a few holes of golf, with ultrasmart and modern offices. An eye-catching building that is a dead ringer for the glass pyramid designed by I. M. Pei for the courtyard of the Louvre in Paris turns out to be merely a media center containing TV studios from which Infosys executives can broadcast to investors or to colleagues in other cities. Impressive as it is, however, the Infosys campus is a world away from the noisy, unkempt reality that is India right outside.

Outsourcing is a great business for India, but so far it has had to thrive essentially in enclaves that feel detached from the rest of the country. The flat worlds these firms inhabit are more akin to well-connected high plateaus, each of which is surrounded by rocky mountains and jungles—or, as Dr. Singh put it in his Independence Day address, they are "islands of high growth." Those islands or plateaus contain roughly 1.3 million Indians working in the outsourcing and information-technology industries. Together, that 0.1 percent of the population, or 0.2 percent of the labor force, produces 5 percent of India's GDP. A joint study in 2005 by the McKinsey management consultancy and NASSCOM, the industry's trade association, forecast that by 2010 outsourcing and IT could be producing 7 percent of GDP and yielding $60 billion in exports (India's total exports of goods and services in 2006 were $197 billion).[17] The work and incomes of these 1.3 million Indians are thought to generate indirect employment for about 6 million more people; some enthusiastic analysts, such as the CLSA brokerage, think the figure could be as much as 13 million. But India's workforce contains 450 million people. For the 442.7 million, or even 435.7 million, not benefiting from outsourcing, the world does not feel flat at all.

For it to feel less than mountainous for the bulk of the population, better job opportunities need to emerge in other sectors: manufacturing, construction, mining, food processing and low-tech services such as transport, distribution and retailing. The good news is that, to some extent, that has begun to happen. Given India's low incomes, the country ought also to be one of the world's cheapest places in which to do things that require a lot of hands: It ought, in other words, to be highly competitive with China in labor-intensive manufacturing.

It hasn't been competitive, until now, for a host of reasons. India's trade barriers have been higher than China's, depriving manufacturers of the cheapest inputs and reducing the amount of competition in the domestic market. Its roads, railways, ports and airports have been outdated and grossly inefficient, adding to the costs of any firm wanting to import components, export finished goods or simply ship their goods to Indian buyers. The electricity supply has been unreliable, forcing firms to take on the cost of producing their own power, which leaves them with a lot of wasted capacity. India's labor laws have penalized large companies while rewarding small ones, making it costly for big firms to lay off workers and so encouraging industries to remain small and fragmented. And many industries suitable for labor-intensive manufacturing have since 1967 been reserved by law for small-scale producers, supposedly to protect craftsmen.

These obstacles have not disappeared. But they have diminished. When the main phase of economic liberalization began in 1991, peak import tariffs on nonagricultural goods were 300 percent and many imports were subject to quantitative controls; in 2006–07, the peak tariff was down to 12.5 percent. That is still higher than China's equivalent tariff of about 5 percent, but it is being reduced a little every year with a declared aim of matching the 8 percent tariff levels set by the members of ASEAN by 2009. This makes it feasible for manufacturers to import components and thus do what China has done so successfully, namely to take part in a transnational production chain, and it also increases the competitive pressure on Indian producers, forcing them all to become more efficient. The number of products subject to the small-scale industry reservations is being whittled away, though it remains large: Since its peak in 1984 the number has dropped from 873 to 326, according to the Planning Commission. Imports of all of these products are now permitted, with the perverse effect that foreign firms are allowed to compete in these markets in India on the basis of their economies of scale but Indian ones are not.

The difficulties in eliminating such perversions explain why the current, Congress-led government tried to introduce the Special Economic Zones that were mentioned earlier in this chapter and which caused violent reactions in West Bengal: SEZs are essentially a way to introduce new rules favorable for business in specially designated areas but not for the country as a whole. SEZs might, on the face of it, have been expected to be uncontroversial.[18] Such facilities are known to have played a successful role in encouraging export-oriented investment in China in the 1980s, and they have been flirted with for years in India, too. India boasts that it set up the world's first "export processing zone" in 1965, but it did not take the idea very far. The country has had difficulty financing the construction of new infrastructure and in attracting multinationals to locate their factories there, so when the government announced in 2005 that it planned to boost the incentives available in special zones it looked like a way for India to sidestep some of the obstacles to its growth. Companies would be exempt from corporate income tax for five years, with further concessions for another ten, and from all customs duties, as well as enjoying faster approval for their investments

under a special procedure. But SEZs drew attack both from supporters of economic reform and from diehard anticapitalists.

Reformers said the zones would simply relocate investment that
would have occurred in any case, thus depriving the state of tax revenue: It would be better to be bolder, cutting taxes and streamlin-
ing regulations for everyone and leaving businesses to decide where
best to invest. Anticapitalists said the zones would tear farmers from
their ancestral land. This latter criticism would not have had much
bite but for another flaw: that although SEZs are approved by the
central government, land acquisition for the zones is handled locally. And in many cases, rather than leaving the investors to negotiate directly with the existing landowners, state governments have
been acting as intermediaries. The result, not surprisingly, has been
both corruption and, just as damaging, suspicion of corruption, as
state governments and politicians themselves have obtained land
cheaply before selling it on at higher prices once an SEZ has been
approved, or may have taken bribes in return for the provision of
land. At Nandigram, the state of West Bengal had acquired the land,
and many farmers felt they had not been properly compensated or
consulted.

Protests about allegedly unfair or illegal seizures of land are one
of the things that unite Communist China, democratic India and
Communist-run West Bengal. A normal assumption is that in democratic India resolving these disputes holds up the process of development much longer than in decisive, autocratic China. Yet that is
not strictly true. Land disputes have not held up the building of
roads in India, for the country has had a Land Acquisition Act since
1894 that has provided powers and compensation rights for the compulsory purchase of land for a public purpose—what in America is
called eminent domain. The problem with road building has been
principally financial, not legal or democratic: A chronic government
budget deficit, reaching 10 percent of GDP at its peak in 2001–02,
driven high by subsidies and ineffective tax collection, left too little
room for spending on infrastructure.

The difficulty with SEZs is that the land acquisition law should not really apply to them. The purposes involved are private—real estate, factories—even if they occur with public encouragement. Following the Nandigram violence, the SEZ program was suspended while a review of the land purchase procedures was carried out. But it was soon resumed. By August 2007 a total of 362 proposals had been approved, with almost 180 more given approval in principle. The Commerce ministry reckons that the proposals so far approved and begun will be generating 1.7 million jobs by the end of 2009; if all the proposals are implemented, they will generate 4 million jobs. How many of those jobs are really new, rather than just relocated in response to the tax incentives, remains a matter of controversy. The SEZs look like they are having a mildly positive impact on economic activity and on infrastructure development, but not a radical one.

Infrastructure has nevertheless been improving—albeit, like many things in India, from a low base. During the first fifty years after independence in 1947, the government built just 334 miles (537 kilometers) of four-lane roads. Between 1981 and 1998 the national highway network grew by just 1.2 percent annually.[19] A huge road scheme was launched in 1998, called the National Highways Development Project, which is intended to build some 14,692 miles (23,646 kilometers) of new four- and six-lane highways. The first phase, known as the Golden Quadrilateral, became fully functional in 2007 and added 3,625 miles (5,846 kilometers) of highways, forming a large ring that connects together India's main cities of Delhi, Kolkata, Chennai (formerly Madras), Bangalore and Mumbai. Due for completion in 2008 is a north-south trunk route from Kashmir to Kanyakumari at India's southernmost tip, and another one passing across the country from east to west between Silchar and Porbandar, adding 4,536 miles (7,300 kilometers) between them. Also under construction are fast road connections between these networks and the country's main seaports.

This road expansion is far too little—parts are already congested, and the network pales in comparison with China's highways.

In 2001–05, China was building nearly 3,000 miles (4,800 kilometers) a year of new highways, while India was building only a little over 620 miles (1,060 kilometers). But it is never too late to build new roads, and when they are completed they do make a difference. As stretches have opened, they have reduced transport costs for industry by cutting travel times and fuel costs, have enabled firms to use larger vehicles for freight, and have stimulated all sorts of further economic activity along the new arteries.

New airports are being built at Bangalore and Hyderabad, while old ones are being rebuilt at Delhi and Mumbai, and are planned to be rebuilt at Chennai and Kolkata. The airline business has been liberalized, allowing new low-cost carriers to spring up, including Jet Airways, Kingfisher and Deccan, cutting the cost of domestic air transport dramatically; Jet is also now flying some international routes, too. Seaports have become more efficient thanks to permission being granted to private firms, including foreign ones such as Peninsular & Oriental (now part of Dubai Ports World) and Port of Singapore Authority, to build new facilities and to compete with the existing state-owned port operators. Again, these ports are miles behind China's in terms of efficiency and volume of cargo handled. Shanghai alone handled 21 million twenty-foot container units in 2006; the whole of India handled only 5 million. But they have improved.

That could be India's mantra when describing her economic progress: Things have improved, but far from enough. Nevertheless the overall improvement in business conditions explains why manufacturing and other industrial output has begun to expand rapidly in the past few years. Productivity, which was falling for a period in the late 1990s, has been growing by more than 4 percent a year.[20] Much, though not all, of the manufacturing growth has been in fairly capital-intensive industries, however, as those restrictive labor laws have led companies to prefer machines to India's multitudes.

Employment growth in industry in 2002–04 was 4.7 percent a year according to Goldman Sachs, which was faster than in either agriculture or services. But it is still not fast enough to raise incomes across a wide area of the country by pulling large numbers of workers out of agriculture. Much more needs to be done before those multitudes feel that their world is flattening.

Can it be done? It is easy to list the problems that need to be overcome, and the list can feel daunting, even pessimistic. To sustain and even enhance its economic development, India will need to do the following and more: further reduce the regulations hampering commerce; reform the judicial system; control corruption; reform its labor laws; boost infrastructure, especially the power supply; radically improve its education system; break up the rigidities and inequalities caused by the caste system; boost incomes and opportunities in agriculture; constrain environmental damage; and all the while prevent political conflict or instability from derailing progress either at the national level or in particular states.

Daunting though this list is, it can be seen in another way: as an indication of India's potential. The process of economic growth is in part a process of removing obstacles, rather as the dredging of boulders from a river will permit the water to flow more smoothly. There are a lot of obstacles to be removed, so there is a lot of potential for improvement. Bit by bit, as long as successive governments remain committed to achieving economic development, these obstacles can and will be dredged away and growth will come.

There is a further important variant: In the best Indian states things have improved a lot, but the worst states drag down the national averages. The poorest states—Bihar, Orissa, Uttar Pradesh, Madhya Pradesh and Rajasthan—were already falling behind the richer ones during the slow growth 1970s but have fallen much further behind during the past twenty years. That is not much different from the picture in other developing countries: Regional disparities are even bigger in Indonesia, China and Brazil, for example. But in India the gap widened especially sharply during the 1990s. And in India's decentralized, federal system, local politics and local regulations complicate the process of reform.

The World Bank publishes a regular study on how easy or difficult it is to do business in different countries. According to the 2007 report, many things have gotten better: The time it takes to register a company in Mumbai has fallen from eight-nine days in January 2004 to thirty-five days now; the corporate income tax has fallen from 36.59 percent to 33.66 percent; new procedures in customs helped lower the time taken to import goods by two days (to forty-one from forty-three) and the time to export by nine days (to twenty-seven from thirty-six).[21] Even so, India ranked a dismal 134th on the bank's ten criteria, well below its immediate neighbors in Pakistan, Bangladesh and Sri Lanka, and forty-one places after China. If each Indian state were to adopt the country's best practice in each of the bank's indicators, however, India would have ranked seventy-ninth in the world, fifty-five places higher. Many of the regulations that hamper business are imposed at state rather than national level.

The dismantling of the license raj, and of its ugly sister the inspector raj, have made it easier for businesses to make their own decisions and have reduced the burden of regulations and bureaucratic inspections. Some states are competing with one another to attract businesses, both through deregulation and by offering direct incentives such as lower taxes, cheap land and subsidies. But not all, and the dismantlement of barriers is far from complete. The most frustrating sort of statistics are those that represent self-inflicted wounds. In the World Bank's rankings, India stands an extraordinary 158th on the ease of paying taxes. Companies have to make fifty-nine separate payments every year, and all the taxes combined make up more than 81 percent of commercial profits, according to the bank. Not surprisingly, tax evasion and avoidance are rife. Trading is also strangely difficult: The time and number of documents required to import and export goods may have been trimmed, but India's ten documents and twenty-seven days for exporting compare with an

East Asian average of seven documents and twenty-four days. Importing takes fifteen documents and forty-one days, compared with an East Asian average of nine documents and twenty-six days.

Even India's fabled advantage of the rule of law, which ought to be the flip side of overregulation, is actually a weakness. The court system resembles Dickens's *Jarndyce v. Jarndyce* in *Bleak House,* a tale of an interminable legal case. It takes an extraordinary average of 1,420 days to enforce a contract in India, or almost four years; that compares with 450 days in Malaysia, 351 days on average in OECD countries and just 292 days in China. Court costs and attorneys' fees add up to 36 percent of the value of the claim, compared with a South Asian average of 26.4 percent. It may take time to open a business but it takes even longer to close one: going through bankruptcy takes ten years, which is a tie with Chad for the longest in the world, and compares with four years in South Asia on average and just two years in East Asia. Claimants recover less of their money (13 percent) in India than in South Asia (20 percent) or China (32 percent).

Fewer licenses, inspections and other regulations should mean less corruption. Here the news is better. In the annual surveys compiled by Transparency International, the Berlin-based private organization that monitors corruption worldwide, India's scores have been improving.[22] Only 12 percent of Indians surveyed by TI's Global Corruption Barometer for 2006 reported that they had paid a bribe during the previous year; Indians questioned also felt that corruption was lessening in education, the judiciary, the media, parliament and utilities. It remained a problem, but a diminishing one. The same organization's Corruption Perceptions Index, which assembles numerous polls and surveys to rank countries according to how corrupt businesses believe them to be, also showed an improvement in India: from 88th place in 2005 to 70th in 2006 (both out of about 160 countries), which merely places India level with China.

Two other big and sadly resilient obstacles are India's labor laws and its power supply. Both suffer from a combination of politics and corruption. The problem with the labor laws is, first, that they are complex: forty-seven national laws and 157 state regulations currently apply to labor markets, with the result that neither workers nor employers can possibly understand their rights and obligations. The second problem is that they make it extremely difficult to lay workers off if business conditions worsen, requiring any firm employing one hundred or more people to get permission from the state government before they can reduce the workforce or close a plant. The Industrial Disputes Act also makes labor disputes last interminably, as the act encourages adjudication rather than compromise, but the dispute-adjudication system is grossly overloaded: More than 500,000 disputes are waiting to be adjudicated, nearly 29,000 of which have been waiting for more than ten years.

The result is that most firms do their best to avoid being subject to these labor laws, which end up protecting only a tiny proportion of the labor force: about 8 percent of the total, or about 20 percent of nonagricultural workers. They do so by remaining small, which is inefficient, or by using only casual labor, which hinders training and productivity. The encouraging figure for employment growth in recent years of 4.7 percent a year, cited earlier from Goldman Sachs, is growth taking place only in the unprotected or "unorganized" sector: "Organized" labor is slowly shrinking. The biggest firms, such as Reliance, Tata or Mahindra and Mahindra, manage to absorb the costs of these labor laws; what India loses is the growth of small firms into medium-sized ones, which is typically how labor-intensive manufacturing has developed in East Asian countries. As long as the government depends on support from Communist and other left-wing parties, however, as has been the case since 2004, the labor laws will not be reformed. Mind you, the previous government, a coalition at one time of twenty-two different parties led by the Bharatiya Janata Party, did no better.

Power supply is a worse problem than other forms of infrastructure partly because it is basic to all industrial activities, but also because it is a tempting target for populism, corruption and theft. Too many state governments give electricity away, either explicitly or by not enforcing payments, and do too little to discourage theft and bribery. As a result, more than 40 percent of the electricity that is generated is not paid for. Not surprisingly, the power utilities do not make adequate returns on their investments and are not rushing to waste more money. The 10th Five-Year Plan, covering 2002–07, was supposed to cut power losses to 15 percent but failed. Some states do better: Tamil Nadu and Andhra Pradesh, for example, lose only 20 percent. The 11th Plan has now set an objective once again of reducing losses to 15 percent. One improvement that has been made is that under the Electricity Act of 2003 all power producers will be permitted from January 2009 onward to supply to large customers. This will add helpfully to competition in the distribution system and allow firms that have built "captive" power plants of their own to sell spare electricity to the grid. The 11th Plan lays down an objective of adding about 60,000 megawatts of electricity capacity during its five-year span; during the 10th Plan only 26,000 were added.

Safe to say, the objective will not be met. Nor is it likely that India's overall spending on infrastructure will be raised during those five years, as the Plan says it needs to be, from 4.6 percent of GDP to 8 percent of GDP. In India, enough is never done. It is frustrating. But more is being done than in the past, and things are still getting better.

The most optimistic Indian commentators think they could soon get better still. They point to a coming "demographic dividend" as a reason why the country is likely to grow rapidly during the next few decades. While China is growing old before it becomes rich, India will—it is hoped—become richer thanks to its relative youth. Its labor force will be boosted by a big influx of young adults during the next few decades, while there will be fewer children to support and no big bulge of elderly people to take care of.

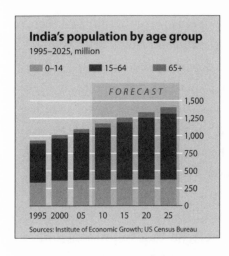

India's population by age group
1995–2025, million

0–14   15–64   65+

FORECAST

1,500
1,250
1,000
750
500
250
0

1995 2000 05   10   15   20   25

Sources: Institute of Economic Growth; US Census Bureau

The trouble is that, as Tarun Tejpal says of India, the opposite could also be true. The country's large, young population will not be an economic advantage unless it can be educated to the standards required by manufacturers and service companies. Right now, India's education is grossly inadequate for that task, and putting that right will be costly. Adult literacy rose from 49.3 percent in 1990 to 61 percent in the latest census in 2001; the Planning Commission claims it will reach 75 percent in 2007–08 as literate teenagers come of age. That overall figure conceals a huge disparity between men and women: While 27 percent of adult men were illiterate in 2001 (i.e., 73 percent were literate) the figure for women was an appalling 52 percent (i.e., 48 percent were literate). And while India has improved its literacy rate, its record remains poor compared with other Asian countries: In Malaysia 92 percent of adult men and 85 percent of adult women are literate; in Vietnam the figures are 94 percent and 87 percent; in China, the figures are 95 percent and 87 percent, though some think these official numbers exaggerate the true level of rural literacy.

Basic education in India faces a litany of problems. Enrollment of six- to fourteen-year-olds in schools is now over 93 percent but the drop-out rate, according to the Planning Commission, was 31 percent for the country as a whole in 2003–04 and is much higher in many states. Only 28 percent of India's schools had electricity in 2005; only half had more than two teachers or two classrooms. Only 40 percent of primary school teachers are graduates and 30 percent have not even completed their own secondary education. So, as the Planning Commission put it, "For a large proportion of our children, school is therefore an ill-lit classroom with more than one class being taught together by someone who may not have completed her own schooling." States rather than the central government pay for more than 80 percent of the education budget, originally on the theory that a decentralized system would be more efficient. It hasn't been. Indian education is rife with stories of teachers who collect their salaries but never turn up for work, and even of local politicians who collect the money for schools and use it for their election campaigns or just pocket it.

Private schools have burgeoned in response to these problems: They account for about 25 percent of pupils at both primary and secondary level, with much higher percentages in the cities, often reaching as high as two-thirds. Improving all of this will be costly, both for private purses and for the taxpayer. Education accounts for more than 10 percent of combined central and state government spending, but is only 3.5 percent of GDP. With the general government budget deficit still at more than 6 percent of GDP, it will be hard to increase public spending on education by very much: the 11th Five-Year Plan talks about adding 0.5 percent of GDP for secondary education and a further 0.25 percent for higher education. Private spending, through tuition fees and philanthropic organizations, will need to add considerably more resources if education is to be improved substantially.

The most common belief about Indian education is that at least the training of the elite—in the top private schools, the best universities, the six Indian institutes of management and the seven Indian institutes of technology (IITs)—is world class, giving India a prime position in the so-called knowledge economy. The irony of Nehruvian socialism, you might say, is that educational spending has been concentrated on the few rather than the many. But even here the picture is not all that good. A report for the Indian Council for Research on International Economic Relations (ICRIER), a private think tank, lamented that only three Indian universities made it into the widely cited Shanghai Jiaotong University ranking of the world's top 500 universities in 2004: the Indian Institute of Science in Bangalore, the

IIT at Kharagpur and Calcutta University.[23] In the ranking published by the *Times Higher Education Supplement* in London in 2006 of what it considers the world's top 200 universities, based chiefly on peer review and citations, again only three Indian institutions qualify: this time Jawaharlal Nehru University in Delhi, and (taken as single multicampus entities) the IIMs and IITs. The THES top 200 included six universities from China plus four from Hong Kong. As the ICRIER study says, "It is a matter of concern that only a few universities in India compete favorably with the world's best institutions. Their number is not only small; these are not in the top rung."

Nevertheless, the government does have plans to expand at least the number of such institutions, even if the quality may be another matter. Dr. Singh emphasised in his 2007 Independence Day address that the government plans to set up thirty new universities, five new Indian institutes of science education and research, eight new Indian institutes of technology, seven new Indian institutes of management and twenty new Indian institutes of information technology. The aim is to ensure that a fifth of Indian children attend tertiary education as compared with about one-tenth now. And he promised a big increase in the number of vocational training bodies for improving the skills of people later in life: 1,600 new industrial training institutes and polytechnics, 10,000 new vocational schools and 50,000 new skill development centers. In India, education is a growing business.

Higher education in India is already large. The country has 348 universities and 17,625 colleges affiliated with universities, educating 10.5 million students at any one time. Each year, 2.5 million emerge with qualifications. Far from all being engineers, the largest group take arts degrees: 1.15 million graduates in 2004. About 285,000 graduated in that year with engineering degrees and diplomas, while 540,000 took science degrees and 480,000 commerce degrees. Nearly half of the cost of higher education is raised privately, which suggests a high level of motivation. Public spending per student is low at around $400 per year; China, according to the ICRIER report, spends about $2,700 per student. On the face of it, that might suggest that India ought to be spending more, just as Dr. Singh promises. If taking higher education does end up yielding higher salaries for graduates, however, then people might well be willing to pay for it themselves. Primary and secondary education might be a better priority for public money.

One common belief about India is true, however: that English, the language of globalization, is widely spoken and even more widely understood. English is the primary language of instruction in all India's universities, and is learned as a second language in schools. It is surprisingly hard to find a figure for what proportion of the population actually can speak and read English. The census asks about first languages (Hindi is by far the most widely spoken, by 40 percent of the population) and not about second ones. *Language in India,* an online journal devoted to the study of languages spoken on the subcontinent, publishes an implausibly low figure: 3 percent.[24] That is 33 million people, or almost twice the population of Australia. But it is a tiny proportion of a country as vast as India and doesn't fit with the evidence of one's own eyes and ears, or the annual output of universities, or the fact that in effect English provides the means by which India's dozens of language groups manage to communicate with one another. Alternatively, TESOL-India, which is a private organization for teachers of English as a second language, gives a figure of about 100 million, or 9 percent of the population, as speakers of English, but up to 350 million as "users" of the language.[25] That higher figure seems implausibly high, given the extent of illiteracy and the high proportion (72 percent) of Indians who live in rural areas. The truth must lie somewhere in between. Nevertheless, the number of Indians who can speak English is increasing every year, with each fresh generation of schoolchildren and graduates.

If you compare India to China, India comes up short on almost every measure except for that ability to use English. However the comparison only provides extra detail for the basic fact: that India's

Health outcomes in selected Asian countries

	Infant mortality, per 1,000 live births, 2003	One-year-olds immunized for measles, %, 2002–04	Maternal mortality, per 100,000 deliveries, 2000	Population with sustainable access to improved sanitation, %, 2002
India	60	58	407	30
Sri Lanka	13	99	92	91
China	30	84	56	44
Vietnam	19	93	130	41

Source: "Towards Faster and More Inclusive Growth", Planning Commission December 2006

income per head is little more than a third as high as China's, because in the past twenty-five years its economic growth has been much, much slower—regardless of how distorted China's GDP statistics may be. The table above, taken from the Indian Planning Commission's own document on its Five-Year Plan for 2007–12, provides one such tragic detail: how health care in India has fallen dreadfully short of the standards even in neighboring poor countries.

As with education and infrastructure, putting that right will be costly, and mainly for the public finances. The deficits of the central and local governments in India have long been a severe constraint on progress, especially progress on improving public services such as health and education. The combined central and local deficit exceeded 10 percent of GDP in 2001–02. Rising revenues and some public sector reform reduced that figure to 6.5 percent in 2006–07. But that still does not leave much room for maneuver: That deficit, it should be noted, is still more than 6 percent amid India's best-ever economic boom.

That said, the right hope, and target, for India's public finances is that the country may achieve the sort of virtuous cycle that China has enjoyed during the past decade, a period during which the Chinese government has doubled the size of its revenues as a share of GDP, to 20 percent. India already raises almost 20 percent of GDP in taxes, so in that sense its public finances are more advanced than China's, but they have been spent ineffectively. If rapid economic growth of 8 percent or even more can be sustained, then three things can and should follow: Tax revenues should continue to increase; politically, it should become easier to widen the tax base in order to force more affluent Indians to pay income tax; and the pressure of corruption, which siphons away public money, especially at state level, and corrodes tax revenues by encouraging bribes to tax officials, should ease as more people gain sight of legitimate sources of funds. If that process does occur, then more public money will be available to improve health and education, among many other things.

A similar optimism about the virtuous effects of sustained growth can be applied to the caste system, which many outsiders cite as one of India's gravest disadvantages. That reputation is unfair, even though the caste system is indeed an iniquity. About 16.2 percent of the population belong to what are called "scheduled castes," also known as Dalits and once called Untouchables, which means they have rights to special treatment through affirmative action programs in education and for government jobs; and a little more than 8 percent belong to "scheduled tribes," which are poorer still and have a right to some protection in the rural areas in which they live.[26] Urbanization and industrialization are both eroding the relevance of the caste system for jobs, incomes and hence social mobility, albeit slowly. If fast growth and broadly based industrialization can be sustained, that erosion should accelerate. Where castes do pose a problem is in the pressure they wield to get affirmative action extended beyond the scheduled castes and to other groups (known in India as "other backward classes" or OBCs), and their ability to form voting blocks in elections to try to achieve such gains. This is a bigger danger at state level than in national politics, but caste-based parties are on the rise and are further fragmenting Indian politics.

The general problem of rural poverty and alienation is likely to pose a bigger headache for central government, and for anyone seeking to marshal support for economic reforms, than is the caste system—even though castes are more important in the countryside than the cities. The violence at Nandigram in West Bengal in 2007 showed what can happen when farmers feel they are being deprived of their livelihoods, even though the deeper problem in Indian agriculture is that those livelihoods themselves have been so poor. With food prices rising all around the world in response to increased demand for grains and for biofuels, it ought to be possible for Indian farmers, too, to benefit.

The big problem, though, is infrastructure and hence access to markets. A huge percentage of produce—40 percent, on some estimates—is wasted before it can get to market. Changing that, by encouraging wholesalers and retailers to build modern distribution systems with refrigerated trucks, warehouses and the like, will take a long time: perhaps ten years, according to Sunil Mittal, a mobile telecoms entrepreneur whose Bharti Enterprises is beginning to build a nationwide network of cash-and-carry wholesalers in conjunction with Wal-Mart. Mukesh Ambani's Reliance Group is also trying to build what is known in India as "organized retailing," as opposed to markets and mom-and-pop kiosks. They have run up against political obstacles, however, as left-wing parties have seen advantages in attacking American giants such as Wal-Mart. Even the Congress Party's leader-in-the-shadows, Sonia Gandhi, has seen a need to defend small shopkeepers. Nevertheless, organized retail is getting organized. Indian politics may muddy the waters. But still they are flowing.

The process of economic and social change is not going to be easy or happy. India, like China, is going through a period of disruptive transformation, and such periods are never calm or uneventful. The transformation, though, is well underway, and it is changing India's approach to the world and to its region. The compliment is being returned.

If you want an approximate road map for how India's relationship to the world and to Asia are likely to change during the next decade, just look at China's evolution during the past decade. As

China's economic development gathered momentum, especially the development of manufacturing and heavy industry, so the country's need for imports of resources and components, and for markets for its exports, expanded, leading China to seek steadily better and deeper relations with resources suppliers in Africa, the Middle East and Latin America, and to find ways to guarantee that export markets would remain open. The level of exports of goods and services as a share of India's GDP in 2006 was roughly the same as for China in 1996 (just over 20 percent). China's is now almost 40 percent. In ten years' time, India's exports may well be at that level. It used to be said of Britain's empire that "trade follows the flag." Nowadays, the flag of foreign policy follows trade.

As a poor country in which trade accounted for much less than 20 percent of a small GDP, global commercial interests did not count for much in India as it entered the 1990s. Now trade in goods and services accounts for more than 40 percent of a much larger GDP, and the share is rising rapidly. In 2000–06 India's exports of goods and services grew by 17.5 percent a year on average, and its imports by 23.4 percent. That growth is a little slower than China's 24.9 percent and 23.8 percent

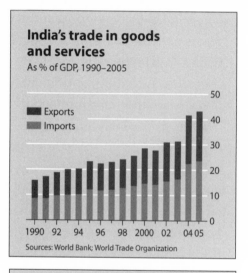

India's trade in goods and services
As % of GDP, 1990–2005

- ■ Exports
- ■ Imports

Sources: World Bank; World Trade Organization

India's main trading partners
$bn (% of total trade), 2005–2006

United States
26.8 (10.6)

European Union
43.3 (17.2)

Middle East & North Africa
27.5 (10.9)

Others
86.8 (34.4)

Total: $252.3bn

Other Asia
60.9 (24.1)

South Asia
7.0 (2.8)

Source: Department of Commerce

annual average rates respectively, but is equivalent to the sort of trade growth China experienced during the 1990s.

Much attention has been given to the growth of China's trade with Africa, its companies' investments in Africa, and the consequent increase in China's diplomatic and other official attention to that continent. The same, with a time lag and hence, so far, on a smaller scale, is happening with India. African exports to China grew from $5.5 billion in 2000 to $28.8 billion in 2006; African exports to India grew from $3.1 billion to $12.6 billion.[27] In the same period, Africa's imports from China grew from $5.1 billion to $26.7 billion; Africa's imports from India also grew, from $2.2 billion to $9.5 billion. In 1995–2004, 16 percent of all the foreign direct investment by Indian companies, or $2.6 billion, went to Africa. Like China, India is becoming a big investor in natural resources in that continent, including oil fields in Sudan. But also, thanks to traditional ties with Indian immigrants in East and South Africa, Indian investment has increased in services and manufacturing, too.

As with China, India's pursuit of its national interest has also led it into nasty places and tricky situations. One example is India's investment in Sudanese oil despite the international condemnation of the genocide underway in Darfur, with the connivance of the Sudanese government. India's Oil and Natural Gas Corporation (ONGC) owns a 25 percent stake in the Greater Nile Oil Project in Sudan. Another is India's changed approach to a neighbor, Myanmar. The Indian government's condemnation of the Burmese junta's treatment of the country's prodemocracy heroine Aung San Suu Kyi, and of protesting Buddhist monks, has become muted; meanwhile India is building roads and fostering trade in Myanmar's western region, and ONGC is active there, too: It owns a 20 percent stake in a big offshore gas field in Myanmar, the Shwe field.

Where India has not yet followed China's example is in clearing up troubles and tensions around its borders. India has fractious relationships with its South Asian neighbors, especially Pakistan,

Bangladesh, Sri Lanka and Nepal, which get in the way of commerce and which also (to China's benefit) distract India with concerns over border security and terrorism. It ought to be plainly in India's interest to encourage more trade with those neighbors as well as to build warmer political ties, but historical enmities and the sectarian politics of India's domestic disputes between Hindus, Muslims and other religions get in the way. Hence the fact that those South Asian neighbors make up a paltry 2.4 percent of India's trade.

India's growing commercial ties with Southeast Asia, and interest in fostering further trade, lay behind Narasimha Rao's "Look East" policy in the 1990s, and its extension during the current decade to talks with the Association of Southeast Asian Nations about a free-trade agreement with ASEAN to match the one that body signed with China in 2002. Commercial interests also contributed to India's eagerness to get involved in regional affairs by accepting the invitation to become a member of the East Asia Summit when that annual meeting was launched in 2005. It is unclear whether the sixteen countries taking part in the East Asia Summit will be willing to use that body to boost their commercial relationships as well as their political ones, but India now wants to be present, in case they do.

The change in India's approach is most obvious in the country's self-confidence. But it is not just a creation of the past four highly successful years. With the end of the cold war, Indian political leaders began in the 1990s to seek a new place and role for India in the world. Hence the "crossing of the rubicon," in C. Raja Mohan's book, on Indian foreign policy, by achieving a rapprochement with its old cold war sparring partner, the United States, that found its culmination in the 2005 civil nuclear agreement signed by Dr. Singh and President George Bush. The testing of nuclear weapons in 1998 was a rather stark declaration that India expected to be taken seriously as a global power, one that estranged it again temporarily from the United States. Another such declaration was the country's un-successful campaign to secure a permanent, veto-wielding seat on the Security Council of the United Nations in 2004–06. A perma-nent Security Council seat would bring with it awkward obliga-tions. But it would also give India equality of status with China, Russia and the Western powers that it believes it deserves.

India has become more open in economic terms, and more open-minded in political terms. It is no longer defined in its own foreign-policy thinking by its longtime policy of nonalignment, nor by its leadership of the anti-Western Nonaligned Movement, nor by the memories of colonialism. Increasingly, its foreign stance is not defined by any philosophy or ethical considerations at all. It is defined by India's national interest.

That national interest, however, should now dictate a consider-able further change in India's foreign and economic policies over the next decade. One change dictated by that interest should be a concentration on improving relations—both political and com-mercial—with the country's South Asian neighbors. Another change would be to deepen India's new openness for trade by en-tering into meaningful (i.e., comprehensive and radical) free-trade agreements with ASEAN or, better still, all the members of the East Asia Summit; and by changing the country's stance at the global level of the World Trade Organization toward being an initiator of trade liberalization and away from being a heel-dragger. A third change is likely to be a new energy in India's diplomatic relations with far-flung parts of the world, such as Australia, Latin America and Canada, from where the resources needed for industrialization will be bought. By the end of the next decade, there should be vir-tually no country in the world that does not believe that India mat-ters, a great deal. That is already true of China. It will soon be true of India, too.

6. A PLANET PRESSURED

IF YOU ADD THOSE THREE powerful countries together, what do you get? Perhaps fortunately for those of us who love language, there is as yet no neologism that blends together China, Japan and India. Some who see the rapid industrialization taking place in two highly populous but poor countries as a combined phenomenon like to use the word *Chindia,* although if you accept the argument of this book that the phenomenon is in fact a much broader one that originated in East Asia, sending geese flying all over the region, then you will instinctively shun the term.[1] Moreover, you will not spend time dreaming up a neologism for Asia's big three for, as subsequent chapters will show, the things that divide Asia's great powers from one another currently far outweigh the things that unite them. There is, however, one issue for which it does make sense to think of these three countries jointly. It is the issue of their impact as consumers of resources and as producers of pollution. If you add the three together, and have China and India develop as Japan did, some would say that you will destroy the planet.

Japanese readers, and devotees of Japan, will blench at that statement. Japan is a rich country with clean air and is a world leader in the efficient use of energy. It has proudly given the name of one of its most historic cities, albeit one blighted by hideous commercial development during the past twenty years, to the first global agreement about how to deal with the problem of climate change, namely the Kyoto Protocol, for the deal was struck there in December 1997. Clean Japan could not be more different from China, with its dreadful smogs, its acid rain and its uncontrolled outflows of toxic waste; or India, with its dying rivers and its disease-prone urban slums. In 2007 China overtook the United States as the world's biggest single emitter of the greenhouse gases that scientists believe are causing global warming and climate change; its emissions are more than four times larger than Japan's, in absolute terms, and twelve times larger per unit of GDP. The growth in demand for energy, iron ore and other commodities in China and India is driving up the prices for all of those resources as available reserves are limited, causing economic suffering in Japan along with the rest of the rich world. Yet the link with Japan is not bogus. Japan is connected to the environmental problems posed by Chinese and Indian growth in two crucial ways: through its own historical experience of the same problems, and through its possible role as part of the solution.

Here are some sentences from two books that have been written about such environmental problems:

> Most of the beautifully scenic [lake] was hopelessly polluted by the so-called red tides of polluted waters from the factories on its shores. Smog warnings became regular and asthma sufferers began trekking to the hospitals. Regional complaints and petitions about pollution, about 20,000 five years [earlier], had risen to 76,000 as this decade began. In the south, hundreds of people fell ill from eating the local fish. Many died. Similar problems occurred in the north, with mercury-filled drainage from one factory and where a painful bone disease was caused by cadmium.

And the other:

> For two decades, the government treated environmental protection as a distraction from economic growth . . . Break-

neck industrialisation produced some of the worst air and water pollution in the world. According to environmental officials, acid rain is falling on one-third of the country, half of the water in its seven largest rivers is "completely useless" . . . one-third of the urban population is breathing polluted air. More than 70% of the rivers and lakes are polluted, and ground water in 90% of the cities is tainted.

Which countries are these books writing about? Either of the extracts could be about China, but only the second one actually is. That extract comes from the book called *China: Fragile Superpower* by Susan L. Shirk that was published in 2007.[2] The sentences in the first extract have been disguised a little. That is because they come from a book about Japan that was published more than three decades earlier, called *Japan: The Fragile Superpower*, by Frank Gibney.[3] Clearly, fragility and Asian superpowerdom go together.

The "lake" I inserted into Mr. Gibney's extract was actually an area called the Inland Sea, a sea channel that lies between the main island of Honshu and the two smaller islands to its south and southwest, Shikoku and Kyushu. Industrial cities such as Osaka, Kobe and Hiroshima can be found on or near that coast. The figure of 20,000 complaints was from 1966 and that of 76,000 from 1971. The place where hundreds fell ill from eating fish was, of course, Minamata Bay in Kyushu, where a Japanese company, Chisso, poured methyl mercury into the sea during the 1950s and '60s with disastrous consequences for local people's health that are still being seen today. The cadmium poisoning was caused by the Mitsui Mining and Smelting Company and produced a disease known as *itai-itai,* or "it hurts, it hurts." The mercury-filled drainage came from a company called Showa Denko, whose effluent caused a second outbreak of Minamata disease, in Niigata prefecture in northwest Japan.

If you look at a photograph taken in a Japanese city in 1965, say, or 1970—in Tokyo or Osaka, or a city with industry right at its heart such as Kita-Kyushu—you will find a strong resemblance to the appearance of most big Chinese cities today, including Beijing, Guangzhou, Shanghai and Chongqing. The air is thick with smog and dust. Days when blue skies can be seen are rare causes for celebration. If you go to any of those Japanese cities now, however, the air is completely different. Blue skies can be seen. Breathing is easy. People need to wear face masks only when they are suffering from colds, not to try to filter out pollution, as they did during the 1960s. It is no longer hazardous to be a traffic policeman.

What happened in Japan to clean the air was a combination of two things. One was popular protest, which even in a democracy dominated by a single party, the Liberal Democrats, forced government policy to change. The country's first proper environmental laws were passed in the early 1970s, limiting emissions from factories and forcing car makers to sell cleaner vehicles. The second was macroeconomic: the revaluation of the yen in 1971 when America abandoned fixed exchange rates, followed by the oil shock of 1973 when the Arab members of OPEC cut supplies of oil and sharply raised the price. This sudden change in Japan's macroeconomic circumstances brought about an abrupt switch in the country's industrial structure and emphasis. Capital investment in heavy, polluting industry began to drop. Energy had become more expensive, and government policy made it more expensive still, by imposing taxes on it even once the market price fell back. Companies adopted energy-saving, more efficient technology and started to make products that fitted the new, cleaner times, especially cars. It was also at this point that electronics companies, encouraged by the government, made big investments in new, high-tech gadgetry, leading the economy in a new direction.

Earlier in this book, China's economic situation now was likened to that of Japan in 1970. Investment as a share of GDP has been soaring, rising toward 45 percent, which is even higher than the peak achieved in Japan in 1970. Booming domestic demand, cheap capital and an undervalued exchange rate have produced fast growth in construction and in energy-intensive, polluting industries such as steel, chemicals and aluminium. China's industrial structure looks odd in that it still includes an abundance of low-tech, labor-intensive companies in textiles and toy making as well as heavier industries and higher-tech ones. The investment boom has produced even worse environmental consequences than were expected. From 1980 until 2002, the amount of energy consumed to produce each unit of GDP had been declining, as grossly inefficient Mao-era industries were replaced by more modern, productive, efficient factories. Since then, however, the trend has gone into reverse. China is not only consuming more energy and producing more carbon-based pollution because its economy is growing: Its energy consumption and greenhouse-gas output have been rising faster even than its GDP.

If Japan's experience is a guide, then at some point in the next few years this can be expected to change. Investment-led growth will fade. The Chinese currency will be revalued. Inflation will raise production costs directly, and will force interest rates to rise, making capital more expensive. Popular pressure against environmental dangers and degradation will force the Communist Party to do what Japan's LDP did in the 1970s and enforce stringent environmental controls. As in Japan, it will take quite a few years before the smog clears and the water becomes useable, since factories and vehicles take time to be replaced or converted. But it can and should happen.

Or will it? There are several reasons why this Japan-shows-the-way story is not quite as reassuring as it looks. One is that in some respects Japan's record is not as good as it may seem if you just wander the streets of Tokyo, Osaka or even Kita-Kyushu. Air quality has improved hugely, as has sanitation and the treatment of drinking water. Those are the things that ordinary people notice and protest about most vociferously. Producing cleaner, more fuel-efficient cars also helped the Japanese car industry, for in combination with a strict vehicle-testing regime that forces old cars to be scrapped quite quickly, it helped to boost new car sales at exactly the time when specializing in such cars proved a great advantage in overseas markets, too, in competition with American gas guzzlers. So business groups were persuaded to support those changes rather than lobby against them. The same is not true, however, of pollution by effluent and in particular by toxic waste.

Companies and business associations in Japan had worked closely with the bureaucracy in Japan throughout the high-growth, postwar period. In the 1970s, although the direction of the economy changed and popular opinion did begin to count, Japan did not suddenly become driven by consumers and voters rather than producers. The business-government nexus remained powerful and successfully resisted many environmental controls. Consequently, even in the 1990s, two decades later, a longtime American resident in Japan, Alex Kerr, could write that "Japan enters the new millennium with only the most primitive regulation of toxic waste."[4]

Many fewer substances are subject to government controls in Japan than in America or Western Europe. Even if they are, breaches of the controls have often been covered up, as became clear in the late 1990s when an outcry developed about disposal of poisonous dioxins along with other waste in incinerators, contaminating the surrounding air and soil. As Mr. Kerr wrote, after television reports on dioxin contamination in the city of Tokorozawa, outside Tokyo, in 1997, it emerged that officials from the city and its prefecture had colluded in concealing data on dioxin discharges from local incinerators and that levels for 1992–94 were more than 150 times the legal limit. Unfortunately, this is but one of dozens of examples.

Japan does enjoy the highest life expectancy in the world (after tiny Andorra) of nearly eighty-three years, so one might argue that the harm done by this poor environmental record has been limited. The Inland Sea remains heavily polluted, and Lake Biwa (a genuine and beautiful freshwater lake, between Kyoto and Osaka) is, like many Chinese lakes, notorious for its algae blooms. Yet people live well, and healthily. That is true, but if you are unlucky enough to be directly affected by toxic effluents you will not live well, and you will have a devil of a problem getting any compensation.

Minamata disease was first discovered in 1956 and was shown definitively to have been caused by Chisso Corporation's mercury discharge from its chemical plant in 1959. The disease killed more than 1,700 people and left countless others crippled and deformed. Yet Chisso continued to discharge mercury into Minamata Bay until 1968. The company concealed its own research that showed that the mercury was causing the disease, and paid minimal amounts of compensation without admitting responsibility. The main victims' group finally won a legal case against Chisso in 1973, securing more substantial sums in compensation, but the group's legal battles with the company and the government continued until 1995. The judiciary and the government proved to be more sympathetic to business interests than to personal safety, and were subject to excruciatingly long delays. It is one of the most shameful stories of postwar Japan. Exactly the same sort of thing could occur in China.

Another reason why Japan's experience is not altogether reassuring is that China has no democracy and an even less independent judiciary than Japan. Popular pressure is building up, as was explained in chapter 3. The issue of dangerous materials hit the headlines in November 2005 when an explosion at a chemical plant in northeast China caused a huge spillage of benzene into the Songhua River, depriving millions of people of their freshwater supply and causing international concern as the river crosses the border and flows into Russia. Popular pressure undoubtedly worries the central government, and can succeed in forcing municipal governments to change their plans—as occurred in Xiamen, a southern coastal city, when demonstrations against a planned new chemical plant in a residential area led to the project's suspension. But redress in the courts is a slow and uncertain process. Environmental NGOs and other groups will succeed in changing local policies consistently only if the central government gives them its backing.

A third reason is that in Japan the switch to a more energy-efficient economic structure took place not just as a matter of deliberate policy but also by necessity: It took the oil shock of 1973 and the currency revaluation two years earlier to force it to happen. Such a series of external events might well occur in China's case, too. But it is not a certainty. If the process of change relies only on government policy, it is likely to be slow.

Meanwhile, China's environment is as Susan Shirk described it: smoggy, dirty and in some places dangerous. So, in fact, is India's on many measures. The Center for Environmental Law and Policy at Yale University, which is one of the most respected and independent monitors of environmental trends, has produced an index to compare the performance of 133 countries all around the world on the basis of sixteen indicators covering six main areas: environmental health, air quality, water resources, biodiversity and habitat, productive natural resources and sustainable energy. On that "environmental performance index" Japan comes fourteenth.[5] China, not surprisingly, comes a lot lower, in ninety-fourth place. Yet India scores the worst of the three, at 118th.

One reason arises from a common problem with attempts to compile international indexes. They can only be compiled using data on things that can readily be measured and that are in fact measured on a fairly consistent basis in all the countries being monitored. Two of China's worst environmental features are thus missed by the Yale index: There are no data on human exposure to toxic chemicals (which lets Japan off, too), nor are there consistent, comparable data on emissions of sulphur dioxide (which come chiefly from coal-fired power stations) and the resulting acid rain. Given that the Yale index includes indicators of environmental health, including mortality rates, India scores badly because of the familiar weakness of its overall health system. Moreover, in India one important source of poor air quality arises from rural poverty rather than urbanization or economic growth: It is the burning of what energy experts call "traditional biomass," often dung but also firewood, as fuel inside homes with the result that indoor air is harmful.

In those ways, India's environmental record is bad because it is poor, rather than because it has made economic growth its priority. Even so, India can hardly be considered immune to the Chinese and Japanese sins of mishandling dangerous materials. It, after all, experienced the disaster in 1984 at Bhopal, in the Indian state of Madhya Pradesh, when a pesticide plant run by a subsidiary of America's Union Carbide accidentally released a huge quantity of a poisonous gas, killing at least 3,800 people straight away and about 20,000 since the disaster, as well as leaving at least 120,000 people still suffering from the ill-effects. In terms of those direct effects, Bhopal was a worse industrial disaster even than the accident at the nuclear power plant in Chernobyl, in the Ukraine, which took place in 1986. Moreover, the Blacksmith Institute, a New York-based environmental think tank, included two Indian locations on its 2007 list of the ten places on the planet that have the worst pollution dangers posed by toxic chemicals: Sukinda, in Orissa, where chromium mines are responsible for the fact that 60 percent of the drinking water contains at least double the level of hexavalent chromium permitted by national and international standards; and Vapi, in Gujarat, where the dangers are posed by mercury, lead and zinc poisoning.[6] China also boasts two picks in Blacksmith's top ten.

Nevertheless, India's worst and most intractable environmental problems lie in the more mundane issue of water, because they affect such a large number of people. The first water problem is simple: lack of access to it. In principle, more than 80 percent of Indians have access to supplies of clean drinking water. In practice, those supplies are unreliable, and getting worse. Most Indian cities can maintain their public supplies of piped water only for a few hours each day. According to the World Bank, in Bangalore in the 1980s water was available through the mains system for twenty hours a day, but now can be had for only two to three hours.[7] In Chennai, it was available for ten to fifteen hours a day in the 1980s, and only less than two hours a day now. In Delhi it is available for only four hours, in Mumbai for five. People cope by obtaining supplies from private tankers or by drilling their own boreholes—or just by filling buckets when it comes through the pipes.

The problem is the same as that outlined for electricity in chapter 5: inadequate investment, low prices that make further investment unattractive, corruption and lack of power for pumping. Demand has risen as India's population has grown and industry has developed, but supply has not kept pace. In some rural areas, the reason is the destruction of ecosystems by deforestation, for example, the tainting of groundwater, or just its overexploitation. More generally, though, the reason is lack of storage and poor distribution systems. Climate change may eventually make the rainfall inadequate, too, but currently there is plenty. It is wasted.

The second water problem is also rather basic: It is sewerage, or rather, the lack of treatment of sewage. China's rivers are dying because of industrial pollution. India's are dying because of human pollution. Even the Yamuna River, which flows from the Himalayas down through the capital city of Delhi, is to all intents and purposes dead once it flows out of the capital laden with 950 million gallons of sewage each day. Somini Sengupta wrote a series of articles in the *New York Times* outlining India's water problems in excruciating detail.[8] As she wrote, a retired Indian navy officer who had once sailed regattas on the Yamuna took his government to the Supreme Court in 1992, accusing it of killing the river and preventing Hindus from performing ritual baths in the river, as is their constitutional right. He won the case, and the Supreme Court ordered the city's water authority to treat all sewage flowing into the river and improve water quality. But in the subsequent fourteen years that instruction has not been met. The city's population has risen by 40 percent in that time, and more than half the sewage that goes into the river does so untreated. New treatment plants have been built, but not enough, and they, too, suffer from power failures.

The Center for Science and Environment, a Delhi-based institute, explains it in this way:

> Treatment capacity has increased almost eight-fold in the last forty years, but wastewater generation has grown 12-fold in the same period. We also suffer from under-utilization. Delhi has a sewage treatment capacity of 2,330 million liters daily—seventeen sewage treatment plants—of its own. But only 68% of this capacity is utilized. The reasons are many: sewage has to be transported over long distances for treatment, through largely defunct conveyance systems. In 2001, only 15% of Delhi's sewerage system was functional. On top of this, almost 45% of Delhi lives in unauthorized colonies, generating "illegal" sewage, which is unaccounted for.[9]

In India, the main environmental issues are lack of enforcement of the law and inadequate spending on infrastructure. Faster economic growth may ease the second of those, by making more tax revenues available. It will not solve the first. In China, the main issue is also enforcement of the law. There is no shortage of money. What there is, though, is a clear pursuit of money at the expense of environmental controls.

If you look at the laws and regulations that have been passed in China to clean up the environment, there is a risk that you will be quite impressed. For example, as a study published in 2007 by the OECD on the country's environment showed, China "has a comprehensive legal framework for water resource and pollution management, with clear mechanisms to control abstractions and to set water quality objectives."[10] A new Water Law was passed in 2002.

Laws on "prevention and control of air pollution" date back to 1995, and were revised in 2000 and 2002. Under Article 6 of the air pollution law, says the OECD, the State Environment Protection Administration (SEPA) is "charged with establishing national ambient air quality and emission standards." Objectives are set for reducing pollution in the regular five-year plans. The rules for vehicle exhaust emissions are as tight as in the European Union: So-called EURO IV emission standards, which were introduced in the EU in January 2005, came into effect in China for gas engines in 2007 and will do so for diesel engines in 2010.

The reality, however, is rather different. SEPA, which is supposed to set standards and oversee their enforcement, has neither the power nor the resources to do so. It has only 300 full-time professionals in Beijing, according to Elizabeth Economy, an expert on China's environment at the Council on Foreign Relations in New York, plus a similar number spread around the country.[11] America's Environmental Protection Agency has 9,000 staff in Washington, D.C., alone. SEPA has no legal authority to force factories that violate pollution controls to close or reform. The authority over pollution and conservation is divided among many different ministries, as well as being delegated to local governments.

China is, of course, an extremely large place. So there are local environmental protection bureaus that are supposed to enforce environmental standards in every province and big city. But SEPA has no direct authority over these EPBs. They report not to SEPA itself but to their local governors and mayors. And the essence of China's environmental problem is that those local governors and mayors do not have an interest in, or much incentive for, enforcing the country's environmental laws. Their interest is in economic growth. They are interested in it partly for its own sake, but also because they and their officials make money from it, through commercial ventures and corruption, and because the business interests that surround the local officials also push in that direction. They are also interested in it for a legitimate, incentive-based reason: Their careers and promotions depend on economic growth.

Supposedly, this is changing. A new contract has been drawn up for local officials, under which their performance criteria will be changed to include their local environments as well as GDP growth. But there has been no agreement on how this should be done, on what green criteria to use. Pan Yue, the vice minister of SEPA, devoted three years of research to producing a set of "green GDP" accounts, which could have been used as the basis for officials' job evaluations. But the effort failed and it emerged in 2007 that it had been dropped. The reason was not a technical one; it was political. The effort was too controversial. Many provinces objected.

SEPA is, by common consent, an island of environmental awareness in a sea of disregard. It cannot achieve much unless the Communist Party's top leaders make up their minds to support it and build a consensus that the environment has to be turned into a priority, equal to that of economic growth rather than subservient to it. Meanwhile, SEPA officials have been experimenting with other ways to exert pressure: by exploiting public pressure, for example, through NGOs and public hearings; by using its limited power to refuse approval for new industrial projects (which tend to be cleaner than old ones) in order to press local governments into closing dirty old ones first; by using banks to exert pressure through putting green conditions on their loans. All of these efforts will remain tentative and ineffective, however, until the party leadership really takes hold of the issue.

Meanwhile, targets are set and laws passed, to great fanfare. The targets are missed, the laws are ignored. One-third of all industrial wastewater in China and two-thirds of household sewage are released untreated.[12] The Yangtze River receives 40 percent of the country's sewage, 80 percent of it untreated; in China's other best-known waterway, the Yellow River, two-thirds of its water is considered unfit to drink and 10 percent is classified merely as sewage.

Impressive targets have been set in the 11th Five-Year Plan (2006–10) to increase energy efficiency by 20 percent by 2010—i.e., to reduce the amount of energy used to produce each unit of GDP by 20 percent—and to cut key air pollutants such as sulphur dioxide and carbon dioxide by 10 percent. In the first year, 2006, that energy target required a drop of 4 percent; the actual result was 1.33 percent. In 2007, according to Yang Fuqing of the Energy Foundation in Beijing, an American-funded NGO, the result was roughly a 2 percent cut. So unless something drastic happens in 2008–10, the targets are going to be missed, by a mile.

Many of these environmental problems are problems for the Chinese and the Indians rather than for the world, except in terms of humanitarian concern and a desire to promote conservation. Unsafe water, toxic spills, smoggy cities: These are domestic issues. Whether they are dealt with depends on domestic politics in each country. Greenhouse-gas emissions pose different, and strictly international, issues. So, in many people's minds, does the depletion of natural resources. A third concern bridges the domestic and the international: If China (and in the future, India) are so bad at enforcing their own environmental laws, will their exported manufactures and food put foreigners in danger, too? That concern hit the headlines during 2007.

The easiest issue to dispose of, quite safely, is the second of those three: the idea that Chinese and Indian development will denude the planet of its resources. This issue is something of a red herring—and by that I do not mean a toxic one. It is clear that if China and India continue to grow at high, even double-digit rates, they will need to consume a lot more energy and other commodities. That is one reason why the price of oil in 2007 was about four times higher than it had been in 2001, and eight times higher than in 1998; and why prices of metals such as copper, nickel and zinc also soared during the past five years or so. But it was not the only reason.

Other reasons, for oil, include production controls by the oil-producers' cartel, OPEC; the wars in Iraq and Afghanistan; and almost twenty years of declining investment in new oil reserves and in exploration and extraction technology, as companies were discouraged by almost twenty years of a declining oil prices. Similarly, for commodities, until 2001–02 prices had been declining for roughly two decades, and as a result so had investment in new mines. It takes a long time to increase investment and to open new mines or oil fields, partly in the nature of the business but also because when everyone wants mining engineers and equipment suddenly and simultaneously, the cost of those assets soars. So although Chinese and Indian demand will continue to buttress energy and commodities prices for as long as demand keeps on growing rapidly, supply will also increase.

Known, recoverable reserves of coal are sufficient for 147 years of consumption at current rates, according to the annual *BP Statistical Review of World Energy;* the figure for natural gas is sixty-three years and that for oil is 40.5.[13] What has happened in the past is that reserves figures decline or grow more slowly when prices are falling, as exploration declines, too, and start to rise when prices are higher. By definition that cannot go on forever: At some point the resources will genuinely run out. That point is far ahead, however, and keeps on receding. The same is true of the other commodities that China and India are devouring eagerly, especially metals. According to the U.S. Geological Survey, world output of copper in 2006 was 15.3 million tons; but the world's known reserves are 480 million tons, covering more than thirty years at the current rate of mining.[14] At 2006 rates of output, the world's known reserves of nickel will last forty-one years, of zinc twenty-two, of tin twenty-two, of iron ore ninety-five, of bauxite (which is used in aluminium smelting) 141 years and of platinum 318 years.

Given that China and India are becoming, on balance, consumers of more of these resources than they can produce domestically, they share an interest in investing in new mines and discovering new reserves.[15] That is also what Japan did during its high-growth period of the 1960s, when its appetite for commodities also expanded rapidly. Fortunately, China in particular has plenty of capital with which to do this investment. Chinese state-owned companies are showing themselves to be willing to explore for resources and build mines in especially inhospitable places, ones where Western companies prefer not to tread. In November 2007, for example, China Metallurgical Group (CMG) won a tender for the right to develop a potentially huge copper deposit in Afghanistan, which may prove to be the world's biggest, with a bid of $3 billion. To get at the copper, CMG will have to build roads and power stations, as well as dealing with Afghanistan's unstable politics.

Similar investments have been made all over Africa. In another 2007 deal, China pledged at least $5 billion of investment in the Congo, in pursuit of copper, cobalt, nickel and gold, but which will also require the building (or rebuilding) of roads and railways. In Gabon, a Chinese consortium is building a railway, a port and a hydroelectric power station to serve an iron-ore mine. China imports more oil from Angola than even from Saudi Arabia (its second-biggest source). Investments in Sudan have landed China in diplomatic hot water, as was outlined in chapter 3. Investments in Ethiopia and Somalia have led to Chinese casualties, as a result of kidnappings and in the crossfire of war. China's overseas aid program has begun to evolve in the same sort of way as Japanese aid did during the 1960s and '70s: It is being used as an adjunct to commercial investments, especially in resources development. The country's overall aid budget remains small though also mysterious: Estimates place it at somewhere between $2 billion and $3 billion a year, much of which is tied to the use of Chinese companies to build infrastructure and new mines.[16] Japanese aid remained largely tied in this way until pressure from other rich countries forced it to change during the 1980s. Indian firms are also engaged in the development of African resources, though without the backing of a similar aid budget, and so far on a smaller scale.

Reserves are not the only issue, admittedly. Access to them is also important. In part that means access at an acceptable cost, which is also a question of technological developments. But more critically, especially for oil, the point is that access to reserves is a political matter. As exploration declined during the 1990s, so the share of known global oil reserves accounted for by members of OPEC increased, and access to those reserves is primarily confined to state-owned oil firms in the countries concerned. As a result, investment in new production is determined by government policy, not by market-led exploration, which is likely to slow down the rate of expansion both of reserves and of production. OPEC members would prefer to keep the price high. Nevertheless other reserves are being found: In November 2007, for example, Brazil announced the discovery of one of the world's largest offshore oil fields which, if it fulfills its apparent potential, is likely to make Brazil (which is not an OPEC member) as large an oil producer as Venezuela, which is one of OPEC's most militant states.

During the oil-price boom there has been much talk about "peak oil," the notion that even if reserves remain large, the rate of production from those reserves is likely to reach a peak, for geological, technological and economic reasons, and then decline. Again, this must logically be true, eventually, but there is no evidence that the peak is imminent: It depends most crucially on technology and cost. Alan Greenspan, the sainted former chairman of the Federal Reserve Board, argued in his 2007 memoir that oil production is unlikely to peak before the middle of this century, and probably much later; and he argued that just as oil superseded coal at a time when coal reserves remained abundant (as they still do), oil, too, will be superseded by new energy technologies well before it runs out.[17] This is a variant on a saying popularized by Sheikh Ahmed Zaki Yamani, who became famous as Saudi Arabia's oil minister during the 1970s: He said that just as the stone age did not end because the world ran out of stones, so the oil age will not end because there is no more oil.

Globalization has produced a constantly evolving list of popular nightmares. During the 1990s, once scares about the world being flattened by the Japanese juggernaut had faded, the main fear was of Americanization, symbolized by the spread of branches of McDonald's and of Starbucks on every urban street. That at least provided convenient plate-glass windows to throw stones at or, in the case of France's antiglobalization champion José Bové, whole restaurants to destroy. In 1999 Mr. Bové, a radical farmer and political activist who spent part of his childhood in Berkeley, California, where his parents were university researchers, led a group that stormed a site in the southern French town of Millau, where a new McDonald's was being built. Mr. Bové was (and still is) campaigning against what he sees as the "industrialization of food," whether through genetically modified crops or hormones in beef. His choice of an American retail outlet to symbolize the enemy found an echo in Beijing in 2007, when Starbucks was forced to close its branch in the grounds of the Forbidden City (the former imperial palace) after an online campaign led by a Chinese TV news anchorman, Rui Chenggang, who said the coffee shop "undermined the solemnity of the Forbidden City and trampled on Chinese culture."

Perhaps it did—and its closure, after the campaign petition attracted 500,000 signatures, also reflected efforts to reduce the overall commercialization of what is Beijing's top tourist attraction. Nevertheless, for a rather squeaky-clean American coffee chain to be targeted as an alien threat was somewhat ironic in 2007 of all years. For that was the year when attention shifted at least temporarily away from abstract economic statistics such as the size of China's trade surplus or the undervaluation of its currency and toward the more down-to-earth question of whether Chinese exports might in fact kill you.

The story of dangerous Chinese goods began in March when American pets started to die after eating pet food that had been made in China and turned out to have been laced with melamine, an industrial chemical. It moved on to Chinese-made toothpaste that was found (in Panama) to contain diethylene glycol, a toxic ingredient normally found in antifreeze, to allegedly faulty truck tires (in America) and to nightclothes (in New Zealand) that were found to have been treated with too much formaldehyde, which can be carcinogenic. An interesting diversion occurred as this story was unfolding when Zheng Ziaoyu, who had been head of the Chinese State Food and Drug Administration and so responsible for the regulation of foods and medicines, was prosecuted and then executed. It looked at first as if this might show how the Chinese authorities were cracking down on all these faulty exports, but it then emerged that he had been executed for corruption instead. The story reached its high point in August when Mattel, America's and the world's biggest toy firm, had to recall huge numbers of its products from stores and customers after its toy vehicles were found to be covered with lead-based paint, while millions of its other toys contained loose magnets that could choke young children. The toys were made in China, like most of the toys sold in rich countries all around the world, including 65 percent of all those sold by Mattel. This story also produced a fatality, though not yet, as far as is known, among children: the manager of a factory that supplied Mattel with toy cars committed suicide.

In all these tales, it was not quite clear who should be blamed. The Chinese manufacturer, for using cheaper and potentially dangerous materials or ingredients, in violation of the buyer's specifications? The Chinese regulators, for failing to enforce their laws properly? The foreign multinational that had subcontracted its production to China in order to exploit that country's much lower costs, one component of which is its weaker and less burdensome regulations, but then failed to check that the resulting products met the safety standards of the countries in which it was planning to sell the goods? Or the regulators in the importing country, who were failing to enforce their own laws sufficiently rigorously, and thus allowing importers to neglect their responsibilities?

The answer has to be all of them, but the greatest blame should surely be placed on the shoulders of the company importing these products and proposing to sell them to foreign consumers. In the end, if the products turn out to be deadly or even just risky, it is that company's reputation and future sales that should rightly suffer. Regulators and customers alike are entitled to expect companies like Mattel to shoulder the main responsibility in ensuring its products are safe. The chief accessory to the crime, though, was also clear: globalization. With so many products being made so far away by people we cannot control, was it any surprise that those products are becoming dangerous? Or so ran many thoughts, as the thinkers and worriers sat sipping coffee made from beans imported from Colombia, or mango juice made from fruit in Southeast Asia.

This is not, in other words, a new phenomenon. For as long as there have been imports, especially imports of basic items like food, clothes or children's toys, there have been extra questions about how to make sure that those imports are safe to eat and use—extra, that is, to the questions already raised by production inside your own country. It was also true in the 1950s when Japan was the low-cost country from which many toy firms bought their products, and it was true in the 1960s and '70s when such subcontracting moved to Hong Kong and South Korea.

Evidence that standards are not being enforced adequately could, in principle, bring about a genuine change in consumer behavior, leading people to shun dubious products and thus hurting specific companies and even a whole sector. When some Austrian wine was found in the mid-1980s to have been laced with diethylene glycol the whole country's wine exports were hit badly. In that case, although few consumers could remember the specific wineries that had been at fault, it was fairly simple to boycott the whole country: There is plenty of other wine to choose from, after all. In Japan, however, Australian wine also suffered from the scandal for a while, such are the vagaries of pronunciation and linguistic misunderstanding. It is more doubtful, though, that a general shunning of products bearing the label MADE IN CHINA will last for long. Moreover, set against China's total exports in 2006 of $969 billion, the likelihood that safety scares would have any noticeable macro-economic impact is close to zero. At a macro level, the only significance of the scares is probably the confirmation it brings that it is time for China to leave behind some of the lower-cost and lower-technology activities that helped launch its export growth in the 1980s and '90s. Indeed, as rising wages have eroded China's cost advantage in making toys and similar products, it could be that some companies have resorted to desperate and devious means to try to keep prices down and profits up.

The episode did, however, provide some new ammunition for critics of globalization and especially for those in rich countries seeking fresh reasons to try to control the flow of cheap imports from China. This reflects a natural and eternal political reality, especially in democracies: that foreigners don't vote, and so can safely be treated as scapegoats during election campaigns. Japan enjoyed that honor during American election years in the 1980s, and so did China in 1992 (after Tiananmen) and in 2000 (for being, in George Bush's words, America's "strategic competitor"); India got a walk-on part during the 2004 presidential campaign thanks to the then-new vogue for outsourcing IT and other service operations to that country. In 2007–08 the role was not surprisingly returned to China, given the huge rise in China's trade surplus.

There is, however, one fear about globalization, and about the implications of industrialization in China and India, that looks justified. It is that lifting hundreds of millions of people out of poverty in those and other emerging economies is going to have a huge and dangerous side effect: If policies do not change, it will make it much, much harder to control the rise in global temperatures that scientists believe is a result of industrialization and consumer affluence, and thus to limit the pace of climate change.

The facts about current trends of emissions in India and China are clear; ideas about future trends depend on assumptions about the prices of different sorts of energy and about government policies. A

The world's top emitters of CO_2

	Emissions, m tonnes, 2005	Tonnes per capita, 2004	Per unit of GDP*, 2004
United States	5,957	20.18	0.55
China	5,323	3.62	3.14
Russia	1,696	11.70	5.13
Japan	1,230	9.91	0.26
India	1,166	1.04	1.88
Germany	844	10.46	0.46
Canada	631	18.09	0.74
Britain	577	9.62	0.36
South Korea	500	10.26	0.81
Italy	467	8.35	0.44

*Tonnes per $1,000 of GDP, 2000 $ at market prices

series of tables and charts is the easiest and quickest way to depict them. First, emissions.

China became already the world's largest emitter of greenhouse gas in 2007, overtaking the United States according to estimates by the International Energy Agency, but comprehensive and internationally comparable figures are not yet available for such a recent year. Nevertheless, the figures for 2005 offer a good guide. The growth in China's emissions make it much dirtier than the rich world in terms of emissions per unit of GDP, but cleaner if your preferred gauge is emissions per head of population. Indian government officials often claim that India is not yet a problem from the point of view of gas emissions, but that is only true if you focus on emissions per head: In absolute terms, India was already the world's fifth largest producer of such emissions in 2005, and probably moved into fourth place during 2007.

Second, energy sources.

The main reason for those high emissions in China and India is inefficiency: old technology, poor controls or enforcement of controls. A secondary reason, though, is the fuels being used. Coal is the dirtiest source of mass energy production in terms of carbon dioxide emissions, as well as producing sulphur

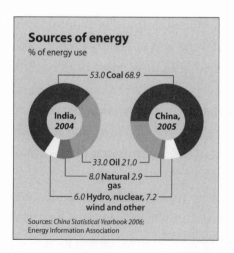

Sources of energy
% of energy use

India, 2004

China, 2005

53.0 Coal 68.9
33.0 Oil 21.0
8.0 Natural gas 2.9
6.0 Hydro, nuclear, 7.2 wind and other

Sources: *China Statistical Yearbook 2006*; Energy Information Association

dioxide and lots of airborne particles, but it is also the most available source.[18] That is especially true for China, which has the world's third largest coal reserves.

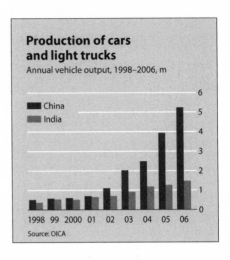

Production of cars and light trucks
Annual vehicle output, 1998–2006, m
Source: OICA

Third, consumer trends amid these countries' still modest levels of affluence.

That long sentence essentially meant a three-letter word: the car. Economic development in Japan, South Korea, Taiwan and other East Asian superachievers brought with it a boom in demand for consumer durables that became known as "the three Cs": cars, coolers and color TVs. The same is happening in China and, with a time lag, India. The OECD's report on China's environmental performance in 2007 contained the following rather surreal recommendation: The country should, it said, "take measures to encourage the use of cleaner transport modes (e.g., bicycles)." Which planet is the OECD on? Bicycles are what the Chinese have just begun to move away from, and they enjoy using cars instead. Indians are doing the same thing, as cars take over from bicycles and, especially, motorcycles. If both Chinese and Indians do continue to get more affluent, they are going to want more cars—a lot more. This simple point was underlined in January 2008 by the unveiling in Delhi by Tata Motors of the world's cheapest car, the Nano, which will cost 100,000 rupees ($2,500) and has an eventual annual production target of one million cars.

So, on current trends, China and India are going to burn a lot more coal and drive a lot more cars, which means that they are going to become far and away the world's biggest emitters of greenhouse gases during the next few decades. When challenged about this, officials from both countries read from more or less the same script: China and India are poor countries that need to concentrate on lifting hundreds of millions more people out of abject poverty; their emissions per capita are much lower than in the rich world; and that even if they are the biggest sources of new emissions, most of the carbon dioxide and other greenhouse gases that are now sitting in the atmosphere were produced by the rich world.

If you take those official positions at their word, the prospect looks rather gloomy. The reason why the United States refused to ratify the Kyoto Protocol, first under President Clinton and then more brazenly under President Bush, is that developing countries like China and India were not required by it to take any action. The successor to that protocol is supposed to come into force by 2012; if it is to have any hope of including the United States, Australia and other rich countries that stayed out of the Kyoto deal then it must include China and India. (Australia belatedly ratified the Kyoto Protocol when Labor regained power in November 2007, removing the Kyoto-sceptic John Howard as prime minister after eleven years in office.) But China and India say that the rich should be doing all the work: in effect, they are saying that the first Kyoto Protocol got it right. It looks like quite an impasse.

Yet the gloom may yet lift. If you take the Chinese and Indian governments at their word on their attitude toward the environment generally rather than on global warming specifically, things start to look more promising. In April 2007, for example, China's Premier Wen Jiabao gave a speech to party officials in which he said that "without faster restructuring and an efficient method of economic growth, China's natural resources and the environment will not be able to sustain its economic development . . . China must take responsibility for reducing polluting emissions."[19]

In his Independence Day speech in August 2007, India's prime minister, Manmohan Singh, echoed those sentiments.[20] "In the rush of modernization," he said, "and the race to develop, we must not forget the value of conserving our resources . . . Let us recall Gandhiji's wise words that nature has given us enough for every-

one's need, but not for everyone's greed . . . People across the world
are increasingly concerned about global warming. And so must
we be. We must be economical in our consumption of fuels and
energy. This we owe humanity and to posterity." Humanity will
be grateful for those words, and no doubt Mahatma Gandhi
(Gandhiji, by his affectionate Indian name) would endorse them,
too. The question is, where might words such as Mr. Wen's and
Dr. Singh's lead?

The answer is that during the next few years, the rich countries
will do a deal with Chinese and Indian leaders, perhaps even Mr.
Wen and Dr. Singh themselves, under which their two countries
will accept targets for the reduction of greenhouse-gas emissions, as
long as the rich countries accept much tougher targets, especially
during the first decade or two of the arrangement. The politics of climate change have altered sufficiently in the United States to make
a deal look possible: In 2007, even President Bush shocked everyone
who thinks of him as the Toxic Texan by declaring a willingness to
take part in negotiations for a successor to Kyoto. Candidates for the
2008 presidential election all felt obliged to come up with a plan
for global warming. Striking a deal will be high on the agenda of the
new president, not only for his or her own sake but because it will
offer a way to emphasize a commitment to multilateralism, and thus
how different the new president is from President Bush the unilat-
eralist, without needing to give ground on security issues.

And why should China and India agree to it? In China's case, the
optimistic but reasonable answer is that the country's leadership, as
was argued earlier, is worried about the country's environment and
its potential to provoke politically dangerous public protests, but is
finding it hard to impose its will on local officials. Just as during the
1990s China's entry into the World Trade Organization was used as
an external pressure to force ministries and local governments to accept economic reforms, so a post-Kyoto deal on global warming
could be used as an external pressure to force local officials to enforce

environmental rules and to justify introducing tough penalties for breaking them. In India's case, that argument does not apply. A financial or technological reward of some kind may be needed to persuade the country to sign up.

This deal is likely to be agreed on initially between America, the EU, Japan, China, India, Russia and Brazil, and then presented to the other 160 or so countries. Its presumption is likely to be that as well as being offered soft targets for emissions in the first decade or two, developing countries will also need to be helped, through money and technology, if they are to become relatively low-carbon economies without foregoing growth and preserving themselves in poverty. That presumption will be a recognition of the rich world's responsibility for the current stock of greenhouse gases. The money might be transferred to the developing countries directly, or more likely by a mechanism linked to a trading system for emissions permits. Permits would be allocated during the international negotiations, within an overall target for emissions reduction, and then rich-country governments and companies would be able to buy them from poorer countries. In addition, mechanisms would be agreed on through which low-carbon technology could be transferred to poorer countries at a considerable discount.

The reason why this deal can be outlined with such apparent clarity is that the options for dealing with global warming are simple and well known. The aim must be to reduce emissions of greenhouse gases. The method of doing so will either be by imposing taxes on carbon-dioxide-emitting activity, or by setting a limit on emissions, and trading permits for those emissions on international exchanges, thereby arriving at a carbon price. Supplementary techniques will include subsidies for research and development of new low-carbon technologies and for methods of disposing of carbon dioxide by burying it in the earth, as well as subsidies for low-carbon energy sources such as wind, solar and perhaps nuclear power. For all that simplicity, however, there are two huge problems to be overcome in arriving at a deal that will actually make the desired difference.

One is inherent in the whole process. The weakness of permit-trading mechanisms is that their beneficial effect on the environment depends on whether governments actually set limits for pollution that are tough; otherwise they are simply a way for excessive pollution to be moved around the planet. In an international negotiation, ultimately involving a huge number of countries, the pressure to compromise on softer targets for pollution will be great. A deal may be announced, with great fanfare. But if its targets are soft, it will make little difference.

The best way around this would be to taper the targets so that those for early years are soft but those for later years become progressively tougher—as long as the rises in global temperature continue to be sufficient to require such measures.

The second problem is more basic. It is one of trust, but also of the international politics of protectionism. Think about the idea that the rich countries should pay money to the poorer ones to compensate them for having to impose costs on their industries by requiring them to reduce their emissions. It makes sense in theory. In practice, it will meet stiff political opposition, at least if it is generalized to include China. After all, during the next few years when this deal is being negotiated, another concern will be high on the agenda of politicians in both the United States and the European Union: that concern is that China, and to a lesser extent India, threatens by unfair trade or by ultra-cheap capital or by some other devious means to destroy the rich world's manufacturing industries and perhaps even services, too.

China has huge amounts of capital. Its foreign-exchange reserves are worth more than $1.4 trillion. It is not tenable to expect Western taxpayers to support further flows of funds in China's direction, or to expect Western companies to be sanguine about paying more to reduce their own emissions than their powerful Chinese competitors pay to do the same. The same politicians who will have been shouting themselves hoarse about China's trade surplus and about the threat of Chinese state-controlled funds buying up Western assets will then be asked to ratify a post-Kyoto deal in which the rich world subsidizes those very "enemies." Such a deal would be dead on arrival.

Even if that prediction turned out to be wrong, a problem of trust will still remain. Imagine that an agreement is signed, targets are set and money starts to change hands, but that a few years later it becomes clear not only that the targets were too soft but also that the agreement is not being enforced in China or India and the soft targets are not being met, anyway. Permits to pollute are being bought by rich countries, but those selling them are still polluting as much or even more than before. After all, we know they are bad at enforcing their own environmental laws, so why should they be any better at enforcing international environmental agreements? At that point, the political row will be vast and noisy: Western money is subsidizing Chinese and Indian competitors, but the planet is still being destroyed.

That is, one might argue, a rather surreal version of a nightmare: If the planet is being destroyed in any case, why worry about a few billions, or even hundreds of billions, changing hands? The row, though, will come well before the planet's destruction; in other words before the climate has changed as a result. As should be well understood by now, the trends that threaten to bring about drastic changes in the climate are trends that cover half a century or even a a century ahead. A political row over money and missed targets would occur during the next decade. Moreover, if negotiations over the Kyoto successor coincide with a period of friction over trade with China and associated job losses, it could happen sooner. It could then overturn the whole effort to grapple with the problem of climate change.

What, if anything, can be done to prevent this problem of trust and protectionism from defeating the whole post-Kyoto enterprise? The basic point is that the idea of a general mechanism to channel funds from the rich to the poor, in compensation for cutting emissions, will have to go. The onus of the deal will have to be carried by the distribution of emissions targets themselves. This will not solve the issue of trust, but it will take away its financial sting.

Removing that mechanism will be unfair for all the poor countries that, unlike China, are not running big trade surpluses and sitting on large amounts of capital. This category includes India, as well as the many even poorer countries of Asia such as Laos, Cambodia, Bangladesh and others. What will have to happen is that financial assistance to those countries will have to be channeled separately from the post-Kyoto deal itself. Within Asia, there is an excellent channel that is already available. It is called Japan.

Japan is close at hand, it has successfully developed advanced technology for controlling air pollution, it is rich and the Japanese government, too, is always looking for ways to burnish Japan's reputation in the region. It would not be appealing to Japanese voters or businesses for it to channel more aid and technology to China, its great strategic and commercial competitor. Where there could be a chance to use Japanese capital and technology is to help the poorest countries of Southeast Asia, such as Cambodia and Laos, a form of assistance that would offer Japan an appealing way to compete with China in those and other countries as a benefactor. Indeed, in November 2007 Japan showed its interest in just such a role when, at ASEAN's annual summit, it unveiled plans to spend $2 billion in 2008–12 to help other Asian countries deal with air and water pollution. That is a small but useful start in what would need to become a much bigger program if it is to have any real impact. But where there could also be a good opportunity for Japan is with India.

India is far poorer than China, and its companies are not yet seen as direct competitors to Japanese firms. Moreover, it is part of the "arc of freedom and prosperity" that the Japanese government has been trying to promote in Asia, to differentiate its own efforts from China's. Most appealing of all, it would offer yet one more way to strengthen India and balance China's rise.

The instinct for political self-preservation and for using external pressure to force internal reforms should be enough to get China into a serious post-Kyoto deal. The way to get India into such a deal would be for Japan to take the lead in providing financial compensation and discounted technological assistance.

If you visit Beijing and take a deep breath at any time other than during the Olympic Games, you will feel not only unwell but also pessimistic about the chances that China will ever succeed in cleaning up its environment. There is plenty of cause for concern, despite the Japanese precedent cited earlier. But there are also some better signs, even if they still remain exceptions rather than the rule. To feel a bit more positive, come to one of those exceptions, around the other side of northern China's Bohai Bay from Beijing, to the city called Dalian.

The most noticeable change in China for anyone who has visited regularly over several decades is physical: the new buildings, the new roads, the switch from bicycles and three-wheelers to cars, and the accompanying increase in smog. My first business trip to China was only in 1993, so I cannot bear witness to the full extent of those changes in Beijing or Shanghai from Chairman Mao's time or from the early period of market reforms under Deng Xiaoping after 1978. On that first trip, however, I did visit Dalian, as a contrast with the then much more modern Beijing.

The immediate impression given by Dalian in 1993 was one of grime, heavy industry and decay. The city is at the tip of the Liaodong Peninsula, which will crop up again in chapter 7 as it was occupied for much of the first half of the twentieth century by Japan, the colonizer that operated the South Manchurian Railway, which carried raw materials from near the Russian and Mongolian borders down to Dalian and beyond to Lushun, the naval base that foreigners called Port Arthur. This made Dalian a natural base for heavy industry, both during the Japanese occupation and under Mao, and much of that industry was located smack in the middle of the city. In 1993 I was not allowed to visit those factories, so my main memories of the trip are three: the aforementioned grime; a tour around a new industrial park that was being laid out to attract light industry, especially through foreign investment by Japanese and South Korean companies, but which looked pretty empty; and a series of glitzy, noisy and sleazy nightclubs, which my colleague at the *Economist* insisted we visit in order to get a glimpse of "the new China," or rather the newly permitted behavior of the tiny number of affluent Chinese, which mainly meant the sons and daughters of Communist Party cadres.

My next visit to Dalian was in July 2007, fourteen years later. By then, the city's population had grown from about 5.3 million people in 1993 to about 6 million. It had thus attracted some migrants from the countryside but had not grown at anything like the pace of China's other industrial cities, many of which have doubled or tripled in size. Although the industrial zones have now filled up and multiplied in number, heavy industry remains the foundation of the city's economy: It has the country's biggest oil refinery and biggest shipbuilding yard, and it is also a center for the manufacture of other heavy equipment. So far so typical. It is unusual, however, in two important respects. Compared to 1993, it looks and smells a lot cleaner. And it has a new, and rapidly growing, element in its economy: information technology.

Dalian's mayor, Xia Deren, is also a harbinger of change as well, naturally, by being a promoter of his city. He has an academic rather than a party-cadre bent, with a PhD from Northeastern University's Institute of Finance, he is in his early fifties and he worked as an assistant to a former mayor, Bo Xilai, when Mr. Bo was governor of Liaoning province in which the city stands. Bo Xilai is an important figure in Dalian's story. He was mayor at the time of my previous visit, and is notable as the son of Bo Yibo, one of the Communist Party's so-called eight immortals, the revolutionary veterans who dominated Chinese politics under Deng Xiaoping in the 1980s. Bo Xilai is now minister of commerce in the central government, but in Dalian and Liaoning he began a clean-up of which Mayor Xia now talks proudly. The city closed more than 100 companies that had very outdated and dirty technology, and has moved more than 200 other polluting companies out of the downtown area and into industrial parks. The land left vacant by those factories has been used for construction of new offices and apartment blocks, but also for public parks, utilities and a swanky new museum. The city plants 100 million trees every year, he says; in 2007, when we spoke, it was laying out sixty square kilometers (twenty-three square miles) of new trees and grassland.

Dalian, in other words, does not quite fit the common image of China's new urban centers. Its air has gotten cleaner, not dirtier, and although heavy industry and manufacturing remain important so, too, does a business more associated with India than China: information technology. Until three or four years ago, Dalian suffered for its cleanliness with growth in output and incomes that was lower than in other big cities. Now, IT and (thanks to its seaside location) tourism are helping it to catch up. Initially, Dalian's IT business depended heavily on business from the former colonial power, Japan: Firms like DHC (which stands for Dalian Hi-Think Computer Technology) and the bigger, older Neusoft (the *Neu* stands for Northeastern University, where the organization was set up in 1988, becoming a company in 1991) got their starts from software and call-center work for Japanese clients. Neusoft's boss and founder, Liu Jiren, also got his inspiration for how research can be organized and commercialized during a spell working at the National Bureau of Standards in the United States in the 1980s. The first Chinese software firm to float its shares, Neusoft has since founded an educational institution linked to Mr. Liu's old university, Northeastern, the Neusoft Institute of Information, which opened in Dalian in 2001 on a new and very monumental campus that is more than a little reminiscent of Stanford University in California.

The IT business has been booming for Neusoft and the much smaller DHC, as well as other firms. Software-design contracts for foreign companies, especially in mobile phones and for Japanese consumer electronics firms, still provide a solid foundation: Overseas revenues provide only 30 percent of Neusoft's turnover but roughly 70 percent of its profits. The domestic IT market, in businesses such as insurance, telecoms, financial services and power utilities, has been growing rapidly but profit margins remain slim. That could well change during the next decade. For a big new source of business is likely to be the renovation and development of government IT systems, with two essential purposes: the establishment of a top-notch IT infrastructure to enable Chinese industry to move upmarket; and, just as important, the improvement of government information systems to bolster official control. Neusoft's Mr. Liu cites a new national monitoring system for natural resources being built for the Ministry of Land and Resources, a new "national product quality monitoring system" and even a new national identity-card system using smarter cards with embedded computer chips. Given the scale of this government IT work, it might not be long before Chinese IT companies such as Neusoft will be able to teach India's outsourcing giants like Wipro and Infosys a thing or two—and even some of America's software superstars.

Dalian is an exception. Most Chinese cities have become grimier during the past fifteen years, not cleaner. Most have increased their dependence on heavy industry, not reduced it. But if China decides to revalue its currency sharply, if inflation forces Chinese industry upmarket and if a post-Kyoto deal enables the Chinese leadership to impose its will and enforce environmental controls, then the rest of China might well start to look—and smell—more like Dalian.

7. BLOOD, MEMORY AND LAND

SO ASIA IS BECOMING ONE, to borrow from Kakuzo Okakura's 1903 phrase, thanks to the growth of trade and the resulting economic integration. That, combined with the rising strength and reputation of what are by far the world's two most populous countries, China and India, and the nervousness but also revived self-confidence of what is still the region's biggest economy, Japan, is leading politicians, foreign-policy strategists, businessmen and investors to think about Asia as a unified whole. In the future, that tendency will only grow. Yet as Asia becomes one, the continent's historical divisions are also becoming more important. These divisions have many causes, first and foremost history itself: history as a source of bitterness and mistrust, history as a source of unresolved disputes.

A sign in the entrance to an unassuming, long, low-built structure in the middle of Ping Fang, an industrial area in the outskirts of Harbin, in Heilongjiang province way up in the industrial northeast of China, makes the point succinctly. It portrays a well-known Chinese idiom: *Qian shi bu wang, hou shi zhi shi*. That is the Pin-Yin transliteration of characters that can be translated into English as:

The past should never be forgotten,
since we can always learn from it.

Then, up the stairs, is a larger illuminated sign in both Chinese and English. Its words are rather more blunt, but also more typical of the way in which history overshadows the relationship between Northeast Asia's three neighbors, China, Korea and Japan, and of how it is expressed and portrayed in memorials and museums:

> Early in the twentieth century, the Japanese militarists flagrantly flouted the international conventions, and clandestinely plotted biological and chemical warfare in an attempt to realize the political ambition of dominating Asia and ruling the world. Very quickly such weapons were used in the battlefield, making the Japanese militants the most vicious Fascist war criminals in human history.
>
> The Manchurian Unit 731, which was entrenched in Ping Fang District, Harbin, for 13 years, was the nerve center of the Japanese militarists in executing the plot. Not only did they conduct big-scale germ weapon research, tests and production here, but they also used healthy humans to conduct germ tests. Just between 1939 and 1945, at least 3,000 people were cruelly terminated in the laboratories. During the whole germ warfare, at least 300,000 people were slaughtered or maimed.
>
> Forgetting about the past means betrayal. By exposing the criminal past of Unit 731, we want to preserve the facts in order to warn future generations. Let history usher in a peaceful, civilized and progressive human society, and prevent a recurrence of historical tragedy.

The museum at Ping Fang, to which that sign is presented as a foreword, is a little reminiscent of Auschwitz, although contrary to the claim in the sign the atrocities that went on at Unit 731 were on nothing like the scale of the genocide at the German concentration camp in occupied Poland, near Krakow. But what was done at Ping

Fang in the 1930s and '40s was nonetheless barbaric, and the site does share some things in common with Auschwitz. The exhibits are in sparse, ill-lit rooms, leading off gray corridors, leaving the visitor with the feeling that the building has barely changed since Unit 731 of Japan's Kwantung Army had its headquarters there, rather as Auschwitz appears as if it has been untouched since liberation in 1945.[1] The Kwantung Army was the division of Japan's Imperial Army that had been based in the area since Japan first arrived after defeating Russia in 1904–05 in the bay near Port Arthur (Lushun, in Chinese) and took control of the Liaodong Peninsula on which the naval base of Port Arthur is built.

The Unit 731 building has in fact been touched: It was used, incongruously, as a school for some years after the Communist Party took power in 1949; and it was merely one building on a large site containing dozens of others, most of which were destroyed by the retreating Japanese troops. But the gray corridors and sparse rooms give the building a utilitarian atmosphere, as if emphasizing, as at Auschwitz, what Hannah Arendt called "the banality of evil." Like Auschwitz, the Unit 731 site has an industrial feel to it, with railway tracks running through the compound, bringing to mind an image of victims being brought in on trains like cargo, rather as Jews were taken to their deaths in that way by the Nazis in Europe. Although there was nothing anti-Semitic about the Japanese atrocities there, and no Jews were victimized, Harbin and the Unit 731 museum have an extra poignancy for a European visitor because the town was such a center of Jewish settlement from the turn of the century until the 1930s. Harbin barely existed until Russians constructed a railway to run southward from there to the city of Dalian and nearby Port Arthur in the early 1900s. By the 1920s about 20,000 Jews lived in Harbin, including the family of Israel's current prime minister, Ehud Olmert. Most fled during the Japanese occupation.

Unit 731 was not an extermination factory like Auschwitz, nor was there any Japanese equivalent of Hitler's plan to eradicate the

Jews, but its victims were similarly dehumanized by the Japanese soldiers and medical staff, who used a slang term for them: *maruta,* or logs. A few are thought to have been Western, Korean and Russian prisoners of war, but most were local Chinese, abducted or just taken prisoner for resistance or other crimes in what the Japanese called Manchukuo, a colony that encompassed chiefly what are now the three Chinese provinces of Heilongjiang, Jilin and Liaoning, along with parts of what are now Mongolia and Russia.

The activities that were centered on that building in Harbin were, among all the things that the Japanese Imperial Army did from 1931, when it took full control of Manchukuo, until it was defeated in 1945, the ones that most obviously constituted a war crime, or crime against humanity. Testimony from Japanese soldiers who served there confirms that Unit 731 carried out biological and chemical experiments on animals and humans, testing germs and toxins, as well as physical experiments on live victims such as freezing, putting them in pressure and vacuum chambers, and vivisection. The work was similar in kind to that carried out by German scientists, under the direction of Josef Mengele, at several of the Nazi concentration camps in Europe.

The statements by those Japanese veterans, made at various times in the postwar period from the 1950s to the '80s, provide the most compelling and convincing exhibits at the museum. For there is little else actually there: a limited number of not very revealing photographs; some relics such as pots, scientific instruments and syringes that could have had many possible uses; and a lot of diagrams and maps, mostly reproductions. Virtually all physical evidence and records were removed or destroyed in 1945; corpses were incinerated or thrown in the Songhua River that flows through Harbin. As a result, the Ping Fang museum does not have the shock value held by Auschwitz's rooms full of human hair and discarded personal belongings. Instead, it represents the horror of what took place there mainly by means of dioramas and declaratory signs such as the one quoted earlier. It is the Japanese confessions, essentially statements of repentance, that make the museum feel real and powerful, and remove all doubt about whether the experiments could really have happened.

That point is ironic, in a number of ways. The most frequent accusation leveled at Japan by Chinese and Koreans—the two Asian nations that feel most strongly that they were the victims of Japanese imperialism in the first half of the twentieth century—is that the Japanese have not adequately repented for their sins. Yet at the museum commemorating the clearest war crime, Japanese repentance forms the principal evidence.

A second irony, however, is that none of that evidence was presented at the principal trial of Japanese war crimes, the International Military Tribunal for the Far East, which was held under American auspices in Tokyo in 1946–48. The reason is that the United States gave the senior Japanese scientists and soldiers in Unit 731, including their leader, Shiro Ishii, immunity from prosecution in return for handing over the findings from their experiments, just as they did for many German scientists.

A third irony is that the shaky basis of that very Tokyo trial provides Japanese revisionists with their strongest grounds for opposing what they call the "masochistic" version of their country's history, for decrying their government's frequent desire to offer public atonement, and for defending the Yasukuni military shrine in Tokyo where fourteen of the leading war criminals convicted in the Tokyo trial are commemorated. It was the annual visits to that shrine by Junichiro Koizumi, Japan's prime minister in 2001–06, that caused the worst chill between China and Japan since diplomatic relations were resumed in 1972.

Chinese war museums are replete with hyperbole, as the statement in that sign at Ping Fang about "the most vicious Fascist war criminals in human history" shows. They are also not beyond some falsification and invention. Nonetheless, as a result of those repentant statements, the claim that at least 3,000 people were used in the experiments at Ping Fang does seem to be well founded. It first emerged during a war crimes tribunal in Khabarovsk in the Soviet Union in 1949, at which twelve senior figures from the Kwantung Army and Unit 731 who had been seized by invading Russian troops in Manchukuo were tried and convicted for their biological experiments.

Soviet officials had been involved in investigations of Unit 731 in Japan itself at the time of the Tokyo trial, but did not insist on presenting any information about it to the court. By 1949, the cold war was underway and Soviet policy had changed. The Khabarovsk tribunal was dismissed at the time by the West as propaganda— presumably because of the immunities granted to Shiro Ishii and his colleagues, and because in cold war conditions everything communist could be labeled as dubious or dangerous.[2] So was a later war crimes trial held in China itself in 1956, at which more veterans of Unit 731 were tried. All twelve on trial in Khabarovsk were found guilty but none was executed: They were given prison sentences of up to twenty-five years but by 1956 all had been repatriated to Japan. By contrast, several thousand Japanese soldiers are thought to have been secretly executed by the Soviet Union in 1945 or soon afterward for alleged war crimes. The twelve on trial at Khabarovsk may well have provided some scientific data to the Russians as a plea bargain.

Communist governments may invent many stories, but not all their stories are therefore invented. Nevertheless, the Chinese declaration that 300,000 people were killed or maimed in actual germ warfare by Japanese forces all over China cannot be verified. No real evidence is provided for it. Testimony at Khabarovsk and subsequent statements by repenting servicemen has confirmed that bacteriological weapons were indeed deployed in various battles, the first of which is said to have taken place in 1939 on the Sino-Mongolian border. But it is impossible to know how many people were killed by such methods, as opposed to conventional weapons or even natural causes, nor the degree to which survivors continued to suffer in later years from the effects of germ warfare, as lawsuits have claimed.

One exhibit at Ping Fang underlines the uncertainty, as well as the prevailing atmosphere of conflict and suspicion in the early 1950s between Mao Zedong's Communist government and the U.S. against whom it fought in Korea from 1950–53. The exhibit is a supposed shell casing for a bacteriological bomb, with four compartments inside, alleged to have been used during the Korean War by the United States. The Chinese and North Koreans accused the Americans in early 1952 of using such bombs to drop diseases, including plague, anthrax, cholera and encephalitis. As evidence, they produced bomb casings, film, flies that survived in unusually low temperatures and so might have been bred especially to carry diseases, and, crucially, confessions by captured American airmen.[3]

The United States has denied vehemently that it has used bacteriological weapons. Some of the airmen subsequently recanted their confessions once they had been released, but not all. A popular scare swirled in America about prisoners being brainwashed while in Chinese custody, a scare that later found its expression in the movie *The Manchurian Candidate.* The truth about these accusations of the use of bacteriological weapons in Korea has never been clearly established, but Russian archives released after the collapse of the Soviet Union in 1991 have indicated that America was innocent and that the story was confected by the Chinese and North Koreans, with assistance from the Soviet Union.[4]

That controversy served to keep the truth about Unit 731 obscure, too. It finally began to emerge only in 1980 when John Powell, a former journalist whose career had been ended in the 1950s amid America's anticommunist witch hunt after he had reported allegations about American use of germ weapons in Korea, managed to use America's then-new Freedom of Information Act to uncover enough hitherto secret documents to be able to reveal the immunity deal done between the American government and the scientists of Unit 731. His article in the *Bulletin of Concerned Asian Scholars* was appropriately entitled: "Japan's Germ Warfare: The U.S. Cover-up of a War Crime."[5]

If you put the Unit 731 museum together with a war memorial in another Chinese city, Nanjing, the story of Japan's historical tensions with China may look quite clear to you: Japan invaded China, turned part of it into a colony, tried to gain control of more of the country and committed many unspeakable atrocities while it was doing so. It therefore ought to apologize and provide a lot of money to China by way of compensation. That is quite a common view in the U.S. Congress, even though Japan is America's close ally and China is plainly some sort of a competitor for the United States. So even before showing how the story is rather more complex than this summation would suggest, it is worth interjecting that the Japanese government has in fact conveyed its apologies to China publicly on at least seventeen separate occasions since diplomatic relations were reestablished in 1972, with statements being made by prime ministers, Emperor Hirohito himself, and lesser officials. Its development aid to China since then has totalled ¥3.6 trillion ($31 billion) in soft loans, grants and technical assistance. China waived claims for formal compensation soon after relations were normalized in 1972.

The museum in Nanjing, a southern Chinese city that was the Nationalist Kuomintang government's capital in 1937 and known to foreigners then as Nanking, is a modern, purpose-built structure that tells the story of the most notorious of those atrocities in a somber, surprisingly subtle and very moving way. A statue you come across quite near the entrance is of Iris Chang, the young Chinese American writer who brought the events back to the West's attention with her 1997 book titled *The Rape of Nanking*.[6] The book was shocking and controversial: It became a bestseller but also drew criticism from independent historians for its alleged inaccuracies as well, more predictably, from Japanese revisionist scholars and politicians. Perhaps as a result of that controversy, or of dwelling too much on terrible deeds, or for other unknown reasons, Iris Chang committed suicide in 2004 at the age of thirty-six.

What happened at Nanking remains fiercely disputed.[7] Unlike Unit 731, the atrocity at Nanking did feature in the Tokyo war crimes trial, and a great deal of testimony and other evidence was submitted about it. The evidence was, however, controversial even then. Among the trial's eleven judges was an Indian named Radhabinod Pal who wrote a vast dissenting opinion condemning the whole tribunal, a section of which was devoted to the atrocities at Nanking. The events began in December 1937 when Japanese forces advanced up the Yangtze Valley from Shanghai and captured Nanking on December 13. The prosecution case for the atrocity was, as Justice Pal wrote in his opinion, that when Nanking fell

all resistance by Chinese forces within the city ceased. The Japanese soldiers, advancing into the city, indiscriminately shot civilians on the street. Once the Japanese soldiers had obtained complete command of the city, an orgy of rape, murder, torture and pillage broke out and continued for six weeks.

During the first few days, over 20,000 persons were executed or killed by the Japanese. The estimates of the number killed in and around Nanking within six weeks vary from 260,000 to 300,000 . . . The accuracy of these estimates is indicated by the fact that the records of the Red Swastika Society and the Tsung Shan Tong [two charity groups] show that these two organizations between them buried over 155,000 bodies. During the same period of six weeks, not less than 20,000 women and girls were raped by Japanese soldiers.

Pal said, however, that he had "some difficulty in accepting the account given in its entirety. There have been some exaggerations and perhaps some distortions." Nevertheless, he went on to write that

> even making allowance for everything that can be said against the evidence, there is no doubt that the conduct of the Japanese soldiers at Nanking was atrocious and that such atrocities were intense for nearly three weeks and continued to be serious to a total of six weeks.[8]

It is important to use the words of Radhabinod Pal on this matter because he is a hero to those Japanese who reject the verdict and validity of the Tokyo trial. There is a monument to him just outside the museum at the Yasukuni Shrine in Tokyo.[9] Yet even Justice Pal did not doubt that an atrocity had taken place at Nanking, such was the volume of evidence presented by foreigners who resided in the city at the time and who were therefore much more independent as witnesses than were the Chinese representatives of the Nationalist government. Pal's doubts centered not on whether there had been an atrocity but rather on whether any criminal responsibility for it should be laid on the political leaders of Japan and on the regional commanders of the division of the Japanese Imperial Army that was involved.

Understated and sophisticated although it is, the Nanjing museum illustrates why and how a historical issue as seemingly plain as the atrocity that began in December 1937 can be open to such fierce dispute. For a start, the overall death toll is debatable, to say the least—but it is engraved in stone at the museum, in large numerals, as 300,000, as if no questions can be raised about it. That number was claimed by the Kuomintang (KMT) in 1938, and then reasserted by the KMT government's representatives at the Tokyo trial. But, like the identical figure for the number of people killed by germ warfare, it cannot be verified. Charities present in Nanking at the time (the Red Swastika Society and the Tsung Shan Tong) made reports of the number of bodies they buried, as Justice Pal cited, but some of the records were not submitted until much later, and there is plenty of room for doubt as to whether these organizations actually were capable of coping with the volume of burials they claimed. No one knows how many people were present in the area, whose fairly small population had been swollen by refugees. Even local Chinese historians, spoken to off the record, express doubts that the figure of 300,000 is accurate.

The displays at the Nanjing museum are problematic, too. There are lists of names of victims engraved in stone, rather as at the Vietnam Veterans Memorial in Washington, D.C., but since records of the deaths are so poor the names cannot be considered reliable. Some of the photographs displayed at the museum have been alleged by Japanese critics to have been doctored. And they may well have been. That does not, however, mean that all are fake, nor that no atrocity took place—as Justice Pal himself wrote in 1948. Whatever the body count was—whether it was 50,000, 150,000 or even the official claim of 300,000—what happened in Nanking was terrible. The Chinese government certainly has no intention of letting the memory of the atrocity fade. The Nanjing museum was closed for more than a year until it reopened on the seventieth anniversary of the seizure of the city, on December 13, 2007. An already large museum was being more than doubled in size.

History is full of ambiguities, of different truths, of different interpretations. There is ample scope to argue about both the facts and their interpretation, especially when war and the chaos of civil conflict make disputes even harder to resolve. In the case of China and Japan, there is also the question of which history and which war are to be argued over. Come, to add to our museum collection, to an even larger institution devoted to the Sino-Japanese War at Lugouqiao, or Lugou Bridge, what westerners call Marco Polo Bridge, a few miles outside Beijing. Whereas the Unit 731 museum at Ping Fang has a subdued feeling about it, and the one at Nanjing is modern and moving, the "Chinese People's Anti-Japanese War Memorial Museum" at Lugouqiao is a garish place of pure patriotic purpose, intended to relate to visitors, especially to hordes of Chinese schoolchildren, the horrors of what the Japanese invaders did in China and the heroism of the resistance against them, led of course by the Communist Party. Beyond the patriotic and partisan tub-thumping, though, it contains three particularly striking features.

The first is the sheer length of what the museum considers to be the Anti-Japanese War. Most people know that Japan took control of Manchukuo in 1931, and that the event on which the museum site is actually built took place on July 7, 1937. Japan had stationed troops at the bridge, supposedly to protect Japanese interests in Beijing, and a clash took place with Chinese government troops. The cause of the clash is somewhat mysterious: It seems to have been occasioned by the disappearance of a single Japanese soldier, who was alleged to have been kidnapped by the Chinese troops but later turned out to have been visiting a brothel. Its importance, though, is that it provided the pretext for Japan's invasion of the rest of China, which led, six months later, to Nanjing: Westerners therefore often date the Sino-Japanese War as lasting from July 1937 until August 1945, or even 1931–45.

The Lugouqiao museum, however, considers the conflict to have begun in 1874. That was the year when Japanese forces first landed on Taiwan, to avenge a massacre there of about fifty fishermen from Okinawa and the other Ryukyu Islands who had sheltered there in 1871. Japan had only just formally defined the Ryukyu kingdom, which is a chain of islands roughly equidistant from Korea, Taiwan and Japan's southernmost main island, Kyushu, as being Japanese territory. That incorporation is also the origin of

Japan's claim to sovereignty over some uninhabited rocks in the area, known in Japanese as the Senkaku and in Chinese as the Diaoyutai, which continues to be disputed. Nowadays its significance is generally attributed to undersea oil and gas resources and competition to define "exclusive economic zones" favorable to either side.[10] But the dispute also runs deeper than that. The Ryukyu kingdom used to pay tribute to the Chinese emperor and was influenced over the centuries by both Chinese and Japanese culture. Okinawa now plays host to America's largest military base in Asia, but it is on the front line of the longer-term historical tussle between China and Japan. The absorption of the Ryukyus and the landing on Taiwan marked the beginning of Japan's challenge to the central position China felt it was entitled to in East Asia.

The second striking feature shakes that assumption about historical tensions. Right at the end of the exhibition, after descriptions, photographs, relics and dioramas depicting invasions, atrocities, battles, acts of resistance and the fourteen class A Japanese war criminals who are so outrageously (in the Chinese view) enshrined at Yasukuni (see below), is a wall of numbers and photographs devoted to a surprising subject. It is the friendship between China and Japan. Statistics are shown for trade between the two countries, Japanese investment in China and even Japanese aid to China, and the photos are of various bouts of glad-handing between the countries' leaders—including that frightful Yasukuni visitor Junichiro Koizumi. It is a refreshing balance against the rest of the exhibition, but must produce some cognitive dissonance among the Chinese schoolchildren who are trooped around the museum. Are they supposed to hate the Japanese, or like them?

The third feature is simply a number, and returns us to the tensions and to the way in which dialogue about history between China and Japan has become more difficult, not less. It is 35 million. This, according to the Lugouqiao museum, is the total number of Chinese casualties caused by the Japanese during their wars in China. Very roughly, it would correspond to about 8 percent of the Chinese population in the 1930s of 450 million. It is, to say the least, pretty hard to see how this number can have been arrived at. By way of comparison, an American academic who has specialized in cataloging macabre statistics of what he calls "democide," R. J. Rummel of the University of Hawaii, came up with a total for the Japanese-inflicted death toll in China of about 6 million.[11] He has no pro-Japanese bias, since his purpose was to show the scale of the murders committed by the twentieth century's worst killers, all of which were governments and among whom he included Japan.

The Chinese figure of 35 million is itself quite a recent one: It became the official government reckoning of the Japanese toll only in 1995 when it was cited by President Jiang Zemin on the fiftieth anniversary of the end of the war.[12] The figure includes both the dead and the wounded, although that is not made clear at Lugouqiao. But also the number has grown. Initial figures submitted to the Tokyo trials in 1946–48 were of almost 1.9 million killed and 1.3 million wounded by the Japanese, making 3.2 million in total. In 1985, China's official figure was an already high 21.7 million total, of which 12.2 million were said to be deaths and 9.5 million wounded.

In the chaos and conflict of China in the 1930s and '40s, firm figures would always be hard to come by. This was a period when nationalists were killing communists, and vice versa, and both Chinese armies were committing their own brutalities against civilians. R. J. Rummel gives a figure of 10 million for the number killed in China by the nationalist Kuomintang armies in 1928–49, both directly and through starvation. It may be that it has become convenient to attribute more and more of that mayhem to the Japanese. It is also worth noting that Jiang Zemin's figure of 35 million takes the Japanese toll neatly up to or above the death tolls commonly attributed to his own Communist Party since it took power in 1949, in various purges, famines and bouts of violence. If there is ever a domestic reckoning of his party's record, it may be convenient to be able to claim that the Japanese were even worse. Time is supposedly a great healer, but in the case of China and Japan it has produced a widening gap in perceptions of history.

Right in the center of Tokyo, quite near the Imperial Palace grounds and more or less next door to a big martial arts center, the Nippon Budokan, stands an elegant Shinto shrine surrounded by cherry trees, the area in front of its entrance bedecked, in the Japanese style, with snack machines and vendors of roasted maize. This is Yasukuni, the shrine that has taken on a quite remarkable notoriety in foreign minds and in some Japanese ones, too. The shrine's name means "peaceful country," but for many it has come to symbolize the idea of an unrepentant Japan, a country where scores of senior members of the ruling Liberal Democratic Party visit the shrine regularly to pay homage to the war dead whose souls reside there, which include fourteen class A war criminals. It has also, though, come to symbolize for many Japanese the idea of being a proud, self-confident, normal nation, one willing to pay respects to its war dead in the same sort of way as occurs in other countries, regardless of whether the wars in which the soldiers died were victories or defeats.

The shrine itself offers little to get excited about, unless of course you have a friend or relative commemorated there. It was founded in 1869 to enshrine those who had died in the civil wars that marked the demise of Japan's 300-year-long Tokugawa shogunate and the restoration of government led by, or at least focused on, the emperor. That demise was in turn prompted in part by the arrival of American warships in Tokyo Bay in 1853, demanding that Japan open itself up for trade and threatening an attack if it refused; such tactics by Britain and other imperialists had forced humiliating concessions on imperial China during the first half of the nineteenth century, confirming that neither Chinese nor Japanese military technology was any match for the Europeans and their American cousins. The exposure of Japan's weakness triggered off a revolt and several years of turmoil that were brought to an end by the restoration of the emperor's status and the formation of a government that sought to modernize Japan in emulation of the Europeans rather than bowing down to them, as the Chinese had done.

Including those who died in the 1850s and '60s, the shrine is now home to almost 2.5 million *kami,* or souls, of those who have perished for their country. Shinto is essentially a religion of ancestor worship and has no formal deities, so the shrine provided a place at which the particular ancestors who died in wars could be worshipped. The name of Yasukuni was granted by Emperor Meiji in 1879 and ever since then the shrine has had a close association with the imperial household, which is natural given the emperor's central role in the Shinto religion, but also the fact that those who died in war since the Meiji Restoration did so in the name of the emperor. Some buildings at the shrine have been financed with money from the imperial family even in the postwar period, and every year a messenger from the imperial household attends the spring and autumn festivals at the shrine. But no emperor has actually visited the shrine since 1975. The reason is that in 1978 the shrine authorities formally admitted to the shrine the *kami* of 1,068 "martyrs of Showa," all convicted and executed war criminals, including the fourteen categorized as class A, who were the political and military leaders of Japan in the 1930s and '40s. The *kami* were admitted by adding their names to the list in the shrine's archives. The names were provided by the Ministry of Health and Welfare.

That seemingly technical point is relevant because officially the shrine is a private entity. It was owned by the state until the new, American-drafted constitution introduced the separation of state and religion into postwar Japan. It is no longer under the direct control of the government, which produces the odd result that the national shrine to the war dead is in private hands. But the shrine's intrinsic connections to the basic institution of the Japanese state, the emperor, make the shrine's status ambiguous. And although the enshrinement of the war criminals was a private act, it involved cooperation by the ministry. Nonetheless, after it took place the then-emperor Hirohito, who was renamed Showa in the Japanese tradition after his death in 1989, chose not to visit the shrine again personally. He realized that the presence of the *kami* of the men who had been his own political leaders in the 1930s and '40s, and who had been executed for what they did in his name, would make any visit by him especially controversial. His son and successor, Emperor Akihito, has not paid a visit, either.

It is the museum in the grounds of Yasukuni, the Yushukan, that is more explicitly controversial, however. This museum is the work of private curators rather than the Japanese government—a fact that becomes clear when you realize that its basic purpose is to repudiate the verdict of the Tokyo war-crimes trial, a verdict that was formally accepted by the Japanese government when it signed the San Francisco Peace Treaty with the United States and others in 1951. The enshrinement of the class A war criminals, among the other "martyrs of Showa," had the same repudiating implication: If Hideki Tojo, Emperor Hirohito's prime minister in 1941–44 and commander of the Imperial Army, was executed as a criminal in 1948, three years after the war had finished, then his *kami* would not qualify for admission to a shrine dedicated to those who died serving their country in war. But if he was executed as a military act of "victor's justice" after an illegitimate trial, then his *kami* would belong at the shrine.

The exhibition at the Yushukan, like that at Lugouqiao, covers the whole period of history from the Meiji Restoration until 1945, with some sections devoted to even earlier periods. But the focus is on the hundred years from 1850 to 1945, with a purpose that is made even clearer if you visit the Yushukan's English language Web site.[13] As you enter the Web site, a slogan appears on your screen: "The truth of modern Japanese history is now restored." There has been a museum at Yasukuni for many years, but until the new Yushukan was opened in 2002, it was mainly devoted to exhibitions of military equipment and other memorabilia in the shrine's collection.

The story the Yushukan's new exhibition tells is rather different from the one in Chinese museums, not surprisingly. It is a story centerd, of course, on Japan, one based on the nation's sense of vulnerability to foreign attack or intimidation, a sense that had been reinforced by the American ships that sailed into Tokyo Bay in 1853 and demanded that the country open itself up for trade. The exhibition tells how, during the subsequent decades of the nineteenth century, Japan felt threatened by instability on the Korean peninsula and by the encroachment into northeast China and into islands around Japan by tsarist Russia, which was feared even to have designs on Korea itself. Britain, France, Germany, the United States and Russia all established footholds in China in the form of "treaty ports" and some surrounding areas that were placed under their jurisdiction in so-called unequal treaties that they forced on the Chinese government. When Japan tried to do the same after defeating China in a short war in 1895, forcing China in the Treaty of Shimonoseki to cede to it the Liaodong Peninsula, a "Triple Intervention" by Germany, France and Russia conspired to force Japan to cede Liaodong back again.

In this colonial, imperialist world, how was Japan to survive? By making an alliance with the most powerful imperialist, Britain; by modernizing itself and importing British battleship technology; and by consolidating first what it already saw as its own territory— the Ryukyus—and then stabilizing or seizing other islands and peninsulas in Japan's neighborhood that could make it vulnerable if anyone else seized them: Korea (1894 and again in 1910), Taiwan (1895), and the Liaodong Peninsula and Port Arthur at a second attempt (1905). Japan was doing simply what the European colonial powers were doing, especially once it had defeated one of them (Russia) in battle in 1904–05. And, as the American ships had shown in 1853, those colonial powers were a threat to Japan itself. Like the Europeans, Japan then developed aspirations for more territory, especially land that brought trade and natural resources, which were becoming ever more important for a newly industrializing power, in a world in which open markets could not be taken for granted.

By virtue of its alliance with Britain, Japan benefited from the Treaty of Versailles at the end of Europe's First World War and was granted some former German territory in China. It already had some of Manchuria, having taken over the running of the South Manchurian Railway from Russia. Manchuria had a lot of resources, and was right next door to Japan's colony in Korea. It had not always been part of China proper, being beyond the Great Wall and home to the non-Chinese Manchus who had invaded China themselves in the seventeenth century and founded the Qing Dynasty. What could be more natural than to take control of the whole of Manchuria? After all, China was in chaos and incapable of running it properly or stably itself. Manchuria would offer a further buffer against the dangers posed by rival powers, especially Russia.

So the museum's story goes on, of Japan becoming a colonial power just like the Europeans, and defending its legitimate interests as it did so. When an oil embargo was imposed on it as pressure to try to force it to cease its operations in southern China in the late 1930s, Japan felt it had no choice but to build an empire elsewhere in Southeast Asia in order to obtain resources, to confront the European colonialists then dominating Asia and ultimately to confront the United States at Pearl Harbor in December 1941.

The story is not untrue, although some parts of the exhibition concerning America's role in provoking Japan into war had to be changed in 2006 after complaints from the United States. What is most striking about the Yushukan exhibition, however, is not so much what it says, but what it leaves out. For starters, it is a story only about Japanese warriors, battles and foreign policy. At times it reads almost as if no one else was involved.[14] Since the museum is at a shrine dedicated to Japan's own war dead, that might perhaps be considered fair enough, although there is a smaller shrine at Yasukuni dedicated to other nations' war dead, the Chinreisha. And it is worth noting that just across the road from the Yasukuni Shrine is another museum, called the Showakan, dedicated to telling the story of how hard life was during the war years of the 1930s and '40s—but it, too, is about life only for the Japanese. It does not even mention life for colonial laborers in Japan, who were mostly Korean, let alone the fact that other countries were affected by war at the same time—war that Japan played a crucial part in provoking, whether legitimately or not. The intended audience for the museum is purely Japanese, so Japan is what it is about.

Secondly, however, the Yushukan's story is highly selective. There is no mention of Unit 731 or of bacteriological warfare. The atrocity in Nanjing is mentioned but not as a happening of any particular severity or controversy.[15] That the terrorist act that triggered Japan's occupation of the whole of Manchukuo in 1931 was carried out by members of Japan's own Kwantung Army to provide a pretext for full occupation is mentioned but glossed over. In fact, blame for the spreading of the conflict is attributed to the Chinese: "After the second Shanghai incident [in 1932], which is again triggered by the Chinese side, Chiang Kai-shek resorts to the strategy of consuming Japanese forces in the vast battlefield covering the entire Chinese mainland." The notorious use of tens of thousands of Asian women as sex slaves for Japanese troops (so-called *ianfu* or "comfort women"), the use of Koreans and Taiwanese as forced labor, the Bataan Death March in the Philippines of 75,000 Filipino and American prisoners of war in 1942, the generally high fatality rate of Allied and Asian prisoners of war: None of these are featured. Indeed British visitors to the Yushukan tend to get hot under the collar immediately after they pass through the museum's turnstiles, since straight in front of them is a locomotive from the Thai-Burma railway, the building of which expended the lives of many British POWs. This is not, in other words, a museum of atonement. It is a museum of rectification: the rectification of Japan's own view of its history, away from the one imposed by the

International Military Tribunal for the Far East—the Tokyo war crimes trial of 1946–48.

It all happened so long ago. The Japanese government accepted the verdict of the Tokyo trial, regained its sovereignty in 1952, became a functioning democracy that renounced militarism and colonialism and was the greatest economic success story of the second half of the twentieth century, at least until China began to emulate its success after 1978. Japan has made many official apologies to its Asian neighbors. Yet the history still matters.

It matters, for example, when conservative groups in Japan write high-school history textbooks along the lines of the Yushukan exhibition. When they are accepted by the Ministry of Education the news causes angry demonstrations in Beijing and Seoul, as they did in 2005—even though such revisionist books will be used by only a tiny number of Japanese schools. The vast majority of Japanese schoolchildren use textbooks that do tell them in detail about the invasion of China, the Nanjing atrocity and other misdeeds by the Imperial Army. It also matters when Chinese textbooks are revised, as they were in the early 1990s, to emphasize patriotic education, and when one of the main measures of that patriotism is the fierceness of the books' portrayals of Japan's sins.

Japan's prime-minister-for-a-year, Shinzo Abe, was persuaded to appease the Chinese and South Korean governments when he entered office in September 2006 by not visiting the Yasukuni Shrine, as his predecessor, Junichiro Koizumi, had to great anger in China and South Korea and to criticism in the United States. Mr. Abe's decision to visit Beijing and Seoul straight after entering office, and to avoid visiting the shrine, drew fulsome praise from abroad for his more cooperative vision of intra-Asian relations. Yet four months later he spoiled that image by publicly denying that there had been any "hard" evidence that the Japanese army had itself coerced Asian women into being comfort women for its sol-

diers, despite abundant testimony from Korean and Chinese survivors to the contrary. He later retracted his statement, after widespread criticism at home and abroad. And in August 2007, when
he paid an official visit to India, Mr. Abe made a point of visiting
the descendants of Radhabinod Pal, the Indian judge at the Tokyo
trial who had taken Japan's side. Perhaps this should not have been
a surprise. Before becoming prime minister, Mr. Abe had made
many public statements criticizing the Tokyo trial. And one should
not forget that his maternal grandfather, Nobusuke Kishi, was the
economic supremo in Manchukuo in the 1930s, and was later im-
prisoned—but never tried—as a suspected war criminal. Kishi
became prime minister himself in 1957–60, and was one of the
architects of the LDP.

If reconciliation is truly to occur between China, Japan and
Japan's also embittered former colony, Korea, it will need to be in-
spired from the top, from presidents, emperors and prime ministers, emulating the way in which the leaders of France and Germany
sought to cast aside the past during the postwar decades. Why, the
European or American observer is tempted to ask, can Japan not
take the lead in this process? Why can Japanese prime ministers such
as Mr. Koizumi or Mr. Abe not see that Japan's image and influence all over the world are harmed by their refusal to do so, that all
the official apologies that Japanese governments (including Mr.
Koizumi's) have offered are undermined in the eyes of their recipi-
ents by visits to the Yasukuni Shrine, and by denials by Japanese
cabinet members that wartime atrocities occurred? A typical Japanese line on the issue is that Japan has freedom of speech, and is
therefore home to many views, which cannot therefore be suppressed. These views, however, are held not just by intellectuals or
right-wing lobby groups but by cabinet ministers. I recall being at
an international conference in Tokyo at which Han Sung-Joo, a former South Korean foreign minister and ambassador to the United
States, put the point especially starkly but admirably frankly: The

problem, he said, is that we do not believe that your apologies are sincere.

Dr. Han is surely right: At least in part, Japan's apologies have not been sincere, especially when they have been voiced by conservative LDP politicians. But although Japan should shoulder much of the blame for that, America is also to blame. At the heart of the problem lies the event that took place over thirty-one months from May 1946 until November 1948: the Tokyo war crimes trial. The lack of sincerity in many Japanese apologies is related directly to the injustice of that trial.

If you read accounts of the trial now, it is hard not to feel ashamed of the way the Americans and their allies conducted the whole event. Some Americans were ashamed even at the time. John Dower, a historian at the Massachusetts Institute of Technology and doyen of Western scholars of wartime and occupied Japan, produces some telling quotations.[16] General Charles Willoughby was head of intelligence operations for the leader of the American occupation, General Douglas MacArthur. In a private exchange with one of the judges at the trial, B.V.A. Röling, General Willoughby described the trial as "the worst hypocrisy in recorded history." Another American serviceman, Brigadier General Elliott Thorpe, who had been involved in choosing who should be put on trial, dismissed the Tokyo tribunal as "mumbo jumbo." As Mr. Dower writes, Thorpe later explained, "I still don't believe that was the right thing to do. I still believe that it was an ex post facto law. They made up the rules after the game was over. So we hanged them because they used war as an instrument of national policy." George Kennan, the State Department official who later became famous as the conceptualizer of the policy of containment of the Soviet Union, described the trials as "profoundly misconceived from the start."

The problem with the Tokyo trial can be seen as soon as you read who the judges were and how the charges were framed. There were eleven judges, whereas the trial of the Nazis in Nuremberg that had started the previous November (and lasted a mere ten months) had just four. Of the eleven judges only three were Asian—one from the crumbling Kuomintang government in China, one from the Philippines and Justice Pal from India—even though it was Asian countries that Japan had occupied and was chiefly accused of having brutalized. The central charge laid against the twenty-eight defendants, under the special charter of the Tokyo trial, was that of committing "crimes against peace: Namely, the planning, preparation, initiation or waging of a declared or undeclared war of aggression." In other words, using military force as an instrument of national policy. Might any other country, just possibly, have ever behaved like that before, or since?

The four European and American judges represented countries that had themselves seized countries or territory in Asia in wars of aggression; some, including France and the Netherlands, were at that very time fighting to retain their Asian colonies. The Dutch had rejected a declaration of independence by Indonesia in 1945 and were fighting a guerrilla war to maintain control; France fought from 1946 until 1954 to try to prevent Vietnam from becoming independent. Britain was about to relinquish India grudgingly in 1947, Burma in 1948 and Malaya not until 1957. The Soviet Union's judge came from a country whose army had recently carried out its own atrocities against civilians in Manchuria. Aborigines and Maoris would no doubt have accused the two judges from Australia and New Zealand of similar crimes.

This was, as Mr. Dower puts it, a "white man's tribunal," which "essentially resolved the contradiction between the world of colonialism and imperialism and the righteous ideals of crimes against peace and humanity by ignoring it. Japan's aggression was presented as a criminal act without provocation, without parallel and almost entirely without context."

That was also the gist of the 12,000-word dissenting opinion by Justice Pal that is now so celebrated by Japanese revisionists. Quite rightly, he attacked the trial as a travesty of justice, which lacked a sound legal basis for the bulk of its charges, and which was covered with a thick layer of the most appalling hypocrisy. He took particular pleasure in attacking the attempts by the prosecution to accuse the defendants of fostering an idea of Japan's innate racial superiority, given that the European empires—especially the British one under whose rule as an Indian he had lived—had done exactly the same thing for centuries. Nevertheless, what Justice Pal also said, and which Japanese revisionists choose to overlook, was that the Japanese army had, in his view, been guilty of atrocious conduct beyond merely the conventionally appalling nature of war.

Following the trial, seven class A war criminals were hanged at Sugamo prison in Tokyo, including Hideki Tojo, the wartime prime minister, and Iwane Matsui, the commander of the army responsible for the Nanjing atrocity, although he had not been present in that city at the time. Two defendants had died of natural causes during the trial, and one was released after suffering a mental breakdown. Sixteen others were given sentences of life imprisonment.

So were the defendants guilty? The real question is, of what? The central charge was bogus and hypocritical. Atrocities such as Nanking were brought up at the trial, yet the main venue for punishing such genuine crimes lay elsewhere: in the trials of class B and C criminals that were held in the theaters of war themselves. The defendants in Tokyo were made to take legal responsibility for what the Japanese army did in their name in other Asian countries, yet the man in whose name the defendants were themselves working, Emperor Hirohito, was expressly excluded from prosecution or blame.

Yet then there is Unit 731. In 1980–81, when information about Unit 731 first came to light in the West in articles by John Powell, Justice Röling—by then the only surviving judge from the Tokyo trial—wrote that as one of the judges in the International Military Tribunal, it is a bitter experience for me to be informed now that centrally ordered Japanese war criminality of the most disgusting kind was kept secret from the Court by the U.S. government.[17]

It might well have been right to find some of the defendants guilty of the barbarous deeds of Unit 731, since those deeds did require central government sanction and direction. Had that occurred, the Japanese revisionist case about the trial and the wartime history would have been far weaker. No wonder that the Tokyo trial still overshadows intra-Asian politics.

The deepest divide, and the most bitter feelings, about the wars of the twentieth century is that between Japan and China. Contrary to the message of the Tokyo trial, there was nothing exceptional— i.e., exceptionally bad—about Japan's choice, as a matter of foreign policy, to join the Europeans and become an imperialist. All the empire builders should apologize for what they did to their colonial subjects, not just the Japanese. But, as Justice Pal said in his dissent, the conduct of Japanese troops was exceptionally bad in many cases. It is that that Japanese political leaders should be apologizing for. They should also, on moral grounds and in the national interest, be condemning any fellow politician who seeks to deny that atrocities took place.

It is also the case, however, that even if Japan's imperialism was not exceptional, those who were colonized by it still bear special resentments toward it, which holds a special weight because of the geographical proximity and shared cultural heritage of the countries concerned. In effect, the Tokyo trial punished the Japanese leaders for having had the temerity to attack the United States and the European empires; neither America nor the European powers had cared much about what Japan did in Korea, Taiwan or Manchuria.

Europe's postwar success at putting history behind it might suggest that Asia should now be able to do so, too, but so far that has not proven possible.[18] That China has an authoritarian government and Japan a democratic one has made reconciliation harder than in postwar Europe; fear of China's rise in the 1990s and 2000s has, if anything, toughened positions on both sides, with Japanese nationalists determined to give no ground to the Chinese upstarts, and Chinese nationalists increasingly confident that they can use history to keep Japan on the defensive. Even when relations improve, as since Shinzo Abe's visit to Beijing in October 2006, they are improved by shelving historical disputes rather than by resolving them.

Japan and China are natural rivals, which makes historical reconciliation at once vital and elusive. But there is also another country in Northeast Asia that is involved, and whose feelings show the complexity of these historical issues, even without that ingredient of great-power rivalry. That other country is Korea—or rather, for the time being, that means South Korea, for we cannot know much about the feelings held by North Korea. South Korea holds bitter feelings toward Japan, for its colonization of the whole of Korea from 1910 until 1945, and for a continuing dispute over an island that lies between the two countries, called Dokdo in Korean and Takeshima in Japanese. But it also retains deep suspicions toward China, over the countries' rightful borders and over the related issue of history.

A good way to get a taste of South Korea's feelings toward Japan is to visit yet another war museum, this time the War Memorial in central Seoul, which is right next door to a huge American military base.[19] The most detailed part of the museum, and much of the hardware and memorabilia, is devoted to the Korean War. But the exhibition also takes its visitors through more than a thousand years of military history, most of which, it seems, was spent fighting the Japanese. Given the two countries' locations, that is not perhaps surprising, just as English history could easily be satirized as consisting essentially of a series of wars with the French, until the Germans came along to take France's place. More relevant is the recent history of Korean-Japanese conflict, which begins in the museum in 1895 when the War of the Righteous Armies began, following the assassination of Korea's Empress Myongsong by Japanese agents. The empress had advocated closer relations between Korea and Russia in order to forestall Japan's growing influence in Northeast Asia. Although Japan did not then annex Korea as a colony, it did so in 1910. A sign at the museum retells it thus:

> **THE NATION'S ORDEAL AND RESTORATION**
> During the 5,000 years of its history, Korea has recovered wisely from many foreign incursions and national crises. However, in 1910, a shameful page was written in our history when the Japanese occupied Korea. Through the activities of the Righteous Armies, various resistance and independence movements both here and on foreign soil, and a strong sense of national unity, the long-awaited liberation of Korea from Japan was realized on 15 August 1945.

The Righteous Armies were essentially bands of irregulars. They established bases first in Manchuria, before Japan took full control in 1931, and then in Russia, and conducted guerrilla attacks from there. A "Korean Restoration Army" fought in China during the Anti-Japanese War after 1937 and was partly absorbed into the forces of the Soviet Union. One of its guerrillas was called Kim Il-sung—who went on to become the founding dictator of North Korea.

Nowadays the relationship between South Korea and Japan is less hostile than that between China and Japan, though emotions still run high—over textbooks, Yasukuni visits and the comfort women issue, primarily.[20] There are many more meetings between historians from the two countries, and nongovernmental organizations, to discuss history than there are between the Chinese and

Japanese, and the discussions are much freer. The closeness of relations waxes and wanes between Korean presidencies. President Kim Dae-jung, who was a famous dissident during the military dictatorship of Park Chung-hee from 1961–79, and who spent several years in exile in Japan and the United States, sought to ease tensions during his presidency in 1998–2003. He accepted a written apology from the Japanese government during a state visit to Tokyo in 1998 and pledged in return to consider other issues from the colonial period to be closed. His successor, Roh Moo-hyun, broke that agreement, provoked, he might say, by Junichiro Koizumi's visits to the Yasukuni Shrine.

At times, the tension between South Korea and Japan verges on the pedantic. Both countries' diplomatic services, for example, have been charged with the task of convincing the world as to the "correct" name for the sea that lies between the Korean peninsula and Japan: To Japan it is the Sea of Japan and to South Korea it is the East Sea. When at the *Economist* we published maps using the Japanese name during the 1990s, we would receive letters and delegations from the South Korean embassy in London seeking to convince us that this was wrong. Having traditionally used *The Times Atlas of the World* as our style guide for such names, we changed our style for that sea when the atlas started using both names: East Sea/Sea of Japan, or vice versa. That in turn provoked long letters from the Japanese embassy, and requests for meetings, to convince us of the error of our ways and to persuade us to switch back.

In that sea, though, the islands of Dokdo/Takeshima raise a more serious issue. Like most such disputed islets, they form a useless set of rocks, important only to fishermen and to nationalists. Japan's legal claim to them is based on the fact that the Meiji government incorporated them formally in 1905. As that came a year after Japan had forced the Korean government to accept Japanese "advisers," Koreans consider the Dokdo annexation as one of the first acts of colonization, and claim historical rights over the island dating back almost 1,500 years. For that reason, South Korea's first president, Syngman Rhee, annexed them himself in 1952 to preempt any decision by the United States to return them to Japan when its sovereignty was restored in that year.[21] Subsequent administrations have reinforced Korean sovereignty by stationing guards there. Japan has never accepted Korea's claim but made no fuss about it until 2005 when the Japanese prefecture to which the islands would belong if they were Japanese, Shimane, restated Japan's claim and provoked noisy protests in Seoul.

Of longer-term importance are two Korean grievances on North Korea's border with China—but Japan is implicated even in those. The current border between China and North Korea, which follows the Yalu and Tumen rivers, is based on an agreement made in 1909 between China and Japan. South Korean nationalists claim that this agreement was invalid, because Korea was still then legally a sovereign country and yet two other countries imposed a border treaty on it. The alternative border, which the Korean nationalists believe should be claimed in the event of a reunification between South and North, would be farther into Manchuria, taking in an area largely populated by ethnic Koreans and called Kando or Gando in Korean.

There is no official claim to Kando by either the South Korean government or the North (which affirmed the current border in 1962). It is, to say the least, unlikely that any future Korean government would want to press the issue terribly hard. Except for one thing: Chinese scholars have recently been producing literature that may be designed to prepare the way for a Chinese territorial claim on part of North Korea.

That literature has concerned what to outsiders seems an arcane historical question. It relates to a kingdom called Koguryo or Goguryo, which ruled over large parts of Manchuria and the northern part of the Korean peninsula for about 800 years until the eighth century A.D. Koreans consider Koguryo to have been one of the "Three Kingdoms" into which Korea was divided before the Silla Dynasty united the country by conquest in 668. Since 1999, however,

Chinese school textbooks have taught that Koguryo was, in fact, part of ancient China, and a project under the aegis of the Chinese Academy of Social Sciences has been producing reports designed to further this claim. South Korean historical dramas are quite popular on Chinese television, but those that depict the Koguryo era have been banned—though, in mitigation, it should be said that such dramas have also tended to lean rather strongly toward the Korean point of view.

On the face of it, the argument over Koguryo may seem to be of importance only to archaeologists—some of the biggest Koguryo tombs are inside China—and to disputatious historians. But that would be wrong. The issue strikes at the heart of Korean identity, which as in all countries is dependant on history. The Chinese claims also accentuate Koreans' sense of vulnerability, which is understandable given the country's position squeezed between two great powers, China and Japan, not to mention Russia to the north and the United States all around.

It is possible that in the event of a real negotiation, the Chinese claim to parts of North Korea would simply be neutralized by a Korean claim to Kando, and that both parties would therefore agree to stick to the current borders. But other, less happy outcomes are also possible. No one knows what might happen if the current regime were to collapse in North Korea, or if reunification were to be seriously contemplated. China, the United States, Korea and Japan would all face tricky choices about what to do, and would have conflicting interests over territory, strategy and influence. At that point, the historical claims might suddenly attain a much greater, and potentially deadly, level of seriousness. For that is in the nature of many of Asia's border disputes and flash points: They look resolvable on paper, given goodwill and the presence of cooperative governments. But neither goodwill nor cooperation can be depended on for as long as memories are bitter, suspicions run deep and ambitions are welling up all over the region. Asia is a dangerous place.

8. FLASH POINTS AND DANGER ZONES

ASIA'S RIVALRIES can be bitter and are keenly felt, both for historical reasons and strategic ones. As China and India grow in strength, so each is becoming more conscious of the other as a potential threat and of the way their respective backyards are being encroached on. Japan is all too aware that having had the leadership of Asia to itself for several decades it now has a clear rival in the shape of China, one that in many ways is better placed to exert influence and defend its interests than Japan is. The United States, quite naturally, sees China as the only country that could, in future, become capable of challenging it as the world's most powerful country, both in economic and military terms. But none of these countries would actually fight one another, would they? There is too much to lose from conflict and too much to gain from peace.

Given that Asia contains four declared nuclear-weapons states, in China, India, Pakistan and North Korea, and that the biggest such state of all, the U.S., is deeply involved in the region's security and is a close military ally of both Japan and South Korea, it is reasonable to assume that the barriers to conflict between the major powers are high. With the possible and important exception of North Korea, the belief that any conflict would be very costly and would risk escalation to a nuclear level would surely deter all the big countries from confronting one another. In any case, the two rising powers, China and India, above all need to maintain the momentum of their economic development for several more decades if they are to satisfy their peoples' aspirations and to pull themselves out of poverty. To confront America or to provoke conflict within the region would be to risk losing that momentum for many years.

Those arguments are logical as well as reassuring. But they do not close the issue. There are at least two possible ways in which conflict could occur, even during the next decade or so. One would be through a miscalculation by one of the big powers, based on a different logic about the high costs of war in modern times. Perhaps, someone might conclude, the real modern reality is that the costs of fighting back or of intervening are now too high. On that logic it may be advantageous to make a first strike, since your opponent and other countries will decide to accept a fait accompli if they believe that to change things back again would be too difficult, too unpopular and too costly. It may have been possible to eject Saddam Hussein's Iraq from Kuwait in 1991, but it would be too costly to confront China if it were to invade Taiwan or North Korea, or India if it were to invade Pakistan. Words of condemnation might rain down on the invader, just as they did on China after the Tiananmen Square killings in 1989, but the pain inflicted by words will soon pass, just as they did after Tiananmen. On that thinking, a country could be tempted to use military means in order to snatch an advantage of some sort.

The second possible way in which a conflict could break out is through an accident, probably an event in one of the region's smaller countries, that either provokes one or more of the big powers to get involved militarily or else tempts them by offering an opportunity, in a move that then draws others in. It could be an opportunity to seize territory that might not be expected to occur again, or it could be an opportunity to make a demonstrative, threatening point about military strength and prowess in order to raise a country's status and achieve other ends without actually having to confront the other major powers. Asia is rife with flash points and danger zones, many right on the borders of the three great powers. A variant on this notion is the proxy war: Just as during the cold war the Soviet Union and the United States did not confront each other directly but struggled for influence and position through smaller wars elsewhere, so the rival powers of Asia could, in principle, be tempted to do the same.

Currently, neither of these sources of conflict looks imminent. Nevertheless, it should be noted that China and India are both raising their military spending and seeking to modernize their armed forces, and Japan has been contemplating an amendment to its constitution to give its armed forces more freedom of action, as well, no doubt, as making it possible to spend more money on strengthening and modernizing its forces. The Chinese government's latest defense budget, published in early 2007, included a 17.8 percent rise in military spending in renminbi terms, to the equivalent of $45 billion, a jump that sent eyebrows rising all over Asia and certainly in Washington. That was the tenth successive double-digit rise in the annual military budget in local-currency terms. The official figure is thought by analysts at the International Institute for Strategic Studies (IISS), a London-based think tank, to understate the true total by 30–50 percent because it omits unofficial revenues earned by the People's Liberation Army as well as weapons bought abroad and much defense equipment research.[1] The Stockholm International Peace Research Institute (SIPRI) concurs, choosing a figure for its military-expenditure database that is nearly 50 percent higher than the budgeted one.[2] On the other hand, Chinese military spending may in some respects be more inflated than budgets elsewhere because of the Communist Party's constant desire to retain the loyalty of the People's Liberation Army, not just through fancy weapons but also cushy lifestyles. For example, retired Chinese generals not only enjoy generous pensions but also retain offices and the same size personal staff as do serving generals of the same rank.

Even at $45 billion China's military spending is more than double the size of India's and is roughly the same as that of Japan, a far richer country. It is, however, less than 10 percent of America's annual military spending of more than $500 billion, which equals about 4 percent of American GDP. China's official military GDP share is 2 percent; since GDP has been growing at a double-digit rate, military spending has also been able to do so. Japan's official figure for military spending, which is capped at 1 percent of GDP in order to remain in accordance with its pacifist post-1945 constitution, also understates its true level of spending, or at least preparedness, for Japanese figures, too, omit a lot of spending on defense research and technology as well, as was noted in chapter 1, as spending on the impressively equipped Japan Coast Guard.

Nevertheless, if during the next decade China's military budget were to continue to grow at 15 percent a year in renminbi terms, slightly slower than in 2007, and if, say, the Chinese currency were to appreciate against the American dollar by an average of 5 percent a year (roughly its recent rate of appreciation), then by 2017 Chinese official military spending would total $286 billion, or $430 billion if SIPRI's 50 percent uplift is applied. If the growth were to average 20 percent a year then official spending would by then be equivalent to $440 billion, or $660 billion with the 50 percent uplift. Of course, America's military budget will also have grown in that time: 5 percent compound annual growth over ten years, for example, would take it to about $815 billion. These numbers also make no allowance for inflation. But they do indicate that during the next decade, China could, if it chooses to, build up a formidable military force that in terms of total spending would be not far behind the United States. No other big Asian country's military budget is currently growing anywhere near as fast as China's.

The table shows that Asia is already a heavily militarized place. As was noted earlier, the continent is home to four of the world's eight declared nuclear-weapons powers, in China, India, Pakistan and North Korea, with a fifth on its borders, Russia, a sixth on its

Capabilities of Asia's main military powers

	Military spending 2006, $ bn	Spending as % of GDP	Active military manpower, '000	Nuclear weapons?	Combat aircraft	Destroyers	Aircraft carriers	Submarines
China	45.0	2.0	2,255.0	Yes	3,435	28	None	58
Japan	41.1	1.0	240.4	Threshold	280	44	None	16
India	22.3	2.8	1,316.0	Yes	883	8	1	16
Pakistan	4.5	3.5	619.0	Yes	368	None	None	8
North Korea	Not known	Not known	1,106.0	Yes	590	None	None	63
South Korea	23.7	2.6	687.0	Threshold	518	6	None	20
Taiwan	7.7	2.3	290.0	Threshold	479	11	None	4

Source: "The Military Balance 2007", IISS

western edge that is working on going nuclear, Iran, and a seventh that is undeclared but universally assumed to have nuclear weapons, namely Israel. Three countries qualify as what nuclear specialists call "threshold" states, meaning that they have the technological capability and resources to develop nuclear weapons quickly if they were to decide to: The three are Japan, South Korea and Taiwan. Ranked by military manpower, five of the world's ten biggest forces are in Asia (China, North Korea, India, Japan and South Korea). China comes fourth after U.S., Britain and Russia in its official military spending and first in terms of military manpower. India, China and Taiwan were three of the six top importers of arms in 2005, and China was the world's fifth biggest exporter of arms in that year.

As was observed in chapter 1, three Asian countries have active and advanced space programs: Japan, China and India. In January 2007 China used a surface-to-air missile to destroy one of its weather satellites in space, the first time such a thing had been attempted since both America and the Soviet Union tried this during the 1980s. Following the test, analysts tried to work out why China had done it, without any advance warning and with no immediate explanation of what it had done. The probable answer is also the simplest one: to show that it could. China will henceforth have to be taken seriously in any thinking about the weaponization of space and how to limit it, and will have to be taken seriously by anyone—i.e., the U.S.—expecting to use satellite-based information systems during a military confrontation. The irony is that Chinese officials are hypersensitive about what they call "the China threat theory," by which they mean claims by foreigners that China has desires to expand its territory or attack other countries. China wants to deny that it is a threat of any sort while also seeking to prove that it is capable of becoming one should it prove necessary.

China has a long border and a long coastline, so it is natural for it to want a modern military force to defend itself. The development of that military force was once assumed to be principally directed at three targets: border security, internal stability and Taiwan, which in China's view are all connected. Now, though, China appears, not surprisingly, to have broader objectives as well. President Hu Jintao has talked about the vital importance of strengthening China's navy, which many have taken to mean the development of a so-called blue-water fleet, which essentially means one equipped with aircraft-carrier groups and nuclear-powered submarines capable of operating thousands of miles away from China's coastline and for long periods. That, after all, is the sort of navy that a great global power might be expected to have.

India, as another aspiring global power with a long coastline, is also investing in its navy.[3] It already has one elderly aircraft carrier, the INS *Viraat*, which was previously the HMS *Hermes* in the British Royal Navy, and is refurbishing another, the *Admiral Gorshkov*, which was bought from Russia in 2004 and will become the INS *Vikramaditya*. Moreover, it is building an aircraft carrier of its own, at Kochi, on its west coast, although it is unlikely to enter service until 2015, and is expected to build another if that construction program is a success.

To some extent, this process is just a natural consequence of economic success: China and India can now afford better and more advanced armed forces and so are spending the money that is necessary for that. They also feel that as aspiring global powers they should have correspondingly smart and impressive military forces, and should probably send them all over the world as proof of their power. Having stronger military forces will also enable China and India to assist more readily in global peacekeeping operations and in emergency rescues such as the one that took place after the Indian Ocean tsunami in 2004. So it would not be all bad.

That may well be the case. Even so, once countries have capable and strong armed forces there will inevitably emerge senior and influential voices that urge that they should be used. Senior and influential ears may even listen to them. How and when that might happen cannot be predicted: Such routes into conflict as were outlined as possibilities earlier are always likely to take us by surprise.

There are at least five known flash points in Asia where it is already clear that conflict could occur that could involve the major powers. The five are: the Sino-Indian border and Tibet; Korea; the East China Sea and the Senkaku/Diaoyutai Islands; Taiwan; and Pakistan. Let us begin with that last one, Pakistan.

This first flash point is the likeliest of the five to see sparks fly, because it is a sparky sort of place and also because it is a place very likely to cause trouble during the next few years for the United States, in particular. But Pakistan is also the least likely to become a regional danger by drawing in more than one other Asian power in confrontation with the others.

My former colleague at the *Economist*, James Astill, who is now the magazine's correspondent in Delhi, summed up the state of the country perfectly at the start of his special survey about Pakistan that was published in July 2006:

Think about Pakistan, and you might get terrified. Few countries have so much potential to cause trouble. One-third of its 165m people live in poverty, and only half of them are literate. The country's politics yo-yo between weak civilian governments and unrepresentative military ones— the sort currently on offer under Pervez Musharraf, the president and army chief, albeit with some democratic wall-papering. The state is weak. Islamabad and the better bits of Karachi and Lahore are orderly and, for the moment, boom-ing. Most of the rest is a mess. In the western province of Baluchistan, which takes up almost half of Pakistan's land mass, an insurgency is simmering. In the never-tamed tribal areas bordering Afghanistan, the army is waging war against Islamic fanatics.

Nor is that all. Pakistan has nuclear weapons, and until recently was selling their secrets to North Korea, Iran, Libya and maybe others. During its most recent big stand-off with India, in 2002, Pakistan gave warning that, if attacked, it might nuke its neighbor. Mostly, however, in Kashmir, Afghanistan and its own unruly cities, Pakistan has used, and perhaps still uses, Islamist militants to fight its wars— including the confused lot it is fighting, at America's request, in the tribal areas. Several thousand armed extremists are swilling around the country. Thousands more youths are being prepared for holy war at radical Islamic schools. Osama bin Laden is widely believed to be in Pakistan.[4]

To this admirable summary can be added the following points relevant to Asia's big-power rivalry. In the sixty years since they were separated from each other in the bloody partition that took place at the time of independence from Britain, Pakistan and India have fought three full-scale wars: in 1947–48 and 1965 over the disputed region of Kashmir; and in 1971, when India fought on the side of the then East Pakistan, now Bangladesh, in its battle for indepen-dence. In 1999 the two fought a more limited war when Pakistan launched an offensive in Kashmir at a place called Kargil, an offensive whose principal architect was none other than General Pervez Musharraf, then head of the army. In 2002, as James Astill said, India and Pakistan again came eyeball to eyeball following a terrorist attack in the heart of New Delhi, at the Indian parliament, which almost ended up killing several members of the cabinet. Despite a huge mobilization of troops, war was averted.

Essentially these have been strictly local battles, between neighbors, between a Muslim state and a multicultural but Hindumajority state—except for one thing. This is that China, especially in the 1970s and '80s, offered a great deal of support to Pakistan: arms, money and, most particularly, assistance with nuclear technology. China's motivation was clear: to balance India in South Asia, and thus to weaken it by keeping its attention focused on the threat from its northwest and the battle for Kashmir. During the 1990s, China changed its stance, remaining formally neutral over the offensive in Kargil, for example. It still, however, ensures that its diplomatic links to Pakistan are warm and seems to seek to balance high-level visits to Delhi by corresponding visits to Islamabad, Pakistan's capital. America, too, has long provided support to Pakistan, seeing it as a bulwark against Soviet influence in Central Asia during the Cold War, much to India's annoyance. Since September 11, 2001, the U.S. has given Pakistan even more financial support, in return for its assistance in the war in Afghanistan and the pursuit of al-Qaeda terrorists. But since the late 1990s, America has managed to establish much closer relations with India, too, especially under George Bush, as we saw at the beginning of this book.

Pakistan is plainly the sort of place in which sparks are always likely to fly. It is unstable and fissiparous, its army acts as a state within a state, its intelligence services are notoriously independent in thought and action and it is home to some of the world's most militantly jihadist Muslims. Those Muslims seeking to pursue their jihad, or struggle, are doing so domestically, across the border in Afghanistan and India, and far away in the West, too. In November

2007, when the man who took power in a coup in 1999, General Pervez Musharraf, imposed emergency rule, arrested thousands of opponents and dismissed the judges on the Supreme Court, he justified his action by pointing to the increasing Islamic militancy within the country. The true reason for his action was that the Supreme Court was about to rule that his latest election by parliament to the presidency had been unconstitutional. Nevertheless, the assassination a month later of Benazir Bhutto, leader of the main opposition party and a former prime minister who had just returned from exile to contest parliamentary elections, lent strength to his argument.

Such occurrences would normally be considered purely domestic matters. But Pakistan has attained a much greater international significance since September 11, 2001: as an American ally, as the new home of al-Qaeda, and as a source of support for the West's Taliban opponents next door in Afghanistan. If there were to be another big terrorist attack on the United States mainland, a second 9/11, then the place likeliest to be considered the source of that attack will be Pakistan, or rather its tribal areas near the Afghan border where Osama bin Laden is assumed to be hiding—which would make it likely that whoever is American president at that time would order a military attack on those areas. With luck, that attack would be made in cooperation with whomever is then in charge in Pakistan. But without luck, it might be against their will and could develop into an American invasion of Pakistan. At such a time, India would be sorely tempted to offer America its full support.

That is all extremely risky, from a global point of view. Even as the next American presidency extracts the U.S. from the debacle in Iraq, it could find itself drawn into a new quagmire in Pakistan. From an Asian point of view, however, the vital question is whether anyone else is likely to get involved. That could mean Russia, since if Pakistan were to find itself friendless then Moscow would be a tempting place to call on, in a neat reversal of the state of affairs in 1971 when Indira Gandhi, India's prime minister, struck a "twenty-year treaty of friendship and co-operation" with the Soviet Union to strengthen India's position in the war of that year. The likelier candidate, though, is China.

That a beleaguered leadership in Pakistan, finding itself without other international friends and in a confrontation with India and the U.S., might turn to China for help is unsurprising. The more difficult question is whether China would respond. For China to move from its present policy of warm relations with Pakistan, bringing it modest but not lavish support, to one of active military backing in the midst of a conflict, would require it to be choosing a strategy of aggressive confrontation with both India and America. The origin of such a choice is unlikely to lie in events in Pakistan itself: the country is not of strategic importance for China in geographical terms, and although China is certainly concerned about events in Afghanistan and its borders it has not so far felt directly threatened by them. More likely, such a choice would have to arise from a view that India and America were becoming a serious threat to China's own aspirations, and that they needed to be weakened by tying them down in a long conflict in Pakistan. Such a view could, admittedly, be born of opportunism: Once India and America have gotten stuck in Pakistan, it could be advantageous to China to make the quagmire worse.

Pakistan is, in short, a potential flash point. Bill Clinton described it and the Kashmiri border with India in 2000 as "the world's most dangerous place," chiefly because by then both India and Pakistan had acquired and tested nuclear weapons. It could well be one of the most dangerous places for the next American president, given the presence there of al-Qaeda and of Osama bin Laden himself. Whether it then turns into a dangerous place for Asia as a whole would depend on decisions taken in Beijing.

Chinese decisions are not easy to predict, even though China's foreign policy has been quite consistent during the past fifteen years or so. Our second flash point illustrates that difficulty. There are two ways in which you can think about the unresolved border dispute between India and China. You can see the dispute as a relic of colonialism, involving two areas that while large are not heavily populated, do not as far as is known contain hugely valuable mineral resources, and whose strategic importance may well have faded. It is hard for either of the protagonists to compromise over this relic, for reasons of domestic politics and national pride, but also there is no urgency to reach an agreement. Troops are no longer lined up along the border glowering at each other. Life would be neater if the matter could be settled, but if India and China are still talking about it in 2020 it will be no surprise and little cause for concern. That, roughly, is the line you hear in the Ministry of External Affairs in New Delhi. The dispute is no big deal. The border war between India and China that took place in 1962 would these days be considered just a "police action," I was told by a senior official at the ministry.

The other way to think about it is that this dispute is not about the specific border demarcations at all. In truth, it is about Tibet. In the early 1950s, having seized Tibet, China encroached on the area of Aksai Chin, a desert plateau claimed since at least 1865 as part of India, in order to build a road connecting Tibet and Xinjiang and thus to facilitate Chinese control over those separatist regions. In 1958–59, when China was faced with a substantial uprising by armed Tibetans, some of whom had been supplied and trained by either the CIA or India, and when Tibet's spiritual and political leader, the Dalai Lama, fled to safety in India after the uprising was brutally suppressed, China became even firmer about the border dispute. It made a proposal for a settlement that India could not accept because it would thus have had to give up Aksai Chin and all hope of regaining influence over Tibet. And then in 1960–62 India tried to push forward its military positions in the disputed areas. In October 1962, China launched attacks in both disputed areas, humiliating the Indian forces, leaving 3,000 Indians dead. China had taught India a lesson.[5] The lesson was not just about whose land it was. It was that India should not mess with China, and with its control over Tibet.

This second explanation is not entirely incompatible with the first. It may be that the dispute *was* about Tibet, in the 1950s and early '60s, but that now only a fool would challenge China's control over that region—and India unfoolishly but formally recognized in 2003 that Tibet is part of China—so perhaps the dispute has been reduced to one that is only about arcane points of history and topography. And that is probably true, as a description of the situation today and the nature of the current negotiations. But imagine how things might be if Tibet were to become seriously unstable once again, if there were to be another substantial uprising by Tibetans against rule by the Chinese. There is no sign of that right now. Yet a possible trigger for such unrest may lie ahead. It is the death of the current Dalai Lama, Tenzin Gyatso, or rather the choice of his successor.

Before exploring that, some history is necessary, both about Tibet and about the Sino-Indian border. China invaded Tibet in October 1950, a year after Mao's Communist Party had taken power, and annexed it to the newly declared People's Republic. The Chinese explanation for this is that Tibet had historically been part of China, so Mao was simply restoring his country's traditional borders. Their unity dates back to Genghis Khan, the Mongol leader who in the thirteenth century conquered both of them and created the Yuan Dynasty in China. The Tibetan reply is that their country had, in fact, subsequently been independent albeit under Chinese influence during the three centuries (1644–1911) of the Qing Dynasty, and had been utterly independent during the four decades since China's Republican revolution that toppled the Qings in 1911–12. A treaty between Britain and Russia in 1907 used the word *suzerainty* to describe the status of Tibet: China, the parties acknowledged,

controlled Tibet like a feudal lord, or
suzerain, and neither Britain nor Russia
would seek to interfere.

That, in the Chinese view, offered international recognition of Tibet's status as
a Chinese dominion. In the Tibetan view,
it shows that China did not have actual
sovereignty over their country. Tibet's relationship to China was similar in this
view to that of its smaller Himalayan
neighbors Nepal, Bhutan and Sikkim to
the British Empire: All three remained
independent, but under some British tute-
lage. India today has that sort of relationship with Bhutan; Sikkim was absorbed
into India as a state in 1975 after a referendum there; and India has a scratchy relationship with Nepal in which the remnants
of suzerainty still play a part. Some other
neighboring countries would agree with
Tibet: During the Qing Dynasty, Korea,
Mongolia and Vietnam were also under
Chinese suzerainty, with their rulers paying tribute to the Chinese emperor and

Border disputes betwee<del>n</del>

being treated as vassals in the same way as Tibet, but they are now
independent. So if China has a claim to Tibet it has a claim over
them, too. They do not press this point very hard.

In practice, the reason why Tibet is now an "autonomous region" within China, i.e., run by the Chinese Communist Party, is
that it is on the eastern side of the Himalayas. Strategically, China
feels safer with the world's highest mountain range as its border.
And in the early 1950s, China had no competitor for Tibet, which
was not the case with the other former vassals. Korea had been oc-

Key

■ Occupied by China, claimed by India

░ Occupied by India, claimed by China

N

| 0 | 100 | 200 miles |
| 0 | 200 | 400 kilometres |

CHINA

TIBET

INDIA   MYANMAR

THAILAND

SRI LANKA

Area of main map

CHINA

TIBET

R. Brahmaputra   •Lhasa

NEPAL

Kathmandu   •

Nathu La pass   BHUTAN   Tawang   ARUNACHAL PRADESH   Nizamghat   Walong

•Thimphu   Sadiya

•Tezpur

R. Ganges   R. Brahmaputra

China and India   BANGLADESH

cupied by the Soviet Union and the United States in 1945, and North Korea had been placed under the leadership of Kim Il-sung, who had fought with China and the USSR. Outer Mongolia was under Soviet influence. Vietnam was a French colony. Newly independent India invited Tibet to attend its Asian Relations Conference in 1947 as a sovereign state, but was not in a position to block China's annexation in 1950. India's first prime minister, Jawaharlal Nehru, said at the time simply that Indians felt "let down" by China's invasion.

The border dispute itself is linked both to the strategic importance of Tibet and the history of the past few centuries. Aksai Chin, 38,000 square kilometers of arid territory in the western Himalayas, was treated inconsistently by the British during the nineteenth century, depending on whether they thought China or Russia was likely to control Xinjiang (then called Sinkiang) and Tibet, and thus whether Russia might pose a threat to British interests. A boundary line drawn by a British officer, W. H. Johnson, on an exploration in 1865 defined Aksai Chin as part of Ladakh, and hence what is now Kashmir; a later line drawn in 1899 divided it, leaving much of it to Tibet; but subsequently the British returned to arguing for the Johnson line and to marking that as the border on their maps. None of these boundaries was ever agreed on by Britain and China, however. Complicating things further, in 1963 Pakistan came to a border settlement with China in which it ceded some smaller areas to China that India considers to be part of Kashmir; since India officially considers Pakistan's share of Kashmir to be occupied illegally, it does not consider the Sino-Pakistani border settlement to be legal, either.

The Indian state of Arunachal Pradesh, 84,000 square kilometers in the eastern Himalayas bordering Tibet, was called the North-East Frontier Tract until 1954 and then North-East Frontier Agency before it was given full statehood in 1987. It became properly part of British India only in 1914 under the Simla Convention, a treaty concluded between Britain and the then-independent Tibet. The Simla Convention laid down a border that stretched along the Himalayas to Bhutan, the North-East Frontier Tract and what was then Burma, drawn by the British official Sir Henry McMahon. Thus the so-called McMahon Line demarcated what had previously been unclaimed or undefined borders between Britain and Tibet and was taken by independent India in 1947 as its legal national border.

China rejects the McMahon Line on the grounds that Tibet in 1914 was not in fact a sovereign country and so had no right to sign a treaty with anyone, let alone handing over Chinese land to a foreign imperialist like Britain. After the Simla Convention, Tibetans themselves continued to claim part of Arunachal Pradesh, an area called the Tawang Tract, for it contains a notable Tibetan Buddhist monastery. That monastery was where the Dalai Lama spent his first night in India when he fled Tibet in 1959, through Tawang.

The history of the border war between China and India in 1962 is also relevant to the politics of today, so it is worth expanding on the earlier account. In the 1950s, despite China's annexation of Tibet, Indian foreign policy treated China as being likelier to be a friend than a foe, given that both countries were newly liberated from colonialism. The discovery that China had built a road through Aksai Chin, territory that India claimed as its own, shocked India into changing its approach: Faced with China creating what Israelis in their occupied territories later called "facts on the ground," India decided to do the same by setting up small manned border posts at the perimeter of what it considered was its territory, and did the same in the North-East Frontier Agency (NEFA). India did not think that China would fight over the territory, and so it deluded itself into thinking its very weak detachments in the border areas would do the trick: It had small border posts in Aksai Chin, and sent armed divisions to the NEFA that had only ancient equipment, poor supply lines and little winter clothing. Just as India was planning a small attack in the NEFA to establish its own line, China launched a comprehensive assault all along the NEFA border and in Aksai Chin, and overran both areas.

For the Indian Army and for Nehru personally it was both a shock and a humiliation. It was such a shock, indeed, that thought was seriously given to the possibility that China might be planning not just to seize the disputed areas but to invade India as a whole through Assam, the area neighboring the NEFA. Nehru dumped a fifteen-year policy of nonalignment and appealed to President Kennedy for help with arms and even forces: American and British transport planes immediately started to fly in with weapons, and

Kennedy instructed an aircraft carrier to sail to the Bay of Bengal. When the country's survival was at stake, principles of anti-Westernism and nonalignment suddenly seemed unimportant. But then, before this could have any effect, the Chinese pulled another surprise: They announced a cease-fire and laid out a timetable for withdrawal of their forces back behind the lines the two sides had controlled in 1959. China had the territory it needed—Aksai Chin—and had made its broader point, too.

Since then, after long periods of chilliness and some much smaller border clashes, relations between China and India have become warmer. Little progress has been made on settling the border dispute, but there has been little regress either—although in 2007 Indian reports began to claim that China was pushing its border positions forward near the frontier between Arunachal, Bhutan and China, snaffling as much as eighty square kilometers of land. Even so, it is conventional to assume that Aksai Chin and Arunachal Pradesh are no longer flash points, but just unfinished, sometimes irritating business. That is surely correct—unless Tibet were to become unstable again.

China's control over Tibet looks secure. Although the government denies it, outsiders believe it has flooded Tibet with Chinese settlers. It has certainly built roads and railways to ensure that the region does not miss out on the country's economic growth. The traditional Tibetan territory has been divided between several provinces, including Sichuan, Qinghai and Yunnan, in addition to what is officially called the Tibet Autonomous Region.

Religion, however, has the capability of overturning things. Buddhism plays a central part in Tibetan life, and the Buddhist monasteries are the closest things to an alternative organizing force to that of the Communist Party—just as in Myanmar, the former Burma, Buddhist monks were shown in September 2007 to be the most potent danger to the military regime there, both because of their moral stature and because of their organizational capabilities.

In Tibet, the crucial question is what happens to the Dalai Lama, who has traditionally been the top spiritual leader of Tibetan Buddhism and in practice the political leader, too. The fourteenth Dalai Lama, Tenzin Gyatso, who has lived in exile in Dharamsala in India since 1959, has remained the focus of Tibetan identity and memory, in both religion and politics.

The Dalai Lama will have his seventy-third birthday in 2008 and seems to be in good health. Nevertheless, inevitably thoughts have been turning to what happens when he dies. In Tibetan Buddhism, it is believed that the Dalai Lama is reincarnated, so that after the death of the fourteenth Dalai Lama there will be a search for the child who will be his successor. It often takes several years before agreement is reached on who that successor is. Whenever the next succession takes place, however, there will be three extra complications.

The first is that in 2007 the Chinese government announced new regulations to govern the reincarnations of all Tibetan clergy: Essentially, China has said it will have the last word in determining whether someone has been reincarnated or not. Atheist Communist Party officials will govern Tibetan spiritual decisions. The same sort of rule was used by the Qing Dynasty to try to control Tibetan Buddhism, however, and China also controls the Catholic Church's appointment of bishops in China. The question is whether Tibetans will accept China's decision, especially in the case of their spiritual leader, the Dalai Lama. In response to China's declaration, the Dalai Lama said in November 2007 that he is considering naming his chosen successor himself, before he dies. The second complication is that the Dalai Lama has also said that he will not be reincarnated in land under Chinese control. So if his followers abide by that statement, they will not accept any successor who has been found inside China. The third complication is that traditionally the second ranking lama, the Panchen Lama, has played a central role in choosing the new Dalai Lama. But after the previous Panchen Lama died in

China in 1989 two successors were chosen: one by the Dalai Lama's own selection committee and endorsed by the Dalai Lama; one by a selection committee imposed by China. The Dalai Lama's choice was arrested. His whereabouts are unknown, but he is thought to be a political prisoner.[6]

When the time comes for a succession, there is little or no chance that India or any other outsider will try to intervene directly in the process. The reason why Tibet should be listed as a risk, a possible flash point, emerges from the possibility that faced with the loss of their top spiritual leader, and a probable dispute over his successor, serious unrest could then break out in Tibet itself. Most likely, China would crack down hard on it, as it always has in the past. But if the unrest were more widespread and substantial than before, and if it coincided with a period of weakness of the central government—in the wake of an economic downturn, perhaps—then it may be hard to regain control.

Two risks could then arise. One, which is certainly unlikely, is that in the face of Chinese repression, perhaps involving wholesale slaughter of Tibetan militants, India might feel obliged to do something: to send aid, to agitate for collective international intervention or even to try to create safe havens near Arunachal Pradesh or in Tawang. The other risk is that either China or India might decide to send military forces into the disputed border areas. That might be a diversionary tactic; it might be opportunism, in India's case; it might reflect China's sense of insecurity about Tibet; or it might be a Chinese effort to seize the area of Tawang specifically, given its direct associations with Tibet and with Tibetan Buddhism. If any of these events occur, the stakes would be high.

Our third danger zone is quite a bit simpler, and the stakes are lower. But it could be risky partly because of that fact: It could offer a temptation for a country to make a military point without the likelihood of provoking a wider conflict. It is also a place where an accident could provoke a conflict. This zone is the East China Sea, where Japan and China nurture rival claims over islands and over rights to drill for oil and gas.

The territorial dispute is mundane in its nature, and the undersea resources, while valuable, are not hugely significant for countries with economies as large as those of Japan and China.[7] But national feelings are involved, as well as the sense that if ground—literally, even if it is undersea ground—is given to the other side then it will be a sign of weakness that will be exploited on other issues. So in recent years both sides have taken stubborn approaches to this dispute.

The biggest risk in the East China Sea, however, is not one of direct conflict over a patch of water and the right to drill there. It is of an accident taking place out at sea, perhaps at a time of tension, that then leads to the dispute escalating. Both sides have sent surveying and test-drilling ships to the area. In September 2005 China sent a small flotilla of five naval ships, including a guided missile destroyer, to cruise around in the disputed waters. One of the warships pointed its gun at a Japanese reconnaissance aircraft circling overhead. Keizo Takemi, then chairman of the LDP's committee on marine resources, described this in an interview as "the first example of gunboat diplomacy since Japan's relations with China had been normalized in 1972." There had also allegedly been twenty-five incursions by Chinese exploration ships into Japanese waters during the previous six months. There is no routine system of communication between the Japanese and Chinese navies or coast guards to deal with accidental collisions and thus to prevent misunderstandings and escalation.

The gist of the dispute concerns where, under the United Nations Convention on the Law of the Sea (UNCLOS), each country's "exclusive economic zone" (EEZ) begins and ends. The five current potential oil and gas fields lie in an area where the two EEZs overlap. Japan claims its EEZ should be defined as reaching 200 nautical miles (370 kilometers) from its coasts, as specified in UNCLOS. China bases its EEZ on its continental shelf. The disputed Senkaku

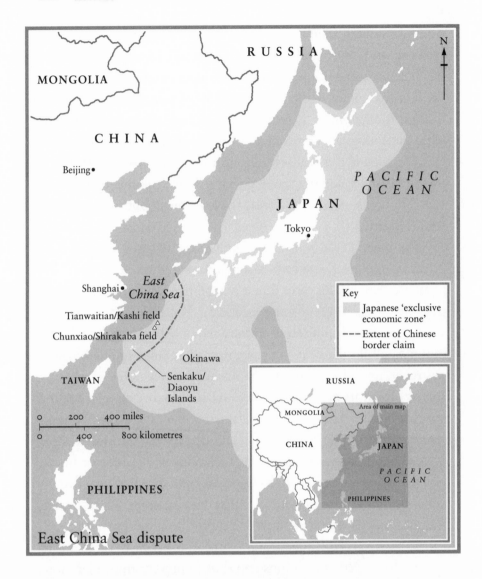

East China Sea dispute

Islands, located to the south of the gas fields, complicate the issue: They are in Japanese hands, and so Japan also considers them a relevant benchmark for its EEZ in the area; China cannot therefore agree on the EEZ without also accepting Japanese sovereignty over the Senkakus. Complicating things further, Taiwan also claims the Senkakus; it argues that they were attached to Taiwan by the Japanese during the colonial occupation from 1895–1945.

In 2006 and 2007, tensions eased over the East China Sea. By November 2007 there had been eleven official meetings between the two countries to negotiate the issue, and one in July 2007 between the Japan Coast Guard and China's State Oceanic Administration to begin discussing ways to manage the risks of collisions and to communicate with each other if one should occur—though no timetable for establishing such a system has been agreed on. In meetings in October 2006 and April 2007 between Prime Minister Abe, President Hu Jintao and Premier Wen Jiabao, the two countries affirmed that they were both interested in finding a way in which the oil and gas fields could be developed jointly between the two countries.

The marine resources issue and the island dispute are thus both subsets of the general relationship between Japan and China. When the relationship chills, as it did between 1998, when President Jiang Zemin visited Japan and the two countries failed to agree on how to deal with their historical bitternesses, and 2006, these sorts of issues tend to be exploited to put pressure on the other side. When the relationship warms up, as it did following Mr. Abe's conciliatory visit to Beijing in October 2006 and in the run-up to the Beijing Olympics in 2008, the oceanic issues fade back into obscurity. Once the Olympics are out of the way, China may no longer be so concerned about keeping a lid on anti-Japanese popular sentiment and so relations may turn chilly again; or politicians in Japan may try to shore up their positions through nationalist posturing. Another risk is that a private Chinese group might decide to take an initiative itself over the Senkakus/Diaoyutai Islands and go and occupy one of the islands and even station some armed guards there for a while. There is no running water, and so the guards would have to take plenty of supplies with them. All Japan has there at present is a lighthouse, which was put there by a nationalist group of its own.

Disputes over rocks and tiny islands abound all over the East and South China seas. Most of those involving China have not yet been formally resolved, unlike the country's land-frontier disputes. An analysis by M. Taylor Fravel of the Massachusetts Institute of Technology in 2005 showed that of the sixteen land-frontier disputes China has had with its neighbors since 1949, it has attempted compromises in all of them and has succeeded in resolving fourteen: with Burma, Nepal, North Korea, Mongolia, Pakistan, Afghanistan, Russia (three disputes), Laos, Vietnam, Kazakhstan, Kyrgyzstan and Tajikistan.[8] The two unresolved disputes are one with Bhutan, and the dispute already outlined with India. The only island disputes it has resolved concerned some islands in the river that forms its border with Russia; and an island called White Dragon Tail in the Tonkin Gulf which Mao Zedong granted to North Vietnam in 1957 as a token of Chinese support for Ho Chi Minh and his Communists. Mr. Fravel's explanation for why the offshore disputes have been left unresolved while the land ones were dealt with quite expeditiously is that the islands had no bearing on the Chinese regime's sense of security, and so did not feel urgent, and that they were not readily assisted by historical precedents.

In addition, China might well have been biding its time: Islands that have not been very important while China has been focusing on domestic security and development and has not been establishing itself as a naval power might in the future become rather more significant. Thus in 2002 China eased tensions with its Southeast Asian neighbors over the Paracel and Spratly Islands in the South China Sea, but not by actually resolving the question of sovereignty: The various claimants (China, the Philippines, Vietnam, Malaysia and Indonesia) simply signed on to a code of conduct about the islands, promising not to seize them or use them for military purposes. The dispute has been stabilized but not resolved.

The same sort of approach could be used with Japan if relations remain warm: A code of conduct could be drawn up, along with a formula for joint development of the marine resources, to leave the question of sovereignty for future generations to solve, if ever. The dispute is not large, or of great value. But it is exploitable when times are tense for other reasons, even offering a chance for one side to make a preemptive point by military means. And the big risk, especially but not only at such times, is of an accidental collision between ships or even accidental firing of weapons.

Accidents are not the big concern with regard to Taiwan, China's "renegade province." There the risk is of what might be done deliberately, most likely following a period of planning and careful thought. The likelihood is that any crisis over Taiwan would arise over a period of several months, during which there would be a lot of time for thought, discussion and second thoughts, a prospect that reassures. So does the fact that China and the United States have had a stable framework of language and understanding about the issue ever since Richard Nixon and Henry Kissinger made their historic visit to Beijing in 1972, a framework that has been maintained by all the subsequent American presidents. The U.S. accepts that there is only one China and that it is ruled by the government in Beijing; it calls for a peaceful resolution of the status of Taiwan; and, through the Taiwan Relations Act passed by Congress in 1979, it pledges to sell to Taiwan the hardware it deems necessary for its defense. Two things, though, have changed in those three-and-a-half decades: the politics of Taiwan, and the capabilities and reputation of China.

Like Tibet, Taiwan is regarded in China as a domestic issue, not a matter of foreign policy. The island is considered a part of China and the duty of the Chinese government is to ensure that China can eventually become reunified, with the parts that it lost during the nineteenth and twentieth centuries restored to the motherland. The return of Hong Kong from British rule in 1997, under a formula that gives the city-state a special and pretty independent status for fifty years, and of Macau from Portuguese rule in 1999 under a similar formula, were two parts of what is expected to be a three-part process. That said, the emphasis has been on "eventually": China has not shown any urgency about the matter.

What it has shown is an unwillingness to accept moves by Taiwan in the opposite direction—in other words, it will not accept any attempts to turn the de facto independence that the island has had since 1949 into formal, de jure independence, following a unilateral declaration.

There is, in fact, some room to debate how strong China's historical claim to Taiwan really is. The island, named Formosa by Portuguese explorers, was inhabited for centuries by aboriginal people, unrelated to the mainland Chinese. Settlers from the mainland came from time to time. China's Qing Dynasty considered it part of its domain—but then for a similar period Britain occupied and ruled Ireland, which doesn't make the Irish want to be British (except the Protestants in Northern Ireland, but like the Taiwanese they are the descendants of settlers). When Japan occupied Taiwan as a colony in 1895, after a brief war with China and the signing of a treaty, it could be argued that China was ceding control of a vassal state rather than a part of its sovereign territory. In 1945, when Taiwan was returned to China after Japan's defeat, Chiang Kai-shek's Nationalist Kuomintang started to prepare the island as a base in case they lost the civil war to Mao's Communists. They took over almost as if they were colonizing the island themselves, seizing businesses and property. In 1947 a revolt against their rule broke out and was repressed ruthlessly, with the loss of somewhere between 5,000 and 20,000 lives, according to Chiang's recent biographer, Jonathan Fenby.[9]

Such a debate is pretty pointless, however. China does have a historical claim, even if it is not watertight. But in any case the reasons why Taiwan matters so much to China are different. They start with the fact that Japan colonized Taiwan, just as Britain colonized Hong Kong, Portugal Macau, and everyone took treaty ports and other Chinese land. So reunification is needed to bring that colonial humiliation to a final closure. Just as important, though, is the fact that the defeated Chiang Kai-shek set up his Republic of China on Taiwan as a rival government for the whole country, and was recognized as the legitimate government of China by the United States and many others until the Nixon-Kissinger trip to Beijing in 1972. The return of Taiwan is needed, in Chinese eyes, to bring that episode—and thus China's civil war—to an end, too.

Taiwan is not just a technical issue for China; it is highly emotive. I recall in 2001 having an interview with a senior Ministry of Foreign Affairs official named Sha Zukang, who was then in charge of arms-control negotiations. (He has since had a spell as China's ambassador to the UN institutions in Geneva, and is now one of the undersecretaries general at the United Nations itself.) The interview was surprisingly calm and cordial, given that the topic was China–U.S. relations, and it took place in the midst of the furor over a collision between an American spy plane and a Chinese fighter, following which the American plane had had to land on Hainan Island, part of China. Mr. Sha is a confident man and totally fluent in English, including the use of it in jocular banter. But when the subject of Taiwan came up, he used a different sort of language. He banged the coffee table next to him hard with his fist. It was a theatrical gesture, and it had the desired effect of making me jump. He then raised his voice and shouted: "I want you to know that I am prepared to die, personally, to ensure the return of Taiwan to the motherland!"

Would China—and so other Chinese as well as Ambassador Sha—fight for Taiwan? In recent decades the principal cause of tension between China and Taiwan, and of worry about a Chinese attack, has been domestic Taiwanese politics. Taiwan has been a democracy since 1992, a process prepared by Chiang Kai-shek's son, Chiang Ching-kuo, but brought about by Chiang Ching-kuo's successor, Lee Teng-hui. In the 1990s, proindependence politicians emerged and became popular, appealing to a sort of Taiwanese nationalism. Lee Teng-hui became the first directly elected president in 1995, and although he never declared a clear plan to seek de jure independence, he made hints in that direction. Mr. Lee had been born on Taiwan while it was a Japanese colony, is fluent in Japanese and has strong links with senior Japanese politicians, none of which will have enamored him to China. In 1995–96 China responded in a saber-rattling way by conducting missile tests in the Taiwan Strait that separates the island from the mainland. Bill Clinton took the threat seriously and sent two aircraft-carrier battle groups sailing to the area as a warning to China not to seek a military solution. Both sides backed down.

Nothing of that severity has happened since. Lee Teng-hui's successor as president in 2000 was Chen Shui-bian, whose pro-independence Democratic Progressive Party crushed Mr. Lee's long-ruling Kuomintang. President Chen has been even more provocative than Mr. Lee, talking in recent years of introducing a referendum on reforming Taiwan's constitution, for example, to change the country's name simply to Taiwan, and applying for readmission to the United Nations, which can only be done by a sovereign country. China, however, has reacted more calmly. A law was passed by China's National People's Congress in 2005 granting the government the right to go to war to prevent Taiwanese secession—which everyone assumed the government could do anyway, if it wanted to. More short-range ballistic missiles—about one hundred each year—have been added along the coast opposite Taiwan, making the total there about 1,000. But those sabers have not been rattled. President Chen has been politically weak, damaged by corruption and other scandals, and so unlikely to be able to carry the day on independence. And China has adopted a shrewd policy of seducing the opposition, inviting leaders from the conservative Kuomintang party, the descendants of Chiang's supporters, to visit the mainland, in the hope that they will win power back from President Chen's Democratic Progressive Party and then be friendlier to China.

The result is that conflict is now less likely to occur as a result of Taiwanese moves to declare independence, at least during the next electoral cycle, than it was during the 1990s and early 2000s. Meanwhile, economic integration between the island and the mainland has proceeded apace. Taiwan's population is about 23 million, and by the Chinese government's reckoning roughly one million Taiwanese are on the mainland at any given time. Taiwanese companies are among the biggest "foreign" investors. Trade between the two, which has to be indirect, generally via Hong Kong or Dubai, is estimated to have reached $108 billion in 2006, or 26 percent of Taiwan's total trade.

In that way, it is often said, reunification is occurring organically. There is no need to negotiate about it, let alone enforce it. That, however, is too sanguine. The people of Taiwan, and certainly the businesspeople there, know that their future depends on close links with the Chinese market. But that is a matter of geography, not politics. The same is true of Korea, but that does not make Koreans want to become a province of Communist-controlled China. If China were to follow Taiwan's example, of course, and introduce some form of democracy, then the path to reunification would get easier. But that is not, shall we say, an imminent prospect. And even democracy would not guarantee unification. Ireland and Britain are both democracies, with a shared cultural heritage and highly integrated economies, but they have no desire to reunify.

Along with Taiwan's democratization, the other factor that has changed in recent years has been the capabilities of the Chinese military and, perhaps equally important, China's reputation and prominence around the region and the world. The military balance of power has long been clear: With 1.4 million men under arms, 400,000 of them stationed near Taiwan, the People's Liberation Army could defeat Taiwan in a straight fight. Taiwan's army has 130,000 men. China's air force has 1,550 fighter aircraft, according to the Pentagon's annual report to Congress, 425 of them within range of Taiwan; Taiwan has 330.[10] Taiwan's four destroyers and twenty-two frigates face sixteen destroyers in China's East and South Sea fleets and forty frigates. A head-on clash is not a likely scenario, however, since it would risk destroying the very province, and people, that China would be seeking to take back.

Much likelier would be an assault, or series of assaults, designed to force Taiwan's government to the negotiating table; or a blockade, or seizure of assets on the island by Chinese special forces. No one can know in advance how capable the PLA is of carrying any of these out, including probably the PLA itself. One part of the balance does seem to have shifted in China's favor, however, and that is the balance between the two air forces. It used to be assumed that Taiwan's air force could deny China control of the air space over the Taiwan Strait. But that is no longer clear, as Professor Bernard Cole of America's National War College has showed.[11] Over the past decade, China has brought new fighter aircraft into operation, improving its capabilities, while Taiwan's air force has stood still.

America showed in 1996 that in a crisis it is prepared to send its navy to stand guard. That signal may have encouraged Taiwan's government to worry a bit less about its own defense spending and capabilities. But the American navy cannot get there very quickly, either from bases in Japan or Hawaii. And another important aspect of Chinese progress has taken place under the sea. In 2004, as was outlined in chapter 4, a Chinese submarine circled Guam, way out in the Pacific, and then turned up in Japanese territorial waters. It had been tracked by the American and Japanese navies, and the Chinese apologized for the submarine's "error." But most analysts believe the submarine's voyage must have been a deliberate attempt to show off the Chinese navy's capabilities. In October 2006 another Chinese submarine suddenly surfaced just five miles away from an American aircraft carrier, the USS *Kitty Hawk*. Both exercises, whether deliberately or not, served to show how Chinese submarines are ranging more widely and becoming harder to detect—which means that their ability to deny American ships access to the area around Taiwan is improving. American naval commanders would have to sail there with even greater care and caution than in 1996, which would also slow them down.

Whether the U.S. would in fact send its navy again is something that cannot be known in advance. It would be hugely controversial

in the U.S. if the country were simply to stand back and allow
a democracy to be overrun by China. The Pentagon and most
foreign-policy strategists would also argue that it would be strategically disastrous for America to allow China to use military means to
get its way over Taiwan. A successful takeover would raise China's
prestige and damage America's. It would also give China naval bases
farther out into the Pacific than it currently has. On the other hand,
an assault or blockade, to create a fait accompli, would be hard to
respond to: For the U.S. not to send forces to liberate Taiwan would
be strategically disastrous, but to send forces to do so would be
hugely costly and would risk a nuclear exchange. The U.S. might
even find that it was short of friends in such a time of crisis: Japan
would support it, as probably would Australia and the far-distant
European powers. But whether any other Asian countries would do
so is doubtful.

The hope must be that no American president ever has to make
that decision. That depends on no Taiwanese president succeeding
in declaring independence and no Chinese president deciding to
call America's bluff.

Kim Jong-il, the chairman of the National Defense Commission of
the Democratic People's Republic of North Korea, is also his country's political and spiritual leader, even though the chairmanship is
his principal formal title. His father, Kim Il-sung, built his dictatorial control of North Korea after 1945 on an ideological cocktail of
communism, Confucianism and the philosophy of *Juche,* or self-
reliance, in a process in which he and his eldest son took on a quasi-
religious status. Perhaps cruelly, given Korea's colonial history, that
status has been likened to that held by Japanese emperors until
Hirohito renounced his divinity in 1946. Koreans would prefer to
emphasize an analogy with the peninsula's own Choson Dynasty
(1392–1910), whose monarchs adopted a Confucian style and language that has also been used by the Kims: Their self-description

as supreme and benevolent leaders, as teachers of the nation, is firmly Confucian even as it is also based on a personality cult. Nevertheless it was ironic—and apparently controversial in North Korea—that Kim Il-sung chose to create the first dynastic succession in a nominally communist country.

The question now is whether this dynasty will last for just two generations, or whether there can and will be a third. The question is best answered briefly: No one knows. North Korea is the world's most isolated country, with little information able to enter it and even less coming out.[12] So there is not much detail to add to that ignorance. Kim Il-sung appears to have first designated Kim Jong-il as his successor in 1972 or '73, when the father was sixty or sixty-one years old, but only announced this to the nation in 1980, when he was sixty-eight. Currently there is no designated successor to Kim Jong-il. It is possible that someone has been named secretly within a very small, loyal ruling group, but there are no clues that this has occurred and some clues that it hasn't. Kim Jong-il was born on February 16, 1942, according to his official biography, or 1941, according to other versions based on Russian records, for he appears to have been born at a Soviet military base near Khabarovsk near the Manchurian border. In 2008 he is thus either sixty-six or sixty-seven. That makes it high time that he designated a successor, especially if he wants to perpetuate the dynasty. His father lived until he was eighty-two, but that is no reason for the son to assume he will live that long.

Little is known about Kim Jong-il's own sons. His eldest, Kim Jong-nam, is known outside Korea mainly for having been arrested at Tokyo's Narita Airport in May 2001 after a tip-off, while traveling on a fake Dominican Republic passport along with two women and a child, probably his son. They said they had been planning to visit Tokyo Disneyland. Outsiders debate inconclusively about whether or not this incident will have been considered a disgrace by Kim Jong-il. Kim Jong-nam seems to have traveled widely outside Korea, which is not incompatible with being a successor since he might be garnering useful experience, and there is nothing wrong with wanting to go to Tokyo Disneyland. But if it is true that he is now essentially living in exile in Macau then that might well rule him out, since if so he cannot be gradually taking up day-to-day management of the country, as his father did during the 1960s and '70s under Kim Il-sung. Kim Jong-nam is the eldest son, but was not borne by the woman now recognized by Kim Jong-il as his first official wife: Jong-nam's mother was dumped in about 1973 for another woman and exiled to Moscow, where she died in 2002. There are two sons by the "recognized" wife: Kim Jong-chol and Kim Jong-woong, both in their twenties and hence rather young and inexperienced. Another dynastic possibility would be to pass control to a half-brother, such as a son of Kim Il-sung born to a mistress in his old age. Or it is possible that the appointment of Kim Jong-il's brother-in-law, Jang Song-taek, in November 2007 to a position that gives him responsibility for North Korea's police, prosecution service and judiciary, may be a harbinger of higher things to come.

That's enough exploration of ignorance. The point is, no one knows and as far as one can tell that includes the elite of North Korea, too. Another thing that no one knows is whether the North Korean regime of Kim Jong-il might collapse, presumably because of economic frailty. Such a thing has often been predicted. At any given time, forecasters generally judge that the regime can last for only another ten years or so. Indeed, it is said that when America's Clinton administration struck its deal with the North Koreans in 1994, the year of Kim Il-sung's death, the White House assumed the regime would collapse during the subsequent decade, and it was just buying time until then.

Under that deal, North Korea suspended its nuclear-weapons program in exchange for aid, fuel oil, and the eventual supply of a type of nuclear reactor that could not yield fuel for military purposes.[13] Both sides reneged on the deal, blaming the other. Since then, the North Koreans have developed and tested long-range missiles, have resumed their nuclear-weapons program in the early

2000s and tested a nuclear device in October 2006, have endured a famine that killed several million people (out of a population thought to be 23 million) and have hosted a summit meeting between Kim Jong-il and the then-president of South Korea, Kim Dae-jung, in 2000. One thing that hasn't happened, in other words, is the regime's collapse. Indeed, analysts in South Korea think it looks stronger now than it did in 1994. Not that they really know, of course.

The Kim regime controls power, it is thought, through a mixture of fear and favors. The elite in the Korean People's Army and in the Korean Workers' Party have been made dependent on the leadership and kept loyal by means of purges but also the granting of privileges and money. As a result, what matters is not simply the overall economic situation of the country, dire though it is; the important thing is access for the Kim regime to the resources necessary to keep the elite both loyal and dependent. In 2006–07, the U.S. successfully brought about a freeze on North Korean accounts at a bank in Macau, Banco Delta Asia, on charges of handling the proceeds of counterfeiting and money laundering. That freeze appears to have grabbed the regime's attention and brought it back to the negotiating table over its nuclear program. It wasn't the freezing of the $25 million itself that hurt the regime; it was the danger that no banks, anywhere, would in the future handle North Korean money, not even in China, if the American charges were made to stick. That threatened the regime's basic tool of power. At least that is what American officials claim happened.

This may or may not be true. What is clear is that there was then a seemingly benign development in February 2007. North Korea again agreed to freeze its nuclear program, closing the facility at a nuclear plant called Yongbyon where it had been producing weapons-grade plutonium and allowing in inspectors from the International Atomic Energy Agency for the first time since 2002. A schedule between North Korea and the other five countries engaged in what are known as the "six-party talks"—America, South Korea, China, Russia and Japan—was agreed on, under which the U.S. would unfreeze the $25 million; North Korea would undertake the aforementioned actions; and the U.S. and North Korea would start bilateral talks about how to "normalize" their relations. Officially the two countries (and South Korea) are still at war, since the Korean War ended merely with a cease-fire in 1953, and have no diplomatic relations. North Korea did not agree to give up its nuclear weapons just to start discussing what its nuclear programs have actually consisted of.

Where the February 2007 agreement will lead is unclear, except that all precedent suggests that progress, if any, will take place in fits and starts with the North Koreans, using brinkmanship to try to extract concessions, especially money, and looking for opportunities to divide the Americans and Japanese, who take relatively hard lines, from the South Koreans and Chinese, who take softer positions. Dealing with North Korea is always a risky process: It has an army of at least one million, 70 percent of it near the border with South Korea; it has used sabotage, terrorism and missile tests to intimidate its opponents. The best that can be said is that it has not tried to blow up the South Korean, or any other, cabinet again since it did so with bombs in the Burmese capital, Rangoon, in 1983, nor has it committed a major terrorist attack since it blew up a South Korean airliner in 1988, killing 115 people. The return in 2007 to the six-party process and some sort of nuclear deal with the U.S. was greeted with sighs of relief, since five years earlier the Bush administration had labeled North Korea as being part of "the axis of evil," and only four months earlier North Korea had conducted its underground nuclear test.

The Americans have been much criticized for making public statements in favor of "regime change" in North Korea, just as in Iraq and Iran. But the really risky moment is likely to come when North Korea's regime changes of its own accord. In other words,

when Kim Jong-il dies—particularly if he does so without any clear
succession. The life of Fidel Castro shows that you cannot frame
policy around an expectation that a dictator will soon die. But
equally, you cannot sensibly ignore the risk that it will happen, both
soon and without warning.

When it does, there are two questions: What happens inside
North Korea? And how will the neighbors react? Naturally, the two
questions are related. There is a benign scenario for both. It is that
if Kim Jong-il were to die of a heart attack tomorrow, power would
be assumed by a small junta of senior military officers. They would
realize that North Korea needs to copy China's market-based economic reforms if it is to survive. Well accustomed to dealing with
North Korean matters in the six-party talks, the neighbors would accept this amicably. Probably, this would begin a roughly thirty-to-
forty-year process of reunification of the North and the South, the
cost and danger of which would be reduced as North Korea emu-
lates other East Asians in achieving rapid economic growth and nar-
rows the gap in living standards between the two countries. That
gap-narrowing is, in particular, the assumption that lies behind
South Korea's policy of "engagement" with the North, or the "sun-
shine policy" as its inspiration, President Kim Dae-jung (1998–2003)
called it. But since Kim Dae-jung launched the policy the gap has,
in fact, become wider.

This benign outcome is conceivable. But is it likely? It is impossible to know what might happen inside North Korea if Kim
Jong-il dies without a clear and accepted succession plan, but a
power struggle has to be a plausible alternative scenario. The reason
he will not have produced a succession plan presumably will be because one has not been agreed on; or he might by then have announced a dynastic plan that the elite will then try to overturn.

The power struggle could take place between different factions
inside the senior ranks of the army and party, or it could be a
struggle between the senior elite and the unprivileged but armed

junior officers and regular army, or both. North Korea is one of the most militarized nations on earth. Amid the disruption, refugees might well try to leave, and the easiest way to do so is across the Yalu and Tumen rivers into China, or across the short border in the northeast with Russia, or perhaps by boat. There are already thought to be about a million North Koreans living in northeast China, with much movement back and forth across the border. Although knowledge of the outside world is limited in the North, it does exist: Videos, and to a lesser degree cellular phones, are thought to have circulated quite widely. It is anyone's guess what part North Korea's nuclear, chemical and probably biological weapons might play at such a time.

If there were to be a civil war, the crucial question is how the neighbors will react. The six-party talks have made it tempting to think that the five outsiders now share a basic interest in preserving stability and averting nuclear disaster, and so would cooperate in the event of disorder. But the alternative needs also to be contemplated. Chaos in North Korea could provide a once-off opportunity to be exploited. The obvious country for which that opportunity might beckon is China. Under the Qing Dynasty, Korea was treated as a vassal, a buffer state like Tibet. Chinese leaders would have to choose between trying to reestablish that control and hoping that the alternative outcome, likely to be reunification, can be turned to China's advantage.

A reunified Korea, one that emerges in a German manner as a South Korean takeover of the North, could potentially be in China's interests if American bases are then withdrawn and if Korea's growing trade links lean toward China. Huge injections of Chinese aid could help in that process. But there is also a risk that a unified Korea would not lean China's way; that amid reunification it might retain its nuclear weapons; and that it could make common cause with the United States against China just as India is beginning to today. If that worry were to prevail in China, then an attempt might be made to keep North Korea a separate country. If the instability were severe, Chinese troops might even invade, to "restore order," and all the better to dictate terms.

Collapse in the North would be a huge headache for South Korea: Think of the risk of refugees arriving, of possible military attack by a northern faction, of the eventual financial cost of unification. But it would also be an opportunity, one that whoever is president at the time would feel he could not afford to miss, just as Germany's chancellor Helmut Kohl swept aside talk of a gradual unification of the two Germanies in 1989. The idea that a South Korean president would press for gradual reunification, over several decades, looks like a delusion. Any sign, however, that China wished to prevent unification, or risked doing so by sending troops across its border, would put South Korea's president in a terrible quandary. Does he stand back and watch China absorb half his country? Plenty of South Koreans have been worrying in recent years that the 150 or so Chinese companies that are operating in North Korea, and the roads that have been built, might be the beginning of the absorption of the North as a new Chinese province. And there have been those ominous Chinese historical claims about the origin of the ancient Koguryo kingdom, outlined in the previous chapter. Could the South Korean president stand back and watch those warnings come true?

Russia has only a short border with North Korea and has since the 1960s had quite a distant relationship with the former Soviet ally, so it would be fairly unlikely to get involved. Japan would be extremely concerned, since it has for centuries considered Korea as a sort of dagger pointing in its direction and would not want China to dominate the peninsula. Japan has 600,000 citizens of Korean descent, many of them from the North, and would be worried about disorder, about intra-Korean conflict on its soil, and even about sabotage in Japan by North Korean agents, which could occur if one faction in Pyongyang were trying to shore up nationalist credentials. But as the former colonial power, Japan knows that neither North nor South would welcome its intervening, except possibly with its checkbook.

That leaves the United States. It has almost 40,000 troops in South Korea, and a larger force of Marines not far away in Okinawa. If this scenario were to take place after 2009, the American force in South Korea will by then have been reduced to 25,000 and moved out of its base in central Seoul to a base south of the city. Chaos in the North would leave the U.S. in a quandary. It would know it should allow South Korea to take the lead in reacting. And it would want, as in the Korean War, to rally a United Nations effort rather than acting unilaterally. But it would also know that nuclear weapons and missiles might become involved, and it would be concerned about China's strategic intentions.

It is all speculation. But the final, vital point is that this scenario could come about extremely quickly: in hours, days, or just a week or two. There would be little time to think, to discuss, to calculate. It is at such moments that a move by one country can be misinterpreted, or that a country might decide that it has to move quickly if it is to move at all and by doing so could miscalculate and bring the great powers into conflict. It is all an extremely risky business. It is also why many American policy makers, and probably even more South Koreans, hope that Kim Jong-il stays healthy—however much they dislike him.

If you want to find more possible scenes of future conflict in Asia, there are other candidates, too. Myanmar, the former Burma, stands sandwiched between India and China, and the pair are tussling for influence in that poor, benighted military dictatorship. If the military junta were to collapse, perhaps as an eventual result of the demonstrations led by Buddhist monks that took place in September 2007, you could wonder whether one or both of the giants next door might try to step in. To see monks leading demonstrations must have been particularly troubling to China, given the precedent it may set for Tibet. Or, at a time when booming trade volumes no longer salve all wounds, there could be a scrap over the effects of Chinese dams on the countries lower down the Mekong River, which flows from Tibet, through China's Yunnan province, into Myanmar, Laos, Thailand, Vietnam and Cambodia. Anti-Chinese riots in several Southeast Asian countries after the 1998 financial crisis prompted some speculation that China might intervene in some way, but it largely kept its own counsel: On the occasion of some future economic crisis, worse scapegoating of Chinese and their businesses in Indonesia or Malaysia could, in theory, draw a stronger response from a by then much stronger and more confident China.

Many things are possible. But the five flash points that have been listed here and explored in detail look not just possible but positively dangerous—especially that last danger zone of the Korean peninsula. The most worrying point is this: that communication between China, India, Japan and the United States is poor—poorer, for example, than the communication links between America and the Soviet Union during the cold war. In 2001, when the American spy plane incident caused the first foreign-policy crisis of the Bush presidency, the most shocking thing for the new policy makers in the White House, Pentagon and State Department was the difficulty in getting the Chinese government to respond to phone calls and other communications. In early 2007, when China launched its antisatellite missile test, again there was no channel of communication available for America or anyone else to ask what had happened.

There have been plenty of talks about hotlines between China and America, or indeed China and Japan, but no action. The latest declaration of intent to set one up between America and China was made during a visit to Beijing by Secretary of Defense Robert Gates in November 2007, but it is anyone's bet when or whether it will actually happen. Nor is there any military hotline between India and China. If one of the flash points starts to take flame during the next few years, the chance of misunderstanding, of miscalculation, of simple miscommunication is high. That is what happens when great powers gain great strength and see great opportunities, but also harbor a great sense of rivalry.

9. ASIAN DRAMA

A FAVORITE TOPIC among columnists and scholars during the past five years has been the fact that the world's politics and economics seem to have been inhabiting different planets. Politically, the world has been going to hell in a hand basket ever since the terrorist atrocities in New York, Washington, D.C., and Pennsylvania on September 11, 2001. Wars in Afghanistan and Iraq, confrontation with Iran, friction with Russia, further terrorist attacks all over the globe—events such as those have made observers of international politics wring their hands in despair. The United States of America, patron saint of globalization, democracy and free-market capitalism, has lost prestige and influence, having even violated its own declared values through its acts at the Guantánamo Bay and Abu Ghraib prisons and through its culpability in the use of torture. The notion that had commonly been held since the fall of the Soviet Union that America is the world's most powerful hegemon since ancient Rome has been consigned to the waste bin of deluded ideas. The quagmire in Iraq has placed a large question mark alongside America's future leadership.

Observers of economics, meanwhile, have been clapping their hands in joy, as the world enjoyed in 2003–07 the best four years of growth that it has had in the past four decades. Trade has boomed, and the fruits of that growth have been shared on every continent, with even sub-Saharan Africa expanding its GDP at annual rates of more than 5 percent. Asia, naturally enough, has led the way, with average annual growth for the region, including Japan but excluding the Middle East, of 8.7 percent in 2003–07. Even America, troubled though it may be by Iraq and divided though its domestic politics have become, has enjoyed a surprisingly buoyant economy. Predictions that foreign investors would cease to buy dollars and refuse to finance an American current-account deficit of more than 6 percent of GDP were confounded until 2007, and by then rising American exports were trimming the deficit in any case.

How can this be, the columnists and scholars ask? Surely bad politics will eventually have an economic impact, too? When turmoil broke out in the financial markets on both sides of the Atlantic in August 2007, making an American recession look like a real and imminent prospect, they appeared to be getting their answer: The good times were coming to an end. Except for one thing: The turmoil had no obvious link to the world's bad politics, unless in some peculiar way the actions of al-Qaeda in Iraq had weighed down on America's subprime mortgage market and on a suddenly weakened British bank, Northern Rock. They hadn't of course. Economics had remained separate from politics and had passed through its own cycle of confidence, excess and readjustment.

The real explanation for why political woes and economic joy could coexist for so long should be divided into two halves. One half consists of the point that the war in Iraq actually helped to amplify global growth and to spread it out more widely than ever before: It did so by contributing to the tripling, quadrupling and eventually quintupling of oil prices, which caused a huge boom in oil-producing countries, including but not only the Middle East itself. At the same time, shortages of mines and worries about political instability interrupting supply also helped bring about sharp rises in commodity prices, with the costs of materials such as copper, nickel, iron ore, zinc and uranium rising anything between three- (iron ore) and fourteenfold (uranium) in 2003–07. That in turn has boosted growth in commodity-producing countries, be they in Africa, Latin America, Asia or elsewhere.

In the past, economists would have called a rapid rise in oil prices a "shock," one that together with costly commodities would hurt growth in the rich, consuming countries and probably cause inflation. But that hasn't happened, because energy and commodities now matter less in rich, developed economies that are all led by services, because control over inflation by central banks is more secure and credible, and because the open markets of globalization have restrained overall price rises and enabled economies to be more flexible and adaptable than in the past. In the 1970s, the transfer of wealth from consuming countries to producing ones—which is what a price boom means—proved to be a drain on economic growth because the money sat in producers' bank accounts rather than being recycled through further trade or investment. This time, much more of the producers' windfall has been swiftly spent, boosting trade and investment flows in all directions.

That is the first half of the story: Political turmoil boosted growth by making resources scarcer, rather than harming it. The other half of the explanation depended on luck, geography and history. The turmoil has taken place in a part of the world—the Middle East and Central Asia—in which today's great powers are either neutral or on the same side, and none is located right nearby. There has been war, terrorism, instability and a lot of name-calling, but it has not pitted the big economic powers of the world against one another. Those big economic powers are the United States, the European Union, Japan, China, and increasingly India, Russia and Brazil. They may have had disagreements about Iraq, and even more about Iran, but not disagreements that threatened conflict or, crucially, that put investors and traders in any doubt about the future openness of these economies to one another. The world was lucky that Osama bin Laden had set up his al-Qaeda headquarters in Afghanistan rather than in North Korea, Myanmar or Pakistan, any of which would have been right next door to China and India; and it was lucky that Iraq and the rest of the Middle East are no longer the scene of superpower rivalry as they were during the cold war. So the political and economic planets have remained separate.

Such fortunate separation is likely to continue for as long as the main arenas of political tension or conflict remain distant from the main arenas of growth, trade and investment. Essentially that means for as long as political tension stays away from Asia. For although in the four golden years of 2003–07 other parts of the world have also prospered, Asian growth has been the locus of that prosperity. It has been the fast-rising demand for energy and other commodities in China and India when supplies are scarce that has resulted in booming prices, which in turn have transferred wealth to Africa, Latin America, Russia, Australia, Canada and the Persian Gulf countries. During those four years, the so-called war on terror, and what Samuel Huntington of Harvard called "the clash of civilizations" between the West and Islam, have caught the world's attention. But meanwhile the much deeper and long-lasting trend has been the economic development of Asia, the emergence in that region of three global powers in the form of China, India and Japan, and the associated increase in the influence, interests and even power of those countries.

The war on terror, or by terrorists, will wax and wane. The first year in office of whoever is elected in November 2008 as America's forty-fourth president will be a nightmarish one, devoted principally to extricating the United States from Iraq and finding some way to pacify or contain that whole region, including Iran. But while the forty-third president's principal legacy will be that Middle Eastern nightmare, the true long-term task for the next president, the probable source of that president's legacy, will lie in Asia.

The *Asian Drama* that is the title of Gunnar Myrdal's famous book of 1968 was, as his subtitle put it, *An Inquiry into the Poverty of Nations.*[1] That Swedish economist's drama was about overpopulation, poverty and the danger of what we now call "failed states." Today's Asian drama is an inquiry into the prosperity of nations, and into what happens when several big neighboring countries become prosperous at the same time. They have done so in a process that is less associated with Myrdal's ideas than with those of the man with whom he shared the Nobel Prize for economics in 1974, Friedrich Hayek, an Austrian economist who settled in London in the 1930s and who in the 1970s and '80s became the intellectual idol of Margaret Thatcher.

Today's Asian drama is a much more upbeat and inspiring story than the one that preoccupied Myrdal, for this drama is lifting hundreds of millions, eventually billions, of people out of the squalor in which they and their forebears have lived for centuries, it is lengthening and enriching lives, and it is generating new wealth and ideas and confidence. It is knitting Asia together into a single, vibrant market for goods, services and capital, one that stretches all the way from Tokyo to Tehran. If that process of integration and economic growth continues, as it should, it will form the single biggest and most beneficial economic development in this twenty-first century, providing dynamism, trade, technological innovation and growth that will help us all. In the second half of the twentieth century, the world's most advanced country and biggest economy, the United States, benefited hugely from the growth and development of both Western Europe and Japan. Now, in these early decades of the twenty-first century, the rich countries can expect to enjoy a similar boost from the growth and extra trade that will be provided by Asia.

As well as knitting them together, however, this drama is also causing friction between Asian powers that had previously kept a strict economic and political separation from one another. China, India and Japan are grinding up against one another because their national interests are now overlapping and in part competing, because each is suspicious of the others' motives and intentions, and because all three hope to get their own way both in Asia and more widely. Recall the quotation from a very senior official at the Ministry of External Affairs in Delhi, which was cited at this book's outset: "The thing you have to understand is that both of us [India and China] think that the future belongs to us. We can't both be right."

Actually they can, but not if they want the future to be exclusively theirs. To have three local great powers all at the same time may be unprecedented for Asia but it is not unprecedented for the world. There was a similar situation in Europe during the nineteenth century, when Britain, France, Russia, Austria and, until German unification, Prussia existed in an uneasy balance in which none was dominant and none was entirely comfortable, but which nevertheless coincided with a period during which Europe prospered and became firmly established as the world's dominant region.

Like Asia's powers today, the European powers of the nineteenth century were rising, scratchy, aspirational and at times unstable. Following the defeat of Napoleon Bonaparte's effort to secure dominance of the continent for France, relations between the powers were managed through the "Concert of Europe," a loose organization set up by Britain, Russia, Austria and Prussia, which France later joined. International congresses, the equivalent of today's summits, were held at intervals to resolve disputes and maintain peace. They were successful at least until the 1850s, when Russia fought Britain, France and the Ottomans in the Crimea, and the 1860s, when Austria and Prussia began the wars that culminated in German unification. The great powers in effect ran Europe, but the consequences for smaller countries were quite beneficial: Belgium was created in 1830 as a compromise to balance the interests of neighboring powers; Greece gained its independence from Ottoman Turkey under European protection; and Italy emerged as a nation-state thanks to the absence of any continental hegemon.

Whether you consider Europe's nineteenth-century experience with balance-of-power politics as a good or bad omen for Asia depends on how long a sweep of history you consider and on what you think are the most crucial differences between modern times and the world of 150 years ago. If you take a long sweep, then the precedent is bad since Europe's power balance ended in two devastating world wars in the twentieth century. On the other hand, it kept the peace on the continent for about half a century, which would count as an optimistic prospect today, and the wars that then took place in the second half of the nineteenth century were skirmishes compared to the Napoleonic Wars that the Concert of Europe brought to an end. That optimism is reinforced if you take the view that nineteenth-century imperialism, with all its military associations, was ultimately what was responsible for Europe's loss of balance, with rivalries between the powers being played out all over the globe and thus beyond the scope of the Concert. A final lesson from Europe in the nineteenth century is that the most dangerous moments in balance-of-power politics come not from direct confrontation but rather when something changes in the peripheral vision of the great powers that stimulates new ambitions, opportunities and suspicion.

Today the barriers against the use of war as a tool of national policy are far higher: Nuclear weapons, public opinion, international law, instant communication and transparency all militate against conflict, though they do not, as was noted in chapter 8, rule it out altogether. The barriers against colonial or quasicolonial ambitions are higher still. China and India may battle for influence over Myanmar, but neither is likely to invade it and turn it explicitly into a colony. Moreover the United States, for all its post-Iraq weaknesses and trauma, is playing a stabilizing role as a global military power, capable of deterring others, of a sort that did not exist during the nineteenth century.

Opinion polls taken since the invasion of Iraq have shown that people all over the world now think of the U.S. as a threat to stability rather than a source of it. But that finding is at best incomplete, at worst misleading. It is a natural response to America's decision to invade Iraq in 2003 in the face of opposition from the UN Security Council. But the reason why even after the Iraq disaster the U.S. should be seen as a stabilizing force is that it is the one country from whom an intervention or retaliation would be feared if another major power were to contemplate starting its own conflict or invasion. It is the only country capable of such intervention. It is also the only country that, in recent decades, has shown itself willing to undertake such interventions. In Asia, where the United States is an outside power but with extensive military deployments inside the region, that role as an intervener of last resort is especially important.

Nevertheless, as has been already shown, Asia is piled high with historical bitterness, unresolved territorial disputes, potential flash points and strategic competition that could readily ignite even during the next decade. There is cooperation aplenty, too. But imagine that you were a senior defense strategist or planning official in India, China or Japan. You know that your government is professing friendship to all its neighbors, pursuing "smile diplomacy" all round. You also know that your country's economic interests are spreading and deepening, and so are your neighbors', and that your neighbors are likely to get stronger in the future. What would you do?

The answer is that while acknowledging that your fellow great powers' intentions may prove to be entirely honorable and amicable, you would propose that your country should build up its military and technological capabilities, and strengthen its military and diplomatic alliances, as a form of insurance policy against the possibility that times change and that the other great powers' intentions turn hostile. With an eye on the far future, you would propose that your country should have a space program, taking in rockets, satellite launches and, for prestige purposes, moon landings. With an eye on the medium term, you would propose a strengthening of your navy, especially by adding aircraft carriers and submarines to provide the ability to project power throughout the Indian Ocean, China seas and the Pacific; and you would seek to invest in the development of an indigenous aircraft-manufacturing industry in case supplies of imported aircraft and components become harder to obtain. Meanwhile, for the short term, you would propose that your country order more of the most advanced aircraft that your foreign suppliers are willing to sell and that you should keep on improving your offensive and defensive capabilities with and against short- and long-range missiles.

That is what China and India are both doing. It would be too strong to say that they are conducting an arms race, but what they are doing could reasonably be described as a strategic-insurance-policy race. Most recently, China has been expanding its military spending at almost 18 percent per year, while India's military budget has risen by 8 percent; most likely, China's rate of spending growth will ease somewhat while India's will accelerate, as and when its public finances permit. Japan would also pursue such strategic insurance if it did not have constitutional constraints on the size and nature of its military forces, and a close military alliance with the United States to depend on. But like China and India, Japan has its own space program, is doing everything it can to upgrade its navy short of buying aircraft carriers and is doing the same for its air force.

It will be quite a surprise if China does not have aircraft carriers by 2020 or so, and India has already announced that it will have at least three. Both are energetically engaged in buying and improving their fighter aircraft fleets and their missile capabilities. All three are taking part in military exercises with one another, and sending observers to one anothers' war games: that is all part of the smile diplomacy of Asia. In November 2007 China even sent one of its naval ships on a visit to Japan, the first that the Chinese navy has ever sent. Japan and India, though, have been working on a stronger insurance policy, by building a military network among the democracies and quasidemocracies of Asia and the Pacific, formally in

Japan's case, informally in India's, linking the forces of Australia, the United States, Singapore, India and Japan in exercises, interoperability programs and the like. The network is not aimed explicitly at China. But the Chinese are fully aware of what is driving it.

The newest element in Asia is the emergence of three regional powers simultaneously. But the biggest single element is China's rise, as it forms the centerpiece around which everything else is taking shape. China, because of its open economy and low labor costs, is the hub of an Asian production and trading network. Thanks to the new strength of its public finances and a newly confident and sophisticated foreign policy, China is playing a central role in providing development aid to the poorer Asian countries. Japan's aid program is far larger, but it is less strategically focused and is more constrained by the conditions and apparatus of multilateral aid channels such as the World Bank. India's acceleration of economic growth and trade is likely in the future to impinge on China's focal position within the region, but for the moment it is China's growth and the extension of its interests through the Indian Ocean and into Africa that is impinging more on India. Above all, China's political system makes it Asia's centerpiece. An authoritarian government can be more decisive and is freer to act strategically, especially in its aid giving and its arms sales. But it also gives rise to greater fears and more mistrust.

Such fears do not arise because China has acted or even spoken aggressively in recent years: It hasn't, except toward Taiwan. They arise because of China's sheer size, because of its millennium-long history as a regional hegemon that treated many other states as vassals, and, most of all, because its political system and decision-making process are almost wholly opaque. Mistrust and suspicion about China's political intentions are echoed, too, in mistrust about its corporate activities, especially given the involvement of the state and state-owned companies in the sectors in which China has been investing heavily overseas, especially natural resources. There is suspicion, at times, about Japan, largely because of its twentieth-century history, but that suspicion is mitigated by its democracy and by its close relations with the United States. Suspicion of India is held only by its closest neighbors in South Asia. So the main problem in Asia is fear and suspicion of China. It is not going to go away.

What, then, can be done about it? What can be done to ensure that in this new balance-of-power politics that is arising in Asia, suspicion of China does not provoke tension that damages economic and societal relations between the region's main powers, or even actual conflict over one of the many flash points and border disputes? What can be done, in other words, to manage the inevitable rivalry between China, India and Japan, and those three powers' relationships with strong, involved outsiders such as the United States and Russia?

   Many of the specific issues that divide the region's powers and that lie behind those disputes and flash points have been explored in earlier chapters. There are, however, some broader points that can be made about what outsiders, in the United States and Europe, and insiders, in Japan, China and India, should do during the next few years to manage the situation and, it is hoped, to benefit from it. This book will therefore offer nine recommendations. These proposals—i.e., their adoption or rejection—can also be used as indicators of whether, during the next decade or so, Asia's powers are heading toward constructive, cooperative relations or more destructive, competitive ones.

   Recommendation number one is directed at the United States, since this book opened with George Bush's nuclear deal with India and described it as an act of grand strategic importance. The deal, amid a wider rapprochement between the U.S. and India, represented President Bush's recognition of the new balance-of-power politics in Asia and his effort to exploit it. That recognition and that effort make sense for America and also help serve the wider global interest of maintaining stability in the region. A stronger India will, in time, directly counter China's growing strength but will also help to ease fears of Chinese domination of Asia among the region's smaller countries. In other words, in balance-of-power politics it is surely better if the balance is fairly even, and America's support for India's economic development and status serves that objective.

Although President Bush's initiative toward India was strategically sensible, it was not sufficient on its own. To make the U.S.–India rapprochement truly serve both American interests and the interests of global stability, the new American president who takes office in 2009 will need to go further. That president will need to fill in the large gaps that have been left surrounding the deal by President Bush and his secretary of state, Condoleezza Rice. The largest of those gaps is in the global regime that is designed to prevent the proliferation of nuclear weapons and materials, which is centered on the Nuclear Nonproliferation Treaty (commonly known as the NPT) that first entered into force in 1970.

Among the known nuclear-weapons powers, three—India, Pakistan and Israel—have never signed the NPT. North Korea signed the treaty but then withdrew from it in 2003. America's civil nuclear deal with India blows a hole right through the NPT by granting India an exceptional status: The forty-five countries assembled in the nuclear suppliers group have been asked, under the deal, to agree to define India as a permitted recipient of nuclear materials even though it refuses to sign the NPT and has accepted inspections by the International Atomic Energy Agency of only some of its nuclear plants and not all, as is normally required. For President Bush, helping India and getting it on America's side was a higher priority than reforming and modernizing the NPT. For his successor, the nonproliferation regime itself needs to be a priority. If the regime is left to fester, with India's exceptional status unaddressed, other countries will be encouraged to seek and make deals outside the NPT framework, and the risk that nuclear materials could fall into the hands of terrorists will grow.[2]

North Korea's withdrawal from the treaty and Iran's flouting of it while pursuing its own uranium-enrichment program showed that the nonproliferation regime was already failing before President Bush blew a further hole in it with his India deal. His sense of priorities was therefore understandable. The India deal has not made matters any worse in the short term than North Korea and Iran had already managed. But the new American president must think and act for the longer term. He or she should seek ways to bring the world's nuclear-weapons powers and its nuclear suppliers back to the negotiating table in order to agree on a new NPT, one that India, Pakistan and Israel can be persuaded to sign. That will almost certainly require new and credible pledges on nuclear disarmament by the existing nuclear-weapons states, especially the U.S. and Russia. In the same context, pressure can be put on China to rein in its recalcitrant nuclear neighbor, North Korea, to try to get North Korea back inside the nonproliferation regime with tough safeguards around its own proliferation activities, and to bring in Pakistan, whose nuclear program depended on Chinese assistance.

The NPT sounds an arcane issue, one that is unlikely to appeal to the man or woman in the street, which is why it is unlikely to feature prominently during the U.S. presidential election campaign in 2008. But it is no exaggeration to say that when nuclear weapons are involved, the whole future of the planet is at stake. So the nonproliferation regime ought to feature prominently in the briefings given to the new president by their foreign-policy advisors between election day in November 2008 and inauguration day in January 2009. It would also offer a fine way for a new president to gather the world's great powers around the table, under the chairmanship of a newly legitimate and popular American president, to solve a common problem of the mightiest importance. To display a clean break from George Bush, the new president will surely seek every opportunity of that sort that can be found.

Hence the fact that recommendation number two is also directed at the United States and concerns another mighty common problem:

global warming, or climate change as some prefer to call it. To use this issue to gather people around the presidential table would not mark a clean break from President Bush: He began to hold just that sort of meeting in 2007, after he shocked his critics by accepting that the science of climate change indicates that measures need to be taken to slow or reverse the rise in global temperatures. Where there is a chance for a clean break, though, lies in the sort of measures that America can propose and the way in which it could suggest that China and India get involved in the reduction of harmful emissions.

The situation now is that everyone accepts that something needs to be done, but everyone is hoping that others will do it. The U.S. is opposed to firm and binding targets for countries' greenhouse-gas emissions. China and India favor targets, and accept that it is in their interests to try to control the growth of their own emissions, but they argue that their targets should not be stringent. They think the rich world should bear the brunt of emissions reductions both because it is wealthy and can afford to, and because most of the excess carbon dioxide and other warming gases already in the atmosphere were produced by them. As chapter 6 outlined, the conventional idea is that some sort of financial compensation mechanism needs to be set up, so that the richer countries pay the poorer ones to cut their pollution.

Such an idea is not going to get very far, or achieve very much, if China and India are involved. Unless the mechanism transferred money in an incomprehensible or secret way, which is surely not possible for an issue of such high public interest, then the transfers will be objected to by any and all political groups that fear that China and India pose an economic threat to America and Europe.

Chapter 6 argued that the notion of financial transfers needs to be kept separate from that of emissions cuts, and that any such transfers will need to be aimed not at capital-rich China but at poorer countries. Here is another idea: The new American president should

put two offers on the table. The first would say that the U.S., starting anew in 2009, now supports the notion of firm and binding targets for emissions cuts, and volunteers to take the largest cuts itself,
with targets set for each decade from now to 2030. (Much climate
talk centers on 2050, but that is too far ahead to be meaningful either to politicians or to ordinary households; most of the policy-
makers who agree to such targets will be dead by the time the
reckoning comes at midcentury; moreover, the science keeps evolving and improving, so it makes little sense to make commitments so
far in advance.) Each country would be left to work out how it will
meet its targets, whether through pollution-permit trading, carbon
taxes or technology, or some combination of all three. In that way ex-
perimentation and competition would be encouraged, rather than
seeking to impose a single solution for all the world and for all time.

The second offer is that in return for that pledge, the other big
economies should agree to set up a common fund into which all,
without exception, would contribute. The rich, led by the U.S.,
would contribute much more than would China and India, but the
important principle this would establish is that those two emerging
giants will also chip in money, and that the amounts they put in
will rise as they get wealthier during coming decades. The fund
would have two purposes: distribution to the poorest countries, in
Africa and elsewhere, to enable them to adopt cleaner energy as they
develop; and to support the research and development of clean energy technology to advance the day when the fossil-fuel age comes
to an end. There would be a risk that this money would be used to
fund boondoggles, or be stolen or wasted, as is often the case with
big international projects. But the purpose would be grand and the
eyes of the world's media would be trained on it, providing some
restraint.

Recommendation number three would, if it were followed, help
with the process of bringing the world's most powerful countries

together to reform global regimes such as the NPT and to agree on measures to deal with climate change. It is that both the United States and the European Union should, as a matter of urgency, scrap or reform all the top organizations of global governance in which China, India and Japan are not properly and fully represented. That should immediately include the Group of Eight, the annual G8 Summit of heads of government and finance ministers from the rich industrialized countries that is the closest thing the world has to an international steering group. But it should also include the Security Council of the United Nations, the shareholdings and voting powers of the International Monetary Fund and the World Bank, and any other decision-making bodies of global importance. Without the three big powers of Asia, which will also soon all be among the very biggest economies in the world, none of those decision-making bodies makes any sense at all.

The G8 is especially absurd. Japan is among the eight, but also there are Germany, Britain, France, Italy, Canada and Russia, along with the United States, of course. At least Germany, Britain, France and Italy do actually still number among the world's eight biggest economies, which was the original selection criterion when the body was set up in 1975 (albeit as the G6, with Canada added a year later). China's economy is three times larger than Russia's, and almost the same proportion larger than Canada's. These annual summits are held with great hullabaloo in the member countries, by rotation, and the members have in recent years deigned to invite the heads of government of developing countries, including China and India, to join the summiteers for dinner. That needs to change: China and India, along with Brazil, Saudi Arabia and a big African country (probably South Africa or Nigeria) should be made full members, if the group's deliberations are to have any meaning. If the group's deliberations are to be productive, that will also entail kicking out some of the existing members: at the very least Italy and Canada.

Such a reform is necessary for its own sake. But it is also important as a means to help stabilize the Asian drama. As long as any of the three Asian powers feels that it does not have an appropriate status in world affairs, and the appropriate opportunities to voice its ideas and concerns, then resentment will build up. And as long as the three Asian powers have different levels of status in world affairs, resentment, mistrust and suspicion will be engendered between the three. That is why it is also vital that both Japan and India be admitted as permanent members of a reformed UN Security Council.

Such a reform is notoriously difficult, as none of the current five permanent, veto-wielding members (the U.S., Russia, France, China and Britain) wishes to give up or dilute its power. In India's case, exclusion from the world's leading forum for discussions of international security reinforces the domestic political argument for staying outside the global nonproliferation regime and for displaying a sense of grievance against the countries that happened to be early adopters in the atomic age. It feels especially odd to India that China became a founding P5 member when its colonial invader, Japan, was defeated, but India did not, even though it dispatched its own colonial master at the same time—peacefully, as the UN charter would prefer, rather than in war. China has blocked Japan's candidacy as a way to keep Japan on the defensive over its historical record, which in effect stymies the whole process of reform and so keeps India out, too. If China wishes to retain a higher global status (as symbolized by the Security Council veto power) than its fellow Asian powers, then it will continue to block reform. In that case, China had better recognize that it will thus be storing up resentment and opposition to itself within Asia. It should not be surprising if the two lesser Asian powers (as China sees Japan and India) then gang up against it.

Global governance, in both political and economic affairs, would be better served if the world's biggest economies, in the world's most dynamic region, were all full participants in discussions and decisions. The G8 is often rightly dismissed as an annual photo opportunity, a meeting full of hot air; indeed, the *Economist* long ago ceased to send any journalists to cover the annual summit, as it is always devoid of substance and can perfectly well be monitored from afar. Despite that, the habits and relationships engendered by the G8 process make those countries the world's de facto steering committee for global issues such as trade, financial regulation and the environment, as well as for matters of high politics. As long as neither China nor India is given full membership, that committee will do a flawed job of steering.

The fourth recommendation is a general one, and is offered to international businesses by way of a conclusion based on the economic analysis offered in chapters 3, 4 and 5 of the likely future course of China, Japan and India. It is a recommendation that sounds obvious, but is all too often not followed by corporate boards: It is that in shaping a strategy for how to exploit the opportunities likely to emerge in these three huge economies, boards must think about how the countries are going to change during the next ten years, rather than at how they have behaved during the past ten. They must not base their strategies on what they see in their rearview mirror, for the road ahead promises to be very different from the road already traveled. China and India are changing so rapidly that the mirror offers a particularly poor guide; and Japan has been passing through such exceptional post-crash conditions that the past is no guide even for the mature, affluent country that it has become.

The fad in dealing with India during the past decade has been to focus on services, and especially on the outsourcing of business processes. That industry is not going to go away, but the biggest gains are likely now to be seen in manufacturing and in infrastructure, for that is where Indian private investment is heading and where it sees profitable opportunities. As infrastructure gets built, with a mixture of public and private financing, so India will become even more competitive as a manufacturing base. It is not, however, going to become an especially attractive consumer market any time soon: Even urban Indians' incomes remain too low for that, and most Indians live in the countryside and have even less disposable income.

China, by comparison, does look as if it will develop a substantial consumer market during the next decade, and an appreciating renminbi will make that market more and more attractive to those who export to China as well as to companies prepared to manufacture locally. That consumer market is likely to expand for services as well as manufactures, and as it does the level of technological sophistication of both consumers and producers will rise. Indeed, as was suggested at the end of chapter 6, public procurement contracts are likely to fuel a big growth for information-technology providers, mainly local but also international.

Too many international businesses dismiss Japan as yesterday's market, one that was always hard to penetrate but that now is not worth trying. That is likely to be a mistake, especially for services businesses and those interested in mergers and acquisitions. Japan remains the world's second-largest economy, after the United States, and the program of promarket reforms that were begun in the past decade looks set to continue or even to accelerate. Government and the corporate sector alike are going to be desperate to find ways to raise productivity, in order to maintain living standards and to preserve profit margins, in the face of the rising costs of an aging society. That is likely to create a ready market for service companies that can offer ways to boost productivity, it is likely to lead to further deregulation in the still-inefficient service sector in particular, and once Japanese companies find themselves less flush with cash, it is likely to lead to a new spate of consolidation and mergers and acquisitions.

Recommendation numbers five, six and seven are also directed at the prospect of change in Japan, India and China, but this time at causing it rather than exploiting it. For international purposes, governments give most of their attention to their own strengths, to reinforcing them and to boasting about them (a process known in the trade as "public diplomacy"). These recommendations consist of the notion that each of the countries would actually be better advised to look instead at their greatest weaknesses in international affairs, and to make the elimination of those weaknesses a priority.

Japan's greatest weakness is history, and its continued failure to put that history behind it. Right-wingers in the ruling Liberal Democratic Party, such as Taro Aso, the foreign minister in 2005–07 and the losing candidate to be party leader in September 2007, describe the attention given to this topic as "masochism." Japan diminishes itself, in their view, by continually groveling to China and South Korea about the events of sixty to 100 years ago. Yet that is wilful blindness. Every argument and controversy over historical memories, whether over textbooks, the Yasukuni Shrine, compensation for wartime slave labor and forced prostitution or atrocities such as Unit 731 and the Nanking massacre, enables China and South Korea to seize the moral high ground and to push Japan on to the defensive. Both governments can easily stir up, or respond to, their publics' opinion on those issues, and exploit them for their domestic purposes. Even more damaging for Japan is the fact that those historical issues lose it friends and supporters even among its closest allies in America, Europe and Southeast Asia. The diplomatic cost is high, and is paid every year. Unless the issue is genuinely put into the past, Japan is unlikely to gain the full status as a "normal," sovereign country that so many senior politicians, of both the main parties, say they crave.

The list of actions required to encourage reconciliation between the ordinary citizens of Japan, China and South Korea is long, detailed and difficult, given the political interest in both China and Korea in keeping the history issue alive. That is often true even at lower levels, among institutions and advocacy groups that have made an industry out of historical bitterness. But the list of actions required of the Japanese government is quite short.

The smartest thing it could do would be to work to separate the general issue of historical right, wrong and repentance from the question of responsibility, apology and reparation for specific events and grievances. It should, in other words, take heed of the dissenting opinion given by Justice Radhabinod Pal at the Tokyo trial in 1948, in which he made a distinction between the atrocious conduct of the Imperial Army, of which he considered Japan to be guilty, and the general charge concerning the use of war as national policy, which he considered hypocritical and legally absurd.

Japanese prime ministers, and ideally even members of the imperial family, could and should seek to create opportunities to make apologies and statements of condemnation of the army's specific atrocities, including Nanking and Unit 731. If the Chinese government would allow it, such apologies and statements would best be made in Nanjing and Harbin themselves. A special commission should be established to examine and make proposals about the questions of compensation for wartime slave labor and forced prostitution, along the lines of the German commission, chaired by Count Otto Lambsdorff, that in 1999 agreed to set up a $5 billion fund for compensation and research in exchange for protection against class-action lawsuits in the United States. Half of the German fund was financed by the German government, half by German companies.

Such a commission would require the involvement of the governments of China, South Korea and the affected Southeast Asian countries, in order to prevent the compensation issue from becoming one of broader national reparations. Japan's official position on compensation is that it was all settled in the 1951 San Francisco Peace Treaty and in the subsequent treaties with individual countries, and it does not wish to reopen the whole issue. That is fair enough, but as Germany realized the situation can change and the passage of time makes specific grievances more critical, not less. New evidence comes to light and changes the mood or even the moral and legal background: For example, facts about Unit 731 and biological warfare did not emerge until thirty years after the San Francisco treaty; now that South Korea and other Asian countries are at peace, much more information has emerged about forced prostitution and slave labor than was available in 1951.

Meanwhile, two other measures would be extremely helpful. One is the introduction of special legislation to restore the Yasukuni Shrine to public ownership, as an exception to the general separation of state and religion under the Japanese constitution, so that the Yushukan museum can become a proper publicly controlled museum and so that the status of the "martyrs of Showa," the war criminals, at the shrine, can be a matter of public debate and policy rather than under the control of the shrine authorities. Many people instead propose that an alternative national war memorial should be set up, which is a perfectly good idea on its own merits but the fact is that it will not solve the essential problem of Yasukuni, which is that that shrine will always have a special and higher status than any alternative because of its ties with the imperial household.

The other measure would be even harder to bring about, and may be dismissed as opening up too many cans of too many worms. It is that the United States, both Congress and the White House, should set up a special commission of politicians, historians and legal scholars from America, Japan and Europe, to reexamine the status and basis of the Tokyo trial, the International Military Tribunal for the Far East. On its own, this would surely be impossible. But alongside a new Japanese effort to make sincere apologies and offer recompense for the specific atrocities of which its army was guilty, it could be done.

China's main weakness is its authoritarian, unaccountable and sometimes brutal political system, but it would waste space to recommend that that system be changed. My view on that can be taken for granted. Even short of reform and democratization, however, the Chinese Communist Party and its leaders could surely pay attention to an aspect of that political system that damages China in international affairs. That aspect is the system's lack of transparency.

This is a simple problem to describe but a hard one for the Communist Party to solve. The problem is that no one knows how decisions are made, or who really makes them, and no one trusts information published by the government about military spending, other budgets or indeed statistics of almost any sort. Part of the explanation for this lack of transparency is that the Communist Party wants to keep such information secret from the Chinese people themselves, and international mistrust is an unfortunate side effect of that. Another part of it, though, especially for the military budget, is that China wants to keep its potential foes guessing, and among those foes it counts all of America, Japan and India.

Rightly, Western scholars and experts on China often say that the best way to turn China into an enemy would be to treat it as one. Proposals for containment or for countering China's growing strength could end up provoking the country's leadership into bolstering its strength, evading any controls and acting truculently or even preemptively. There is a corollary to this sensible argument for the Chinese authorities, too. It is that by keeping so much secret and obscure, China encourages other countries to believe that it has a lot to hide, that it may be doing or planning many threatening things and even that the Chinese military may be acting independently of the civilian government. The test of an antisatellite missile in early 2007 was a good example of this: The lack of warning or explanation of the test provoked a spate of speculation about what China's intentions were, and about who in China knew about the test and who might not have. The military budget itself is another example, with so much left out of it or concealed that it encourages other countries to speculate that China's true spending and strength may be far greater than the country claims.

If the Chinese government wants to provoke other countries, especially Japan, India and the United States, into suspecting hidden actions and motives, into seeing it as a growing threat and into preparing to defend their interests against that threat, then it should maintain this policy of secretiveness. The chief responsibility for what Chinese officials lament as "the China threat theory" lies with China itself and its lack of transparency. There are welcome signs, however, of a realization that this behavior carries a cost: In September 2007, for example, the Chinese government announced that for the first time it would provide official information about the country's arms exports to the United Nations. Later in the same year, it also agreed to look into the establishment of a military hotline between China and the United States. In China's interest, and in the interest of harmonious relations between the Asian great powers and with the U.S., those positive signs should be followed up by a coherent and consistent effort to become more transparent.

The big weakness of India is, in some ways, the opposite of China's. It is, as is obvious for all to see, that India's relationships with its immediate neighbors are bad, and that it is constantly suspecting Pakistan, Bangladesh and Nepal in particular of harboring or directly encouraging terrorist acts in India. As a result, border controls are tight and barriers both to trade and to the movement of people are extremely high. No effort is made to hide this South Asian reality. It is tragic in its own right, for everyone concerned, as recurrent wars and terrorism have shown only too clearly. It is also, however, damaging to India's national interests and its regional status in Asia in two important ways.

The first is that India's relations with its South Asian neighbors make it inevitable that China will see and seize every opportunity to become more intimately involved with those countries, which is what it has done—aggressively under Mao Zedong, more subtly in recent decades. The Chinese "strategy of concirclement" that Brigadier Arun Sahgal and others from India's defense institutes warn of and demand responses to, is in large part a strategy that is facilitated or even encouraged by India's poor regional relations.[3] Those relations, and that strategy, contribute in turn to India's inevitable suspicion about Chinese actions and motivations, even when they are normal, legitimate and commercial.

The second is that India's economy is weakened by these poor regional relations. Every country's most natural trading partners are its neighbors, as geography makes transport and transaction costs low, and as historical and cultural links encourage commercial trust and exchange. That should be especially true in South Asia, since all the countries were either actually part of British India for much of the past two centuries or were closely associated with it. Yet South Asia accounts for less than 3 percent of India's overall trade, a proportion too small to be explained merely by those countries' poverty. A recent study of trade between South Asia's two biggest economies, India and Pakistan concluded that trade between the two could expand tenfold, from its current level of not much more than $600 million a year, if the existing blocks to commerce were eliminated.[4]

Efforts are underway to build the South Asia Free Trade Area (SAFTA), but in the first phase (2006–08) India's tariffs on its neighbors' goods are falling only to 20 percent, which is a lot higher than the country's average tariff rate with the rest of the world of 12.5 percent. The SAFTA is shallower and less ambitious than other regional trade liberalization efforts in Asia or around the world. This is not solely India's fault, since commerce is impeded on both sides of all the borders, with Pakistan, for example, permitting trade only in a specific list of approved goods. Transport costs are high because border links have been neglected or are impeded. But India is the biggest loser as a result of the lack of trade links with its neighbors.

It is, of course, a chicken-and-egg sort of issue. Better political relations would allow trade to be liberalized, but also better trading links could foster better political relations. Without better relations, however, India is going to be stuck with an unstable, troublesome neighborhood, in which it forever fears Chinese infiltration: Among its neighbors, Pakistan and Bangladesh have both had military coups during the past decade, Nepal has had a Maoist insurgency and Sri Lanka has been fighting a seemingly permanent civil war. The politics are likely to remain sour and dangerous. So it would surely be sensible to work on the economics, in the hope that commerce could have some beneficial effect on the politics. Faster trade liberalization and efforts to open up transport links should be the main tools. Provincial governments in the states along the border—Punjab, Gujarat, West Bengal, Assam, Tamil Nadu and others—could be allowed and encouraged to become contact-makers and cheerleaders for improved crossborder relations, since it is those border states that would reap much of the economic benefit. That is a controversial idea in India because this is a matter of foreign policy, which is held tightly by the central government. But that policy has been unsuccessful and has come at a high and sadly rising cost.

Recommendation number eight returns us to questions of international institutions. As was noted in chapter 2, Asia has many pan-national organizations, with baffling acronyms to match, but none of them has developed into strong institutions with deep integration or cooperation between the members. The main reason for this is political history: the deep divisions between the region's countries and the desire held by many of them to isolate themselves. A secondary reason is economic: that economic development has only fairly recently—i.e., in the past twenty to thirty years—taken hold in a wide range of Asian countries, and most have focused on integrating themselves into global organizations such as the World Trade Organization so as to facilitate access to rich-country markets, rather than on integrating within Asia itself. There is, however, a third reason. It is that American policy has been to oppose or discourage the development of any panregional organizations of which it is not itself a member.

That opposition slowed down the emergence of any economic or political entity linking Japan, China, South Korea and Southeast Asia—what is now known as ASEAN plus three. In the 1990s, when the U.S. opposed a proposal by Malaysia to form an East Asian economic caucus, Japan obediently opposed it, too. Now, more sensibly, America is allowing such entities to emerge, including the East Asia Summit, launched in 2005, that gathers together the aforementioned countries plus India, Australia and New Zealand. The East Asia Summit is the only panregional body within which all the three regional giants, China, India and Japan, are full participants. The potential importance of the EAS is shown by the fact that China tried to block the expansion of its membership to include India and the Pacific countries, to avoid diluting its own position as Asia's centerpiece. China lost that battle and conceded its defeat gracefully. Given that dialogue between the region's powers is getting more important by the day, it is vital that the EAS now emerges as a substantive forum for cooperation and communication, rather than just an annual photo opportunity.

So this book's recommendation is that the United States should take an attitude toward the EAS similar to the one it took toward the European Union during the 1950s, '60s and '70s. It should prominently and publicly state its support for the EAS as Asia's principal political and economic forum, and say that it sees Asian integration and intraregional cooperation as desirable. It should drop the idea that the U.S. must always be at the table when topics such as trade are discussed. It should sideline the rival panregional forum that was set up in 1989 on Australia's initiative, the Asia-Pacific Economic Cooperation group, which includes twenty-one countries from China to Chile but absurdly does not include India. Since 2004, APEC has, at American urging, been discussing its own free-trade zone, though discussions have not progressed very far. It would be far better to drop them, to support the EAS as the best regional framework for a trade-liberalization deal, and to seek to revive global talks under the World Trade Organization as the best way to boost trans-Pacific trade.

The Asian drama, after all, is that this region contains three powerful countries that distrust one another. One of the main solutions for that has to be regular communication with one another, with witnesses present, and the assumption of obligations to one another that act as an obstacle to severe tension or conflict. The East Asia Summit offers the best hope of achieving that: It is broad enough to include all three major powers, but not so broad as to make agreements impractical.

Things are different in defense and security. There it would make no sense for America to leave the room, for it is the only country that can and does provide security across the whole Asian region, and in the eyes of many Asian governments it represents an independent, if imperfect, mediator or ring holder for the continent. So just as the United States plays no part in the European Union but is a pivotal element in NATO, a similar division of labor is required in Asia. There is no fully functioning security forum for Asia. The closest to one is the ASEAN Regional Forum, which is broadly inclusive and does at least encourage communication. The six-party talks over North Korea have produced greater intimacy between China, the United States, Russia, Japan and South Korea, but that format is too localized to be able to have a wider impact.

Thus the other part of this eighth recommendation is that the United States should take a further initiative in trying to develop the ASEAN Regional Forum into becoming a more intimate organization, one that imposes greater obligations on its members. That principally means information and thus transparency, but could also include communication links and operational ties during emergencies. The Organization for Security and Co-operation in Europe (OSCE), the cold-war body that was introduced in chapter 2, could offer a good model for Asia.

Recommendation number nine, the last on the list, follows from the previous one and is again directed at the poor old United States of America, the world's chief bearer of burdens and payer of prices.

It starts with a compliment: It has often been said in recent years that America has neglected Asia, so preoccupied has it been with Iraq, Afghanistan and its war on terror. But that is not true. The Bush administration has raised America's game in Asia in two substantial ways. First, its nuclear deal and defense framework with India provided a big boost to its relationship with one of the world's most important countries, both today and in the future, and was a sensible strategic move given Asia's balance-of-power politics. Second, the "strategic economic dialogue" between the United States and China, instituted by Hank Paulson when he became treasury secretary in 2006, has greatly enhanced the sophistication and depth of exchanges between what are now the world's two most important economies (even if they are not yet the two biggest). That dialogue, it should be hoped, will be maintained by the new president in 2009, as a means to prevent relations between the two countries from descending into the protectionist name-calling that occurred the last time America found itself confronted by a rising Asian economy, namely Japan in the 1980s.

Those have been two very big and important steps. Where America has neglected Asia, however, during the Bush administration, has been through its evident disregard for Southeast Asia, for ASEAN and for Asian summits in general. Woody Allen once quipped that "90 percent of life is just showing up." That surely applies to diplomacy, too, yet meeting after meeting has been skipped by President Bush or, more pertinently, Condoleezza Rice, or else dignified only by a fleeting appearance. America has been doing a good job with the big Asian powers, but a poor one with their smaller neighbors, and should not be surprised if China's influence in the region has been growing to fill that vacuum. In balance-of-power politics, smaller countries also matter. So this final recommendation is that the new American president should follow Woody Allen's sage advice: If you are invited, show up.

How will this Asian drama end? It won't: it is now going to be a permanent feature of world affairs, and arguably the most important single determinant of whether those affairs proceed peacefully and prosperously or not. The Middle East may determine whether the world is peaceful during the next five years; but over the next ten, fifteen or twenty, Asia is likely to be more important. The drama will pit new, rising powers against the world's long-established powers in America and Europe; and it will pit Asia's new powers against one another and against the region's first modernizer, Japan. In economics and business, the competition will have overwhelmingly positive results. In politics, we cannot be so sure.

This book has explored the opportunities presented by this drama as well as the dangers. Its implications can be summarized in two different images of how Asia might look in 2020: The first could be termed "plausible pessimism" and the second "credible optimism."

The plausibly pessimistic view begins with the risk that China will go through its Japanese-style adjustment to a lower-investment economy in a rocky rather than smoothly handled manner. Recovery will eventually come, and the Chinese growth story will resume, but only after a bruising recession and asset-price collapse, perhaps exacerbated by a recession in the United States. Such a bruising experience will lead to public pressure for political reform, posing the biggest challenge to Communist Party rule since Tiananmen in 1989. But that pressure will again be violently rebuffed and the Communist Party will accentuate its nationalist credentials in order to retain its grip on power.

Such a nationalist move would produce increased tension with Japan, a reduction in cooperation with the United States over North Korea and a spate of mutual truculence between China and India over their border disputes and over Chinese support for Pakistan and Bangladesh. Lord only knows what would happen if a terrorist attack on the United States were to prompt an American invasion of Pakistan, since India would be tempted to cross Pakistan's southern border while the U.S. was crossing from the west.

In these awkward times, the deaths of Kim Jong-il and the Dalai Lama could both occur, prompting China to install a new military government in North Korea, rejecting proposals for unification of the peninsula, and to use brutal methods to suppress an uprising by Buddhist monks in Tibet. Pan-Asian institutions would be stillborn in this fractious environment, as would be efforts at serious global cooperation over global warming. Japan, becoming even more worried about North Korea and China, would finally revise its constitution to permit expanded military capabilities. Taiwan would be an ever-present source of worry about an imminent conflict between China, Japan and America. There could even be a short, exploratory exchange of fire over that very issue. The warm glow of the 2008 Beijing Olympics would then be remembered only through a thick smog of tension.

Now look on the brighter side. The credibly optimistic view is that perhaps China will take its economic adjustment in stride, after merely a short sharp pause in growth, resuming expansion albeit at a slower rate than the 10–12 percent of recent years. By 2020 its economy could be at least three times larger than it is today, and the same could well apply to India, too, as it uses its rising tax revenues to build modern infrastructure and a proper system of primary and secondary education. More open trade with other South Asian countries, initiated by a more confident India, would help lift hundreds of millions of Bangladeshis and Pakistanis out of poverty during the twenty-first century's second decade, and hundreds of millions of Indians would be better off, too. Japan, with more market-oriented reforms and a corporate sector galvanized by the prospect of Chinese competition, could experience a productivity surge similar to that enjoyed by the United States during the 1990s, enabling it to overcome the burden of an aging population and, more important still, to become more confident in international affairs.

In such a climate China, Japan and India, encouraged by the Americans and Europeans, would work together to build pan-Asian institutions within which to manage their disputes and differences. All would be made permanent members of the UN Security Council. When the North Korean regime collapses and the Dalai Lama passes away, their first instinct would be to talk and exchange ideas rather than to act unilaterally. A plan would be struck to unify the two Koreas, under the supervision of international peacekeepers and with the help of aid from Japan, China, America and the European Union among others.

The introduction of the election of Hong Kong's chief executive by universal suffrage in 2017, a step made possible by this harmonious atmosphere, could then increase interest in the use of democracy in China itself as a way to ease tensions and resolve disputes. The emerging middle class in China, irritated by its rising tax burden and lack of political rights, will begin to put pressure on the Communist Party, through demonstrations and through the media, to follow Hong Kong's example. The party's fifth and sixth generations of leaders decide it is time to make concessions, reasoning that they can now repeat the success of Japan's Liberal Democratic Party since 1955 and seek to maintain power even in a multiparty system. As the first elections are called, late in the twenty-first century's second decade or early in its third, we will be about to see whether they will be successful.

Whatever happens, Kakuzo Okakura would be happy. In some ways, Asia is already one. In other ways, it is becoming a single entity. How it does so, with three of the world's most powerful countries sitting side by side, undergoing disruptive transformations and subject to huge domestic and international pressures, is going to be quite an adventure. The stakes in Asia are enormous, for all of us.

ACKNOWLEDGMENTS

GIVEN THAT JOURNALISTS were lampooned long ago by the great British satirical magazine, *Private Eye,* as "legends in their own lunchtime," it is fitting that the idea for this book emerged from a lunch I had with my editor at Penguin, Stuart Proffitt, and the chairman of the Penguin Group, John Makinson, in the spring of 2006. I had floated proposals for two books, one of them on the fractious relationship between China and Japan, the other on the economic and political paths being followed by China and India. Stuart and John wondered whether these two books might not in fact be one, which led me to start wondering about the implications for Asia and the world of having three great powers in that region simultaneously.

In his brilliant but brutally clear manner, George Orwell wrote that "every book is a failure," and every writer must surely understand what he meant.* The hundreds of people who were willing to be interviewed and to share their expertise for this book have nevertheless made *Rivals* less inadequate than it would otherwise have been. I cannot and should not list them all, partly because in China in particular many interviewees still prefer to remain anonymous. But I am grateful to each and every one of them.

*In his essay "Why I Write," first published in 1946. Along with three other essays, it was republished in the Penguin Great Ideas series in 2004 under the original title.

In bringing the book from lunch to the library shelves, I have also been blessed by having two unusually sharp, thoughtful and engaged editors in the aforementioned Stuart Proffitt at Penguin in London and Andrea Schulz at Harcourt in New York, both of whom improved the book by pummelling it (i.e., me) in large ways and prodding it in smaller ones. My literary agent, Arthur Goodhart, read so many versions of chapters and the whole manuscript that this might be defined as cruel and unusual punishment, but he did so with energy and good grace while providing countless useful criticisms and suggestions. Oh, and he did his real job, of negotiating agreements with publishers, successfully and efficiently, as did his colleagues Andrew Nurnberg and Manami Tameoki.

All the charts and tables were drawn by Philip Kenny. The data for them, along with other statistics for the book, were compiled by Christopher Wilson, who also did an admirably thorough job of checking as many facts in the text as he could find sources for. Both Phil and Chris are former colleagues of mine at the *Economist,* who did this work for me in their spare time. Further research help came from Martin Adams, a freelance writer in Beijing.

Chang Yiru, whose day job is at China Central Television, helped me enormously by arranging appointments in Beijing and Dalian, by digging out background material for those meetings and by acting as my interpreter. In Harbin, thanks to an introduction by Michael Xuefai Bai of Shenhua Energy who happened to have studied there, I was guided around the city and the nearby Unit 731 museum by Zhu Dan, whose real speciality is teaching English at Heilongjiang University. My guide in Nanjing, during my visit in 2005, was Yang Xiaming, a scholar there who had also shown Iris Chang around while she was preparing her 1997 book, *The Rape of Nanking.* Yang Daqing, associate professor at George Washington University, kindly put me in touch with the department of atrocity studies at Nanjing Normal University, and its helpful director, Zhang Lianhong.

During many visits to China, Xu Sitao, also known as Steven

Xu, who heads the Economist Group operations in that country, was exceptionally generous with his thoughts, friends and dinners. So, for this project as in my previous incarnation, were my former *Economist* colleagues in Beijing, James Miles and Ted Plafker, and Pam Woodall and Tom Easton in Hong Kong. Special thanks for hospitality, introductions and inspiration in China should also go to Hideto Nakahara of Mitsubishi Corporation, Yuan Ming of Dragon TV in Shanghai, Joerg Wuttke of BASF and Francesco Sisci of *La Stampa*. In Hong Kong, Jonathan Anderson of UBS and Christine Loh of Civic Exchange were extremely helpful, while David Li Kwok Po of the Bank of East Asia and Ronnie Chan of Hang Lung were generous hosts and stimulating interlocutors.

In India, Rajiv Kumar, director of the Indian Centre for Research into International Economic Relations (ICRIER) kindly provided an office while I was in Delhi as well as guidance and good fellowship. Vinay Rai, guiding light of the educational Rai Foundation, helped with accommodation and logistics. John Elliott, a long-time contributor to the *Economist,* gave me access to the India International Centre in Delhi, and, at the *Economist* office-cum-home, James and Mian Astill and Shailendra Tyagi were marvellously helpful, welcoming and hospitable.

Special thanks for hospitality, introductions and inspiration in India must also go to Omkar Goswami, Tarun and Geetan Tejpal, C. Raja Mohan, Arun Maira, Gurcharan Das, Vir Sanghvi, Suman Dubey, Bruce Palling, Jo Johnson, Adit Jain, Sunali Rohra, Ranjit and Indu Shahani, Rajesh and Bansri Shah, David Malone, Alex Hall Hall, Aurobind Patel, Ketaki Sheth and Asha Sheth. Nandan Nilekani of Infosys, Ratan Tata of the Tata Group, Anand Mahindra and Dhoshi Bharat of Mahindra and Mahindra, and Shivshankar Menon of the Ministry of External Affairs were all especially generous with their time and ideas.

The Institute for Defense Studies and Analysis, the Institute for Peace and Conflict Studies, the Delhi Policy Group, the National Maritime Foundation, and ICRIER all organized special seminars to enable me to share ideas with local scholars and experts. Takio Yamada of the Japanese embassy in Delhi provided a great deal of guidance on Japan-India relations. In London, Kamalesh Sharma, then India's high commissioner and now secretary-general of the Commonwealth, made many introductions, as did Rahul Roy-Chaudhury, director of the South Asia program at the International Institute of Strategic Studies. On earlier visits to Kolkata, Aveek Sarkar, chairman of the Anandabazar Patrika publishing group, was splendidly hospitable and helpful.

Thanks for Japan are much harder to compile, for to be fair and accurate they would have to go back a quarter of a century. Since the work for my 2005 special report for the *Economist,* "The Sun Also Rises," was also of great benefit for this book, I can begin by repeating the thanks I gave then to Minoru Makihara, Shintaro Hori, Thierry Porte, Martin Hatfull, Yoichi Funabashi, Skipp Orr, Yotaro Kobayashi, Alex Kerr, Keizo Takemi, Geoffrey Tudor, Jeff Kingston, Tadashi Nakamae and the Freshfields Tokyo office. To that list should be added my former *Economist* colleagues in Tokyo, Dominic Ziegler and Hiroko Ofuchi Konno. Several economists at foreign investment banks were also helpful with their analysis and ideas, including Paul Sheard at Lehman Brothers, Robert Feldman at Morgan Stanley, Richard Jerram at Macquarie Securities and Jesper Koll, then at Merrill Lynch and now running his own fund.

Specifically for this book, Tomohiko Taniguchi and Noriyuki Shikata at the Ministry of Foreign Affairs deserve thanks for setting up many interviews with officials both in Japan and in embassies abroad, and for pointing me toward many useful papers and speeches. Two Canadians—my old friend Andrew Horvat and Canada's ambassador to Japan, Joseph Caron—provided many stimulating "working dinners" with an array of Japanese scholars and writers. I am particularly grateful to Joseph, who previously served as ambassador in Beijing, for introducing me to the "China-Pol" discussion forum for China specialists, and to Richard Baum of the University of California at Los Angeles for allowing me to join and to eavesdrop on the many interesting and illuminating exchanges there.

South Korea's ambassador to London, Cho Yoon-Je, helped set up meetings for me in Seoul, as did Catherine Lee, formerly the *Economist*'s correspondent there and now an independent writer. Japan's ambassador to South Korea, Shotaro Oshima, was generous with his time, thoughts and hospitality, as was Robert Einhorn for introducing me to him. In Singapore, similar thanks should go to Peter Ho, permanent secretary at the Ministry of Foreign Affairs, to Singapore's High Commissioner in London, Michael Teo Eng Cheng, and to Jack Burton, of the *Financial Times*.

The biggest and most heartfelt thanks must go to my wife, Carol. When I left the *Economist* in 2006, some said that I was doing so "to spend more time with my family," albeit fortunately not in the euphemistic sense. Carol was aware that things were not likely to turn out quite that way, for she knows how much I enjoy traveling and snooping about, especially in Asia. She did not then know, however, that my first big project as a free spirit would take me away for such long periods to China, India and Japan, but she bore my absences and obsessions with characteristic fortitude and good humour. For her support and love, I shall always be thankful.

ENDNOTES

1. ASIA'S NEW POWER GAME

1. *Surprise, Security, and the American Experience,* John Lewis Gaddis, Harvard University Press, 2004, based on the 2002 Joanna Jackson Memorial Lectures at the New York Public Library.
2. *National Security Strategy 2002,* http://www.whitehouse.gov/nsc/nss/2002/index.html.
3. See *Engaging India,* Strobe Talbot, Brookings Institution Press, 2004; *Impossible Allies: Nuclear India, United States, and the Global Order,* C. Raja Mohan, India Research Press, 2006.
4. Including by the *Economist,* under my editorship: "Dr Strangedeal," March 11, 2006.
5. A mild version can be found at http://www.idsa.in/publications/stratcomments/ AnandKumar171007.htm, "Bangladesh's Quest for Nuclear Energy." A stronger one was in the *Organiser* of October 7, 2007, "China Encircling India: Gifts Nuclear Muscle to India's Rivals" by M. D. Nalapat, at www.organiser.org.
6. "A Friend Indeed," Robert D. Blackwill, *National Interest,* May 1, 2007. See also the same author's "The India Imperative," *National Interest,* June 1, 2005.
7. Napoleon said, "Let China sleep, for when she wakes she will shake the world." The best recent exploration of this theme is James Kynge's *China Shakes the World: The Rise of a Hungry Nation,* Weidenfeld & Nicolson, 2006.
8. Goldman Sachs Global Paper no. 99, "Dreaming with BRICs: The Path to 2050," 2003; and GS Global Paper no. 152, "India's Rising Growth Potential," 2007.
9. "Global Economic Prospects: Managing the Next Wave of Globalization," World Bank, 2007.
10. See "Why India Is Selling Weapons to Burma," Anuj Chopra, *Christian Science Monitor,* July 23, 2007, http://www.csmonitor.com/2007/0723/.
11. Although anyone seeking to find a personal obsession with this topic might take note of the fact that my first issue of the *Economist* as its editor, on April 3, 1993, carried a cover entitled "Asia Unleashed," with an illustration of a dragon whose teeth consisted of missiles and whose spines were covered with tanks and guns.
12. *Securing Japan: Tokyo's Grand Strategy and the Future of East Asia,* Richard J. Samuels, Cornell University Press, 2007.
13. *The World Is Flat: A Brief History of the Twenty-first Century,* Thomas L. Friedman, Farrar, Straus and Giroux, 2005.

14. *The War of the World: History's Age of Hatred,* Niall Ferguson, Allen Lane, 2006.
15. International Monetary Fund, "World Economic Outlook," 2006 and 2007.
16. "Monitoring the World Economy 1820–1992,"Angus Maddison, OECD Development Centre Studies, 1995.
17. PPP measures are often quoted rather breathlessly as if they show the "true" impact of poorer countries on the world, especially Asian ones. But it is important to be clear about what PPP measures mean. They are good indicators of living standards, which are higher in Asia than the raw dollar numbers suggest because costs, especially for services, are lower than in the West. But they do not measure global influence or impact. Such influence or impact on other countries does not arise from domestic living standards but occurs through trade, aid and financial flows, and such things are transacted at actual exchange rates, not PPP-adjusted rates. Moreover, the price data used for PPP measures are notoriously unreliable and the "baskets" of goods and services used are inevitably subjective. The price data used by the World Bank for PPP measures of China's GDP were taken from the mid-1990s until a revision in 2007 made China's economy suddenly 40 percent smaller in PPP terms.
18. "The Unipolar Moment," Charles Krauthammer, *Foreign Affairs,* Winter 1990–1991.

2. A CONTINENT CREATED

1. John Murray, London, 1903; E. P. Dutton, New York, 1904. Now available from Stone Bridge Press in America and Yohan Classics in Japan.
2. Quoted in *Asian Ideas of East and West: Tagore and His Critics in Japan, China, and India,* Stephen N. Hay, Harvard University Press, 1970.
3. Ibid.
4. As quoted in *The Japanese and Sun Yat-Sen,* Marius B. Jansen, Harvard University Press, 1954; speech also available at http://en.wikisource.org/wiki/Sun_Yat_Sen%27s_speech_on_Pan-Asianism.
5. "From Confucius to Kennedy: Principles of East Asian Governance." Conference paper from January 2007, World Bank East Asia Visions volume, available on www.mahbubani.net.
6. *Fukoku kyohei* in Japanese, but a slogan that apparently originated from an old Chinese history of the so-called Warring States Period, from 300–100 B.C., *Zhan Guo Ce* or "Strategies of the Warring States."
7. "A Theory of Unbalanced Growth in the World Economy," Kaname Akamatsu, *Weltwirtschaftliches Archiv,* Hamburg, no. 86, 1961. And in "A Historical Pattern of Economic Growth in Developing Countries." *The Developing Economies,* Tokyo, Preliminary Issue no.1, 1962. See also http://www.grips.ac.jp/module/prsp/FGeese.htm.
8. *Asian Drama: An Inquiry into the Poverty of Nations,* Gunnar Myrdal, Pantheon, 1968.

3. CHINA: MIDDLE COUNTRY, CENTRAL ISSUE

1. The Little Red Book's real name is *Quotations from Chairman Mao Tse-Tung.*
2. Quoted by Dominic Ziegler in his special report for the *Economist* on China and its region, "Reaching for a Renaissance," March 31, 2007.
3. See chapter 8 for more details.

4.   http://www.miafarrow.org/ed_032807.html.
5.   Paper presented at India-Japan-Taiwan Trilateral Meeting held on March 15–16, 2006, at the United Services Institution of India.
6.   As Robert Zoellick, then America's deputy secretary of state, now president of the World Bank, called for China to be in a speech in New York in September 2005.
7.   In 2004 a new economic census provided an occasion and a basis for the National Bureau of Statistics to revise the GDP figures, which it did in early 2006. The NBS announced that China's GDP was at that point 16.8 percent larger than had previously been thought. It then produced revised figures for the whole period since 1993, which appeared to suggest that provincial reporting had in fact been more accurate than the national data, in nominal terms (i.e., before adjusting for inflation). But it then confused matters further by announcing that the inflation-adjusted national growth rates for 1993–2004 had nevertheless been correct; all that the NBS altered in its revised figures was the deflator used to adjust for price changes, which miraculously produced identical results to the previous announcements.
8.   "What's Driving Investment in China?" IMF Working Paper 06/25, November 2006.
9.   "The End of Cheap Labor (Period)," UBS Investment Research, August 9, 2007. Jonathan Anderson also wrote an earlier report, "The Mainland Productivity Muddle," February 15, 2007, which explained how the poor data on employment and output make it impossible to produce authoritative measures of productivity growth in China.
10. *China's Democratic Future,* Bruce Gilley, Columbia University Press, 2004.
11. *China's Trapped Transition: The Limits of Developmental Autocracy,* Pei Minxin, Harvard University Press, 2006.
12. *The Coming Collapse of China,* Gordon B. Chang, Arrow, 2003.
13. *China: Fragile Superpower,* Susan L. Shirk, Oxford University Press, 2007.
14. "The Durable Communist Party," *China Economic Quarterly,* Volume 11, Issue 1, 2007, Q1.
15. *Beyond Liberal Democracy: Political Thinking in an East Asian Context,* Daniel Bell, Princeton University Press, 2006.
16. *The China Fantasy: How Our Leaders Explain Away Chinese Repression,* James Mann, Viking, 2007.
17. See also "The Political Implications of China's Growing Middle Class," Joseph Fewsmith, *China Leadership Monitor,* no. 21, Summer 2001, The Hoover Institution.
18. "The Value of China's Emerging Middle Class," Diana Farrell, Ulrich A. Gersh and Elizabeth Stephenson, *McKinsey Quarterly,* June 2006.
19. http://www.chinadaily.com.cn/china/2007-07/10/content_5424602.htm.
20. "China's Inevitables: Death, Taxes and Democracy," Francesco Sisci, http://www.lastampa.it/, March 2007; also "From Taxation to Representation," *China Economic Quarterly,* vol. 11, issue 3, 2007, Q3.

4. JAPAN: POWERFUL, VULNERABLE, AGING

1.   "The Old Shogun's Hardest Fight," *The Economist,* October 15, 1983.
2.   "Marlboro Country?" *The Economist,* February 25, 1984.
3.   *The Enigma of Japanese Power,* Karel van Wolferen, Macmillan, 1989.
4.   See chapter 8 for more details on this dispute.
5.   See chapter 7 for more on the museum, the Marco Polo Bridge incident in 1937, and the Yasukuni war shrine in Tokyo.

6. "Japan in the New Global Demography," Roger Goodman and Sarah Harper, http://japanfocus.org; "The Unprecedented Shift in Japan's Population: Numbers, Age, and Prospects," Vaclav Smil, also at the Japan Focus Web site; and an excellent but harder to obtain report, "Childhood's End: Seismic Shifts in Japanese Demographics," Peter Morgan (HSBC's chief Asia economist), HSBC Global Economics, December 7, 2004.

7. For more detail, see the author's special survey of Japan in the *Economist*, "The Sun Also Rises," October 8, 2005. An expanded version of that survey was published as a book in Japanese translation under the title *Hiwa Mata Noboru*, Soshisha, 2006.

8. Prices in fact began to fall from March 1995 until March 1996, but then inflation returned until a longer period of deflation set in from 1998 until 2005.

9. "Employment—the Shift to Flexibility," Peter Morgan, HSBC Global Economics, February 25, 2005; "A Nagging Sense of Job Insecurity: The New Reality Facing Japanese Youth," Genda Yuji, International House of Japan, Inc., 2005; "Nonstandard Work in Developed Economies: Causes and Consequences," edited by Susan Houseman and Machiko Osawa, W. E. Upjohn Institute for Employment Research, 2003; also OECD Economic Survey of Japan, 2005, 2006.

10. Measured by the Gini coefficient. See OECD Economic Survey of Japan 2006, table 4.3, page 104. For a discussion of Gini coefficients and inequality, see chapter 5 on India.

11. The best primer to which is *The Logic of Japanese Politics: Leaders, Institutions and the Limits of Change*, Gerald L. Curtis, Columbia University Press, 1999.

12. See "Japan's Stealth Reform: The Key Role of Political Process," Kent E. Calder, Johns Hopkins University School of Advanced International Studies, Asia-Pacific Policy Paper Series, 2005.

13. *Japan's Quiet Transformation: Social Change and Civil Society in the Twenty-first Century*, Jeff Kingston, Routledge Curzon, 2004.

14. *The Economist*, September 24, 1998.

15. See the OECD's Economic Surveys of Japan for 2005 and 2006.

16. *Kaisha: The Japanese Corporation*, James C. Abegglen and George Stalk Jr., Basic Books, 1985; and *21st-Century Management: New Systems, Lasting Values*, James C. Abegglen, Palgrave Macmillan, 2006.

17. Strictly speaking, the company's name is livedoor, with a lowercase *l*.

18. All the M&A figures are from Dealogic.

19. In 2004. That compares with 2.6 percent in the United States, 2.0 percent in the European Union and an OECD average of 2.2 percent.

20. In a new "National Defense Program Guidelines," Defense Agency of Japan.

5. INDIA: MULTITUDES, MUDDLE, MOMENTUM

1. Mark Tully and Gillian Wright provide a good account of *Tehelka*'s sting in *India in Slow Motion*, Penguin Books, 2002.

2. In *The Best of Tehelka 2*, Buffalo Books 2006.

3. See *The Pursuit of Reason: The Economist 1843–1993*, Ruth Dudley Edwards, Hamish Hamilton, 1993.

4. More detail on the SEZ policy can be found later in this chapter.

5. A process ably chronicled and analyzed in *Crossing the Rubicon: The Shaping of India's New Foreign Policy*, C. Raja Mohan, Penguin Books, 2003.

6.   "The Bird of Gold: The Rise of India's Consumer Market," McKinsey & Company, May 2007.

7.   "India: Everything to Play For," John Llewellyn, Robert Subbaraman, Alastair Newton and Sonal Varma, Lehman Brothers Global Economics, October 2007.

8.   The OECD has not previously undertaken a study of India, which is not a member: OECD Economic Surveys, vol. 2007/14, October 2007.

9.   It is no accident that Amartya Sen, India's most famous economist-cum-philosopher, called his recent book *The Argumentative Indian* (Allen Lane, 2005).

10. For a summary of the difficulties involved in redeveloping Mumbai, see "Maximum City Blues," *The Economist*, September 1, 2007.

11. "Development Policy Review of India—Inclusive Growth and Service Delivery: Building on India's Success," World Bank, 2006.

12. "World Development Indicators 2007."

13. Gini coefficients for Japan, America and Britain are taken from OECD Economic Survey of Japan 2006.

14. "Towards Faster and More Inclusive Growth: An Approach to the 11th Five-Year Plan," Planning Commission, December 2006.

15. "India's Rising Growth Potential," Goldman Sachs Global Economics Paper 152, January 22, 2007.

16. Mr. Nilekani was promoted to cochairman of Infosys in June 2007.

17. "NASSCOM-McKinsey Report 2005: Extending India's Leadership of the Global IT and BPO Industries," National Association of Software and Service Companies, December 2005.

18. For an authoritative examination of the pros and cons of SEZs, see OECD Economic Survey of India 2007, pages 37–38.

19. OECD Economic Survey of India 2007, page 209.

20. Conference Board, at www.conference-board.org.

21. "Doing Business in South Asia 2007," World Bank.

22. Available at www.transparency.org.

23. "Higher Education in India: The Need for Change," Pawan Agarwal, ICRIER Working Paper no. 180, June 2006.

24. www.languageinindia.com.

25. http://tesol-india.ac.in.

26. www.censusindia.gov.in/.

27. All figures from World Trade Atlas.

6. **A PLANET PRESSURED**

1.   For example: *Making Sense of Chindia: Reflections on China and India,* Jairam Ramesh, India Research Press, 2005. Mr. Ramesh has been minister of state for commerce in the Congress Party-led coalition government of India since 2004. There is also *Chindia: How China and India Are Revolutionizing Global Business,* Peter Engardio, ed., McGraw Hill, 2006, which is a collection of articles from *Business Week.* For Kaname Akamatsu's theory of the flying geese, see chapter 2.

2.   And cited in chapter 3, on Chinese politics.

3.   W.W. Norton, 1975.

4.   In his book *Dogs and Demons: The Fall of Modern Japan,* Hill and Wang, 2001.

5. Available at http://www.yale.edu/epi/.
6. http://www.blacksmithinstitute.org/ten.php.
7. Development Policy Review 2006.
8. "In Teeming India, Water Crisis Means Dry Pipes and Foul Sludge," Somini Sengupta, *The New York Times,* September 29, 2006, with further articles in the series on September 30 and October 1.
9. http://www.cseindia.org/.
10. OECD Environmental Performance Reviews: China, 2007.
11. "The Great Leap Backward," Elizabeth C. Economy, *Foreign Affairs,* September/October 2007. See also *The River Runs Black: The Environmental Challenge to China's Future,* Elizabeth C. Economy, Cornell University Press, 2004.
12. Elizabeth Economy, *Foreign Affairs,* ibid.
13. http://www.bp.com/productlanding.do?categoryId=6848&contentId=7033471.
14. http://minerals.usgs.gov/minerals/.
15. There have been many scare stories about this investment, claiming that it involves a new "colonization" of Africa by China. For an antidote to such views, see "The Fact and Fiction of Sino-African Energy Relations," Erica S. Downs, *China Security,* vol. 3, no. 3, Summer 2007.
16. For example: Carol Lancaster, at the Center for Global Development in Washington, D.C., available at www.cgdev.org/content/publications/detail/13953/.
17. *The Age of Turbulence: Adventures in a New World,* Alan Greenspan, Penguin Press, 2007.
18. For a particularly good account of Chinese energy trends, see "China Energy: A Guide for the Perplexed," Daniel H. Rosen and Trevor Houser, part of the China Balance Sheet project of the Peterson Institute for International Economics in Washington, D.C., 2007.
19. "Wen Hits at Failure to Curb Pollution," Richard McGregor, *Financial Times,* May 9, 2007.
20. http://pib.nic.in/release/release.asp?relid=29937.

7. BLOOD, MEMORY AND LAND

1. For a full account, see *Unit 731: The Japanese Army's Secret of Secrets,* Peter Williams and David Wallace, Hodder & Stoughton, 1989.
2. *Embracing Defeat: Japan in the Aftermath of World War II,* John Dower, W. W. Norton, 1999.
3. See *Korea: The Unknown War,* Jon Halliday and Bruce Cumings, Viking, 1988.
4. The U.S. State Department's rebuttal of the claims, which continue to be made by North Korea and, more quietly, by China, can be found at http://usinfo.state.gov/media/Archive/2005/Nov/09-262154.html. For a review of the newly released Russian documents, see "Deceiving the Deceivers: Moscow, Beijing, Pyongyang, and the Allegations of Bacteriological Weapons Use in Korea," Kathryn Weathersby, *Cold War International History Project,* Bulletin Issue 11, http://www.wilsoncenter.org/topics/pubs/ACFC45.pdf. Those documents lacked official stamps and seals that would normally prove their authenticity, but Jon Halliday and Jung Chang, authors of *Mao: The Unknown Story,* Jonathan Cape, 2005, obtained an on-the-record statement from the official spokesman of the FSB (the successor organization to the KGB) confirming that they are authentic.
5. *Bulletin of Concerned Asian Scholars* (now *Critical Asian Studies*), October/December,

1980; John W. Powell published a further article, "Japan's Biological Weapons, 1939–45" in the *Bulletin of the Atomic Scientists,* October 1981.

6.   *The Rape of Nanking: The Forgotten Holocaust of World War II,* Iris Chang, Basic Books, 1997.

7.   See, for example: *The Nanking Massacre: Fact Versus Fiction,* Higashinakano Shudo, published in English by Sekai Shuppan, Tokyo, 2005; "Atrocities in Nanjing: Searching for Explanations," Yang Daqing, in *Scars of War,* edited by Diana Lary and Stephen Mackinnon, UBC Press, 2001; *The Making of* The Rape of Nanking, Takashi Yoshida, Oxford University Press, 2006; "The Nanking Atrocities: Fact and Fable," Ikuhiko Hata, *Japan Echo,* vol. 25, no. 4, August 1998.

8.   In *Documents on the Rape of Nanking,* edited by Timothy Brook, University of Michigan Press, 1999.

9.   A statement provided at the monument, under the name of Yasukuni's chief priest and dated June 25, 2005, states that "Dr. Pal detected that the tribunal, commonly known as the Tokyo Trial, was none other than formalized vengeance sought with arrogance by the victorious Allied Powers upon a defeated Japan . . . With, as the concluding part of his judgment foresaw, the Allies' craze for retaliation cooling down and the biased outlook on history being corrected, the insightful view presented by Dr. Pal has now gained recognition which it should deserve in the academic circle of international law."

10.   This will be described in more detail in chapter 8.

11.   In *Death by Government,* R. J. Rummel, Transaction Publishers, 1994.

12.   Cited in *Modern China: A Guide to a Century of Change,* Graham Hutchings, Harvard University Press, 2000. Also see www.chinadaily.com.cn/english/doc/2005-08/15/content_468908.htm.

13.   http://www.yasukuni.or.jp/english/.

14.   For an excellent exploration of this point, see "Yasukuni Shrine: Ritual and Memory," John Breen, London's School of Oriental and African Studies, available at http://japanfocus.org/products/details/2060.

15.   The exhibition's text on the Nanking "incident" says simply: "After the Japanese surrounded Nanking in December 1937, General Matsui Iwane distributed maps to his men with the foreign settlements and the Safety Zone marked in red ink. Matsui told them they were to maintain strict military discipline and that anyone committing unlawful acts would be severely punished. The defeated Chinese rushed to Xinquan and they were completely destroyed. The Chinese soldiers disguised in civilian clothes were severely punished."

16.   In *Embracing Defeat: Japan in the Aftermath of World War II,* John Dower, Allen Lane and W. W. Norton, 1999.

17.   Quoted in Williams and Wallace.

18.   Even in Europe, history has a habit of reappearing: For example, the British press remains seemingly obsessed by the Second World War, to the distress of many German ambassadors to London; and Poland's president, Lech Kaczynski, caused outrage by raising the Polish war deaths at German hands when negotiating over the European Union reform treaty in 2007.

19.   See also "The Aesthetic Construction of Ethnic Nationalism: War Memorial Museums in Korea and Japan," Kal Hong, in *Rethinking Historical Injustice in Northeast Asia,* Routledge, 2007.

20.   See "Northeast Asia's Undercurrents of Conflict," *Asia Report,* no. 108, December 15,

2005, the International Crisis Group, which also has a useful section on the Kando dispute between China and Korea, which is discussed later in this chapter.

21.   Strictly, in Korean, his name is Lee Sung Man, but he became known as Syngman Rhee to westerners.

8. FLASH POINTS AND DANGER ZONES

1.   "The Military Balance 2007," International Institute for Strategic Studies.
2.   www.sipri.org.
3.   "India's Blue-Water Dreams May Have to Wait," Sudha Ramachandran, *Asia Times,* August 21, 2007, available at www.atimes.com.
4.   "Too Much for One Man to Do," James Astill, *The Economist,* July 8, 2006.
5.   See *India's China War,* Neville Maxwell, Jonathan Cape, 1970; and *Protracted Contest: Sino-Indian Rivalry in the Twentieth Century,* John W. Garver, University of Washington Press, 2001, for accounts of the 1962 war.
6.   See *The Search for the Panchen Lama,* Isabel Hilton, Viking, 1999.
7.   See "Northeast Asia's Undercurrents of Conflict," *Asia Report,* no. 108, December 15, 2005, the International Crisis Group.
8.   "Regime Insecurity and International Co-operation: Explaining China's Compromises in Territorial Disputes," M. Taylor Fravel, *International Security,* vol. 30, no. 2, Fall 2005.
9.   According to *Generalissimo: Chiang Kai-shek and the China He Lost,* Jonathan Fenby, The Free Press, 2003.
10.   "Military Power of the People's Republic of China: A Report to Congress Pursuant to the National Defense Authorization Act Fiscal Year 2000," 2007.
11.   *Taiwan's Security: History and Prospects,* Dr. Bernard Cole, Routledge, 2006.
12.   The best account is nevertheless *Under the Loving Care of the Fatherly Leader: North Korea and the Kim Dynasty,* Bradley K. Martin, Thomas Dunne Books, 2004.
13.   For a detailed account, see *The Peninsula Question: A Chronicle of the Second Korean Nuclear Crisis,* Yoichi Funabashi, Brookings Institution Press, 2007.

9. ASIAN DRAMA

1.   As cited in chapter 2.
2.   See *Nuclear Terrorism: The Ultimate Preventable Catastrophe,* Graham Allison, Times Books, 2004.
3.   See chapter 3.
4.   "Trade possibilities and non-tariff barriers to Indo-Pak trade," Nisha Taneja, Indian Council for Research on International Economic Relations, working paper no. 200, October 2007.

FURTHER READING

The literature on China, India, Japan and, indeed, Asia as a whole is so vast and varied that there is little point in attempting to provide a comprehensive bibliography. Many specialized books, papers and Web sites have already been cited in the end notes. The most useful thing to do here is to list the books, organizations and Web sites that I have found especially helpful and that may be of interest to anyone wishing to delve more deeply into the many topics covered in this book.

On modern India, the best recent general book is by Edward Luce, who spent five years as bureau chief in Delhi for the *Financial Times* and is now based in Washington, D.C.: *In Spite of the Gods: the Rise of Modern India* (Doubleday, 2007). An invaluable history of the country since independence in 1947 is Ramachandra Guha's *India After Gandhi: The History of the World's Largest Democracy* (Ecco, 2007), which will probably be unmatchable for many years. To get a sense of Indian society, spirituality, political culture and much more, it is worth reading any of the sets of essays published regularly by Mark Tully, a former BBC reporter who was born in India and is now something of a celebrity there: for example, *No Full Stops in India* (Penguin, 1991), *India in Slow Motion* (Penguin, 2002) or *India's Unending Journey* (Rider, 2008).

To understand the way the country evolved in the decades before and after the economic reform process began, read *India Unbound* (Knopf, 2001) by Gurcharan Das, a writer who worked for many years in management for Procter & Gamble. If you want to explore India's economic development further back into history, the best guide is *The Hindu Equilibrium: India c. 1500 B.C.–2000 A.D.* (Oxford University Press, 2005) by Deepak Lal. If, instead, you want to understand the many peculiarities of Indian economic policy, try *The Oxford Companion to Economics in India,* edited by Kaushik Basu, (Oxford University Press, 2007): the quality and clarity of the entries varies widely, but it is nevertheless a useful reference book.

The best and most accessible authority on Indian foreign policy is C. Raja Mohan, a journalist and scholar. His *Crossing the Rubicon: The Shaping of India's New Foreign Policy* (Penguin, 2005) provides a comprehensive guide to the changes since the end of the cold war; *Impossible Allies: Nuclear India, United States and the Global Order* (India Research Press, 2006) is a more direct look at the civil nuclear-energy deal between India and the U.S. in 2005 and the changes that led up to it. An admirable study earlier this decade was *India: Emerging Power* (Brookings Institution Press, 2002) by Stephen Cohen. Brahma Chellaney, a distinguished and famously hawkish strategic thinker, offers his own survey of Asia's new relationships in *Asian Juggernaut: The Rise of China, India and Japan* (HarperCollins, 2006). A peerless guide to the relationship between India and China is John W. Garver's *Protracted Contest: Sino-Indian Rivalry in the Twentieth Century* (University of Washington Press, 2002).

If environmentalists think China is felling too many trees, they should add to their concerns the huge number of books being written about it. Another former *Financial Times* bureau chief has recently provided one of the best general surveys: James Kynge's *China Shakes the World: A Titan's Rise and Troubled Future—and the Challenge for America* (Mariner Books, 2007). Susan Shirk's *China: Fragile Superpower* (Oxford University Press, 2007), cited several times in this book, is a good up-to-date primer on internal Chinese politics. Excellent background reading on history and society can be found in Jasper Becker's *The Chinese* (Oxford University Press, 2002). On defense and security, *Rising Star: China's New Security Diplomacy* (Brookings Institution Press, 2007) by Bates Gill is well worth studying.

Two biographies of Mao, one recent and hard-hitting, the other older and gentler, are also good ways to read up on China's modern history: the former is *Mao: The Unknown Story* (Anchor, 2006) by Jung Chang and Jon Halliday; the latter is *Mao: A Life* (Henry Holt, 2001) by Philip Short. An invaluable short (-ish) history of the country is by the man who was the doyen of American China scholars, the late John King Fairbank, and his colleague Merle Goldman: *China: A New History* (Belknap Press, 2001).

Far and away the best means to keep informed on China's ever-changing economy is to subscribe to the excellent *China Economic Quarterly* produced by Dragonomics, a consultancy in Beijing (www.dragonomics.net). The best way to mug up on Chinese economic reform and the economy's evolution is to consult the two books, both called *China—the Balance Sheet* (PublicAffairs, 2006, 2007), produced jointly by the Peterson Institute for International Economics and the Center for Strategic and International Studies, in Washington, D.C., although the books also contain useful chapters on foreign policy, legal reform and more.

On Japan, fewer books are being published in English these days because the country ceased to be a hot topic after its financial crash that began in 1990. Despite their age, the two best works on Japanese politics remain those cited in chapter five: Karel van Wolferen's *The Enigma of Japanese Power* (Vintage, 1990) and Gerald Curtis's *The Logic of Japanese Politics* (Columbia University Press, 2000). The best way to bring yourself up-to-date on how Japanese politics and government have been changing is to read *Japan's Quiet Transformation: Social Change and Civil Society in the Twenty-first Century* (RoutledgeCurzon, 2004) by Jeff Kingston, who is director of Asian Studies at Temple University in Tokyo.

The financial and economic crisis of the 1990s was well-mapped by Gillian Tett in *Saving the Sun: How Wall Street Mavericks Shook Up Japan's Financial World and Made Billions* (Harper Collins, 2004), which tells the story of the failure, nationalization and purchase by an American private-equity consortium of the Long-Term Credit Bank of Japan. Alex Kerr's *Dogs and Demons: Tales from the Dark Side of Japan* (Hill and Wang, 2001) explores corruption, environmental damage and bureaucratic knavery in excruciating and impressive detail. To cheer yourself up, try *Japan Remodeled: How Government and Industry Are Reforming Japanese Capitalism* by Steven K. Vogel (Cornell University Press, 2006), and *21st-Century Japanese Management: New Systems, Lasting Values* (Palgrave Macmillan, 2006) by James Abegglen, a management consultant who had been writing about Japanese business for half a century until his death in 2007.

Changes in Japan's foreign and security policy since the cold war ended and China's emergence as a regional power began have been well analyzed by Western scholars. Christopher W. Hughes of the University of Warwick produced a fine report for the International Institute for Strategic Studies in 2004 called "Japan's Re-emergence as a 'Normal' Military Power" (Adelphi Paper 368-9, available from www.iiss.org). *Securing Japan: Tokyo's Grand Strategy and the Future of East Asia* (Cornell University Press, 2007), by Richard J. Samuels of the Massachusetts Institute of Technology, is an excellent guide to the evolution of strategic thinking in Japan in recent years. Also published in 2007 by was *Japan Rising: The Resurgence of Japanese Power and Purpose* (PublicAffairs, 2007) by Kenneth B. Pyle, a veteran Japan watcher at the University of Washington, in which he charts the course of Japanese foreign policy during the past 150 years.

Material on developments across the whole of Asia is harder to find, because most books cover single countries or subregions. The National Bureau of Asian Research, a think tank based in Seattle and chaired by the aforementioned Kenneth Pyle, produces an extremely useful annual book called *Strategic Asia,* that contains a host of essays and data on developments in the region. It also publishes a journal called *Asia Policy.* To look back further into history, a helpful book is *East Asia: Tradition and Transformation* (Houghton Mifflin, 1989) by John King Fairbank, Edwin Reischauer and Albert Craig. On contemporary strategic issues, two useful books are *Power Shift: China and Asia's New Dynamics* (University of California Press, 2006) edited by David Shambaugh, and *The New Asian Power Dynamic* (Sage Publications, 2007), edited by Maharajakrishna Rasgotra.

For economic history, you can't do better than *Governing the Market: Economic Theory and the Role of Government in East Asian Industrialization* (Princeton University Press, 2003) by Robert Wade, now at the London School of Economics. Another invaluable text is *Dancing with Giants: China, India and the Global Economy,* edited by L. Alan Winters and Shahid Yusuf for the World Bank in 2007.

Finally, a few words about data. The World Economic Outlook database of the IMF is a good one for comparisons across countries and periods. Its address is http://www.imf.org/external/ns/cs.aspx?id=28. The governments of China, Japan and India all now have good and easy-to-use statistical Web sites: for China, http://www.stats.gov.cn/english/; for Japan, http://www.stat.go.jp/english/; and for India http://mospi.nic.in/. Regional data can also be found on the website of the Asian Development Bank, http://www.adb.org/statistics/default.asp, though such data excludes Japan as it is not a developing country.

INDEX